North Korea

COVENTRY UNIVERSITY LONDON
University House
109 - 117 Middlesex Street, London. E1 7JF
Tel: 024 7765 1016
www.coventry.ac.uk/london

Michael J. Seth

North Korea

A History

 macmillan education palgrave

First published 2018 by
PALGRAVE

Palgrave in the UK is an imprint of Macmillan Publishers Limited, registered in England, company number 785998, of 4 Crinan Street, London, N1 9XW.

Palgrave® and Macmillan® are registered trademarks in the United States, the United Kingdom, Europe and other countries.

ISBN 978–1–352–00221–8 hardback
ISBN 978–1–352–00218–8 paperback

This book is printed on paper suitable for recycling and made from fully managed and sustained forest sources. Logging, pulping and manufacturing processes are expected to conform to the environmental regulations of the country of origin.

A catalogue record for this book is available from the British Library.

A catalog record for this book is available from the Library of Congress.

Contents

Introduction

North Korea, so menacing, so oppressive, so wildly extreme in its rhetoric, so closed to the world and above all so bizarre to most outsiders, has been the object of fascination and puzzlement. How can we understand such a strange, isolated state? How can we explain the behavior of its leaders, at turns comic, tragic and threatening? How can we account for this society so radically different from the other Korea with which it shares the same peninsula and the same historical heritage?

The purpose of this book is to help provide some answers to these questions by presenting a basic chronological, narrative history of North Korea from its origins in the colonial period (1910–1945) to 2017. It is hoped by doing so North Korea can start to make sense. We can see it as more than an aberrant bit of history or a security issue – not just a weird cult-state, but as a society that grew out of twentieth-century Korea's struggles to regain autonomy and achieve modernization in order to build a prosperous and independent society that could proudly take its place in the contemporary world. These were struggles and goals that it shared with most other postcolonial states. It has been a dynamic, continually evolving society shaped by historical contingencies, by decisions and actions of its leaders and its elites, and by the responses of ordinary citizens. Without defending what has become one the most odious and oppressive regimes in history we can appreciate its achievements and its concerns. And above all we can see North Korea as a society with a hard-working, long-suffering population who made great sacrifices in the hopes for a better future.

There is another reason to examine North Korea's evolution in a systematic way. It is part of the larger story of humanity. North Korea, by its peculiar nature, offers insights into that story. A remarkable fact about North Korea is the way in which it was created. Korea, one of the world's most ethnically homogeneous societies, with 13 centuries of political unity, was suddenly and arbitrarily divided by the USA and the Soviet Union along an east–west line, not based on historical geography or culture, but a line that divided provinces, valleys and families, and partitioned the ancient state.[1] Yet in just two generations North and South Korea, sharing the same cultural and ethnic heritage, evolved into radically different societies. Modern history offers no other example, not even Germany, which while divided at the same time into East and West did not have the same long history of political unity, nor were the two halves so hermetically sealed off from each other, and nor did they have such sharp contrasts in socio-political structures, ideology or living standards.

The 38th parallel that divided north and south was chosen by the Americans in 1945 because it split the country into roughly two equal halves. Actually North Korea, or the Democratic People's Republic of Korea (Chosŏn Minjujuŭi Inmin Konghwaguk) as it is officially called (the DPRK for short) is slightly larger in area than South Korea (officially called the Republic of Korea, or the ROK). The North has 46,000 square miles (120,000 square km) to the South's 38,000 (100,000 square km). Area-wise all of Korea is about the same size as Great Britain; North Korea is slightly smaller than England or New York State. But it has only-half of South Korea's population – 25 million to South Korea's 50 million. The North is colder and more mountainous with less arable land.

Historically, the population of Korea has been concentrated in four main pockets of rich agricultural land: the fertile plains of the southwest corner, the Naktong Basin in the southeast, the Han Basin in the west center and the Taedong Basin in the northwest. Only one of these pockets, the Taedong Basin where Pyongyang (P'yŏngyang) is located, lies in the North along with the northernmost slice of the Han Basin. The limited land suitable for farming and the short growing season have always been a problem in North Korea. The winters are long and cold. Much of the annual rainfall comes during the short monsoon season in the summer months; the rest of the year is mostly sunny and dry. It is a beautiful but harsh environment. The northeast part of the country has traditionally been a sort of frontier area of Korea, only heavily settled in the first half of the twentieth century when its rich mineral and hydroelectric resources were exploited by the Japanese. The northern border runs along the Manchurian region of China. This boundary is defined by the rugged Paektu Mountain, a 9,003-foot (2744 m) volcano with a lake in its crater. Paektu, the tallest peak in their country, has long been sacred to the Korean people. From the mountain two rivers flow: the Tumen north to the East Sea (Sea of Japan), and the Yalu south into the Yellow Sea. The two rivers make up most of the Chinese border and the 14-mile (22 km) border with Russia. The southern border with South Korea is a jagged line that runs roughly from southwest to northeast and marks the July 27, 1953 ceasefire line at the end of the Korean War.

While Korea is not a tiny country, comparable to Britain or Italy in area and Germany in population, it is much smaller than its neighbors. All Koreans are aware of being surrounded by bigger neighbors: China, Russia and Japan. Koreans sometimes call themselves a shrimp among whales. That fact that they have maintained both their independence and their own cultural identity for most of the past two millennia is a source of pride. North Korea has inherited this sense of being a small state, zealously striving to maintain its autonomy. Its perception of being surrounded by more powerful, potentially threatening neighbors is only aggravated by the fact that it has to deal with South Korea with its greater population, a far bigger economy and the presence of US troops.

These geographical factors – its rugged topography, harsh climate, limited cultivatable land, its sense of geopolitical insecurity and its long, somewhat porous border with China – are all important factors in understanding the history of the DPRK.

This history is divided into seven roughly chronologically based chapters. The first deals with the origins of the North Korean regime, which lie primarily in the nationalist and anti-imperialist movement in Korea that took place during the heavy-handed Japanese occupation of the peninsula from 1910 to 1945. The second chapter examines the division of Korea, the Soviet occupation and the birth of the DPRK in 1948. It then recounts the failed attempt by the North Korean leadership to reunite the state, an attempt that led to the extremely bloody Korean War, 1950–1953. The death and destruction visited upon North Korea during the three-year conflict was one the worst suffered by any country. But the regime survived. The third chapter deals with the reconstruction and rapid industrialization that took place in the decade and a half after the conflict. This is when Kim Il Sung, the North Korean leader and his Manchurian guerilla comrades assumed absolute mastery of the state and when North Korea's achievements were impressive even to unsympathetic outsiders. The fourth chapter deals with the further cultural and political evolution that took place in the 1960s and 1970s, and the emergence of North Korea as a dynastic regime.

Chapter five starts in 1980 when North Korea's leadership could still see themselves as on the way to successfully fulfilling their objectives, and goes on to examine the period of economic stagnation and decline that followed. It ends with the series of crises that called into question the very survival of the regime: the collapse of the Soviet Union along with the economic and political rise of South Korea, the nuclear confrontation with the USA and the death of Kim Il Sung. The sixth chapter deals with the decade after Kim Il Sung's death in 1994 and the ascension of Kim Jong Il, a decade marked by one of recent history's worst famines. The famine ended the tightly controlled system created by Kim Il Sung and transformed North Korea into a mixed market and command economy characterized by corruption and competition for resources. The main task of the regime at this point was to survive; and against the prognostications of many outsiders it did. The last chapter covers the regime's retreat from tentative reforms, the reaffirmation of its unique path to socialism, while the marketization of the economy continued; and it examines the passing of power to a third generation of the Kim family. The last part of the chapter looks at the Seventh Party Congress in the spring of 2016 when North Korea's future was uncertain and unpredictable. The original revolutionary vision of its founders had failed but the regime continued to appear well entrenched in power; yet it was difficult to see what path it could take to survive in the long run. Looking at North Korea in 2017, a few observations are made but not predictions. For who could have predicted the course of North Korean in 1950, in 1970 or in 1990?

There are difficulties in writing a history of North Korea. No society is more opaque, more closed to foreign scholars. Its archives are inaccessible; travel to and within the country is highly restricted. Even basic statistics that almost any country provides on population and economic indicators are often unavailable. Western intelligence agencies sometimes describe the country as a "black hole." This is discouraging for historians who have with a few exceptions left the study of the country to political and security analysts and to journalists. However, in recent years more information has trickled out through the tales of refugees, the archives of former communist allies, and through the diligent efforts of scholars including those in South Korea and at the North Korean International Documentation Project in Washington D.C. Some journalists such as Barbara Demick and historians such as Andrei Lankov have managed to penetrate public stereotypes of North Korea and provide an understanding of what it is like to live in that society. As a result we can attempt a systematic historical study. This account is mostly based on these sources and above all the published works of those specialists who have carefully examined the evidence available. Many are acknowledged in the text, others in the notes.

Still many details and some major parts of this story are still missing or no doubt will be in need of revision someday. If and when the barriers that prevent outsiders from entering are lifted and the archives are opened many of our assumptions and "facts" we thought we understood may be overturned. Yet the broad outlines are clear enough to provide a basic narrative account of North Korea's history.

Notes

1 This statement needs some qualification. Regional differences in Korea when compared to such geographically comparable societies as Italy or Vietnam were probably less marked but they did exist. Northern Korea had its regional identities although they did not neatly correspond to the boundaries of the present-day state of North Korea. These regional differences are examined in Sun Joo Kim (ed.), *The Northern Region of Korea: History Identity Culture*. Seattle, WC: University of Washington Press, 2010.

1

Historical Roots of the North Korean State

North Korea was created by revolutionaries driven by nationalism, anti-imperialism and the search for the right path to modernity. All three were the products of its encounter with the modern world that began in the late nineteenth century. An intense nationalism, accompanied by a fierce desire to be free of foreign control characterized not just Kim Il Sung and the builders of the North Korean state but many modern Korean leaders. An ancient, ethnically homogeneous society with its distinctive culture, Korea found itself caught up in the world of nineteenth-century imperialism for which it was unprepared. China, Russia and Japan fought for control over the peninsula, with Japan emerging victorious. In 1910 it was annexed by Japan which governed it as a colony for 35 years. Under direct foreign rule for the first time in their history Koreans responded with modern nationalist and anti-imperialist movements that sought to regain their independence, and secure it by creating a strong and powerful nation that could take its place among the leading states of the world. This was the aim of the DPRK's leaders, and differed in these respects little from that of all Korean nationalists including those that ruled the South after 1948.

Early Historical Background

Much of Korea's long history may seem too remote to be of relevance to the story of North Korea but, in fact, this is not so. As is true of their East Asian neighbors Koreans have been historically minded, and

1

their interpretation of the past is central to their modern identity. North Korea's ideology and the way it sees itself are intertwined with its understanding of Korean history.

Korea as a unified state dates back to the seventh century. Three kingdoms – Shilla (or Silla) in the southeastern part of the peninsula, Paekche in the southwest and Koguryŏ in the North – had emerged by the fourth century and competed for supremacy until Shilla emerged victorious in 676. Thereafter, except for a brief period in the early tenth century one state governed the peninsula. The northern border fluctuated somewhat, but has not changed significantly since the early 1400s. When the country was partitioned in 1945 it ended 13 centuries of unity. Few states in the twentieth century were as old or had such stable boundaries. It was also homogeneous to an unusual degree. Whatever varied peoples may have lived on the peninsula, they had long become a single ethnic-linguistic group by the nineteenth century. North Korea today is possibly the world's most ethnically uniform society, and South Korea would be a candidate for the second most. While China had a profound influence on their society, Koreans maintained a distinctive culture with their own dress, styles of houses, folk art and customs, their own unique alphabet developed in the fifteenth century, and their own cultural identity. Until the late nineteenth century there were no significant Korean communities outside Korea so that it was, uncommonly, a land where political, linguistic-ethnic and cultural boundaries were nearly the same. Korean history was also characterized by a high degree of historical continuity. Three dynasties ruled from the 676 to 1910 without radical changes in the basic institutions. In the Shilla period it was ruled by the Kim royal family. In 935 a new dynasty ruled from Kaesong (Kaesŏng) in what is now North Korea renaming the state Koryŏ. After nearly five centuries of rule the Yi dynasty came to power in 1392 with a new name for the state: Chosŏn. The Yi or Chosŏn dynasty, moved the capital to Seoul and remained on the throne until the Japanese annexed Korea in 1910. During 13 centuries of monarchic rule many of the same aristocratic families dominated politics and society century after century. Only the intrusion of foreign imperialism and the Japanese takeover brought a break in history and even then the old aristocratic lineages controlled much of the countryside until the land reforms after 1945.

Korea has been shaped by its relationship with its neighbors. Korea was part of the Chinese tributary system, with the Korean king a vassal of the Chinese emperor. This was sometimes misunderstood by Westerners to mean something short of full independence, but the reality was that Korea was fully autonomous. Its obeisance to its huge neighbor was usually more ceremonial than substantive. Korean nationalists in the early twentieth century felt ashamed at what they regarded as their subservience to China – which in both North and South Korea is referred to as *sadaejuūi*, literally translated as "serve the great-ism"; in modern times it had the connotation of slavishly serving a great power rather than being proudly independent. Before 1876, however, the educated classes, at least, took pride in being part of the great cosmopolitan world centered in China and in their adherence to "the study of the Way," as the Confucian tradition was sometimes called. Indeed, the rigid adherence to Neo-Confucianism that characterized Korea from at least the fifteenth century exceeded that of China, Vietnam or Japan but enabled the ruling class to see their society as the truest bastion of righteousness.

From Hermit Kingdom to Colony

North Korean propaganda portrays Korea as a victim of imperialist aggression. In fact, in South Korea too Korean history, despite long periods of peace, is often depicted as one of repeated foreign invasions: the Khitans from inner Asia in the tenth century, the Mongols in the thirteenth, the Japanese in the late sixteenth and the Manchus in the early seventeenth centuries. To avoid trouble Chosŏn state sought to limit its contact with the outside world. The aggressive, globalizing Euro-centered world of the late nineteenth century, however, did not make opting out of the emerging international economic system possible. After the British forcibly pried China open to Western trade in the Opium War of 1839–1842, and after the Americans "opened" Japan in 1854, some Western attention was drawn to the hermit kingdom. The British unsuccessfully attempted to initiate trade. Meanwhile, French missionaries sneaked into the country, and following the execution of several of them France sent a punitive expedition in 1866.[1]

North Koreans regard the *General Sherman* incident as the beginning of the modern era of imperialist intervention into their country. This obscure affair, little known to Americans, has been made into a major event, with the official version memorized by all school children. In August 1866 a heavily armed American ship, the *General Sherman*, with a crew of Americans, Chinese, Malays and British sailed up the Taedong River to Pyongyang seeking to open up trade. A local official explained that the country was closed to trade with foreigners but the ship ignored the request to leave. After tense negotiations led to an exchange of fire between the crew and locals, the Koreans burned the ship, which was caught on a sandbar, and killed its crew. For a while the Americans did not know what had happened to the ship. The government in Seoul informed the Chinese of the incident and through the Chinese the USA eventually learned of its fate. In 1871 the US Minister to China, Frederick Low, led five ships and 1,200 men under Admiral John Rodgers on a punitive expedition. The Americans attacked the island of Kanghwa and some coastal forts. The Koreans fought to the death, inflicting a few casualties on the Americans. Without authorization to proceed further, and frustrated by the Koreans' refusal to talk, Low and Rodgers withdrew. The government, proud to have driven off the barbarians, both the French in 1866 and the Americans in 1871, erected stone signs that proclaimed "Western barbarian invade or land. If we do not fight we must then appease them. To urge appeasement own to betray the nation."[2]

But Korea's isolation quickly came to an end. In 1876, acting in imitation of the Westerners that had recently forced them to open their ports to trade, the Japanese sent their gunboats to Korea and intimidated the court into opening up the country to commerce and formal diplomatic relations with Tokyo. Within a few years the USA, Britain, France and others had joined the Japanese. Some members of the *yangban* aristocratic elite as well as other educated non-aristocrats were quick to appreciate the need to carry out modern reforms if the kingdom was to survive. But the Koreans never had the leisure to experiment with adaptations of Western institutions and technologies since China, Russia and Japan aggressively competed for influence and intervened in the internal affairs of their country. These powers were able to take advantage of the internal rivalries within the ruling class which failed to form a united front against foreign aggression. Japan, which was the most committed power in the region and determined to gain control of what they considered to be a strategically important peninsula, first defeated China in the Sino-Japanese War 1894–1895 and then triumphed over Russia in the Russo-Japanese War 1904–1905 to become the master of Korea. In 1905 Korea became a Japanese protectorate with the approval of Britain and the USA; five years later it became a colony. Koreans reacted to these events in varied ways. Some accepted the reality of Japanese dominance and cooperated with their new rulers, others resisted. The latter waged a guerilla war against the Japanese from 1907 to 1911. About 15,000 of these poorly armed, disparate groups called *ŭibyŏng* (righteous armies) lost their lives before the resistance was stamped out. A few Koreans went into exile, fleeing to Shanghai, Hawaii and elsewhere, or crossed the border into Manchuria or Siberia. Most simply went on with their lives and accommodated themselves to the new order.

These years between 1876 and 1910 were important because they marked Korea's entry into the modern world and exposed Koreans to new ideas about their place in it. By 1910 Koreans studying in Japan, and a few in Europe and America encountered a bewildering array of new ways of thinking about society and government. Ideas of modern science, progress, constitutionalism, state sovereignty, popular sovereignty, human rights, international law and equality entered the discourse of the educated most often through Japanese translations. Of course, there is nothing special about this; Koreans were only participating in the global diffusion and evolution of these new concepts. What was unusual was that, unlike many Asian, African, Middle Eastern, Latin American and other peoples, Koreans, owing to their effective isolation until fairly recently in world history, were exposed to these ideas more suddenly. There was no small group of "Dutch Learning" scholars as there had been in Japan, or Western-exposed intellectuals such as in early nineteenth-century Bengal or Istanbul. Yet the younger generation of educated Koreans eagerly embraced these new ideas in what amounted to an intellectual revolution.

Korea's Unusual and Traumatic Colonial Experience

North Korean society, to a considerable extent, is rooted in the colonial experience. The 35-year colonial regime, 1910 to 1945, touched the lives of almost every Korean, often in disturbing and even traumatizing ways. It was during this period that modern nationalist, anti-imperialist movements began and that competing visions of modernity became defined. It would be hard to exaggerate just how profound that experience was in shaping the character of North Korea. Many of its defining features – the militarization of its society, its coercive methods to marshal the population for state goals, its xenophobia, the cult of the ruling family and its intense, fierce nationalism – were shaped by the peculiar features of Japanese rule.

In many ways Korea was a typical colony. The Japanese had modeled much of their colonial administration on that of the major European powers. As in the case of most Western imperialists the Japanese saw themselves as agents of modernization and progress. They created a modern infrastructure with railroads, schools and port facilities; brought about improvements in agriculture; and established certain industries. But economic development was designed to produce raw materials and products needed by the mother country, which directed and controlled its development. Yet Korea's colonial experience was unusual in that Korea was neither a contiguous appendage to a land empire nor ruled by a distant overseas power. Only 115 miles from Japan's shores, Korea had a long history of interaction with its colonizer, including the sixteenth-century invasions and attempted conquest. It was a familiar, often menacing neighbor. Japan shared a common East Asian cultural heritage with Korean Confucian values that included an emphasis on rank, hierarchy, authority and respect for education. This it married to Western concepts of science, industry, technology and bureaucratic efficiency.

Japan's colonial rule of Korea was also unusual in its intensive nature, to the degree it promoted industrialization and to the massive wartime mobilization of the population during World War II. Most colonies were ruled through local indigenous officials or elites. Japan, however, ruled Korea directly. In the late 1930s nearly a quarter of a million Japanese served in Korea as bureaucrats, police and garrison soldiers and as employees of state banks, companies and schools – a contingent ten times that of the French personnel who were sent to administer Vietnam, a country similar in size and population; and equal in number to that of the British in India, which had twenty times the population. The vast bureaucracy and police system penetrated throughout Korean society, including the Japanese village school teacher and the Japanese village policemen who carried out regular home inspections to see to it that health and other regulations were being carried out. After 1931 colonial Korea was also far more industrialized than most colonies. In particular, the northern part of the country, with its abundant mineral resources, hydroelectric potential and proximity to the expanding Japanese empire in China, was rapidly developed. Seeing Korea as an important base for the expansion into China, an elaborate railroad system was built as well as other infrastructure. Thus by 1945 Japan had set much of the foundations for an industrial society in Korea, most of which was concentrated in what became the DPRK.

North Korea was profoundly influenced by Japan's wartime mobilization and indoctrination of the Korean people. World War II began in Asia with the Japanese invasion of China in 1937. From 1938, when Tokyo came to realize that establishing supremacy over China would be a long and difficult undertaking, wartime Japan quickly evolved into a totalitarian society based on the vague, mystical and racial-nationalist ideology of *kokutai* (national essence) – an ideology in many ways similar to the one that evolved in North Korea. The cult of the emperor had been promoted by the state since 1868 and was central to the creation and intensification of a modern Japanese nationalism. By 1940 political parties were abolished and the entire nation was mobilized in various campaigns to support the war effort. Korea fully participated in this wartime ultranationalism and totalitarian mobilization. From 1938 almost all Koreans were organized into various syndicates in support of the emperor and the imperialist expansion into China. Koreans were required to register at Shinto shrines and to participate in ceremonies honoring the emperor. The school day for all children began with the portrait of the emperor being taken out of its sacred case, the imperial instructions being read to students, and, having lined up into a military-style formation, all teachers and students bowing in the direction of the imperial palace in Tokyo.

This wartime mobilization was accompanied by a change in policy to coercive assimilation. In 1940 Koreans were required to adopt Japanese names, Korean-language newspapers were closed and Japanese became the language of instruction in all schools. Few colonial policies left such bitterness. Meanwhile, women, laborers, farmers, students and those belonging to organizations with compulsory membership were mobilized to collect scrap, provide voluntary labor and attend ceremonies such as Rising Asia Day. No Korean could escape the pressure to participate in these activities. These mass mobilization campaigns set a pattern that has continued to be a part of North Korean life to the present day. A massive relocation occurred as people moved from the agricultural south to the newly industrializing north of the country or to Manchuria, Japan or other parts of the expanding empire. Most of this migration was voluntary, but not all, as labor when needed was simply conscripted. The scale of this mass mobilization and movement of labor was huge. By 1945 one-third of the industrial labor force in Japan was Korean.

Thus World War II shook up Korean society, disturbing long-held routines, uprooting millions and giving Koreans their first experience of living in a regimented, centrally controlled society that did not allow for much of a private life. With its mystical, racial-nationalist ideology, its cult of leadership and its mass mobilization of society for collective projects, wartime colonial rule foreshadowed the North Korean regime. Not all of the salient characteristics of North Korea reflect the peculiarities of its colonial experience, and it would be an overstatement to claim that the totalitarian state was made in Japan. But the impact of colonial rule was profound.

Nationalism and Anti-imperialism

No other feature of North Korea is more defining, more central to its ideology or so essential to understanding its aspirations and its relationship with the outside world than its hyper-nationalism and its view of itself as engaged in an anti-imperialist struggle.

Modern Korean nationalism can be traced to the late nineteenth century. Some Korean intellectuals began to absorb the ideas of popular sovereignty, the concept of a sovereign state operating within an international state system, and began seeing their own society as a nation. This new emerging ethnic-linguistic nationalism, symbolized by the promotion among the educated of the use of the Korean alphabet and the recording of national histories, gradually fused with ethnic and local resentments at Japanese rule to create a popular national movement. A turning point in the birth of Korean nationalism was what the Koreans call the "March First Movement" in 1919. This was part of a wave of excitement and anti-colonial activity that spread across the world from Egypt to China, sparked by the end of World War I, the ensuing Versailles Peace Conference and President Wilson's principle of "national self-determination" set forth in his Fourteen Points. While Wilson's formulation was intended to apply only to Europeans, like so many non-Western colonial subjects, Koreans seized upon this principle of self-determination to call for their own independent nation. When a small group met in Seoul to read a symbolic "Declaration of Independence," calling for the end of Japanese rule, demonstrations broke out across the country. It has been estimated that 500,000 to 1 million people participated in the rallies which continued throughout the spring. Hundreds were killed by Japanese police.[3]

Embarrassed by the international attention this protest movement received and reflecting a more liberal atmosphere in Japan, Tokyo allowed the Koreans to establish Korean-language newspapers and periodicals and permitted some freedoms in discussing political and social topics. The result was a burst of creative energy among artists and intellectuals who laid the foundations for modern literary and artistic expressions, but it also brought about a division among Korean nationalists that would profoundly shape Korean history: between the moderate, Western-looking cultural nationalists and the more radical nationalists who tended to look toward the Soviet Union and communist movements abroad for inspiration.

By the 1920s, many Korean intellectuals looked to the West as a model for civilized behavior, much as the Korean intellectuals in the past had looked to China. Ironically, most of these were educated in Japan, where they read Japanese translations of Western works and in some cases where they studied Western languages, usually English or German. They were highly critical of Korea's cultural backwardness, which they saw as responsible for the fall of their country to the Japanese. Many advocated for a moderate agenda, working within the limitations of the colonial framework. The focus of these moderate nationalists, whom historian Michael Robinson calls "cultural nationalists," was on culture, not politics.[4] This was partly based on pragmatism, since any call for independence would result in arrest and harsh repression, and therefore be ineffective. But it was also based on a sincere conviction that Korea must develop spiritually and culturally before it could be ready for independence. It was their duty to work on uplifting society first. Cultural nationalists advocated a gradual approach to development, seeing education as key. They propagated their ideas through the newspapers, a host of new magazines and through various youth, women's, educational and cultural associations.

This moderate, elitist approach to creating a modern nation did not appeal to all Koreans. A number of young intellectuals, many also educated in Japan, came under the influence of socialism, especially in its Marxist interpretation. They looked to the common people as embodying the essence of the nation and to their own role as leaders of the people. They were impatient with the gradualism of the moderate nationalists and rejected the idea of cooperating with the colonial regime. Furthermore, they were suspicious of both the old landowning and the newly emerging Korean entrepreneurial classes, and saw the overthrow of both the colonial regime and the indigenous elite as their aim. These more radical Korean nationalists saw their role less as cultural reformers bringing the masses up to modern standards of civilization than as part of the vanguard of the "people." Most of them, after the 1917 Bolshevik Revolution, became associated with the fledgling communist movement. As a result, the nationalist movement in the 1920s was divided between moderate "cultural nationalists" and radical, Marxist-leaning groups. The ideological foundations of North and South Korea can in part be traced to this split.

This split between cultural and radical nationalists was reflected in the exile community. All the exile organizations suffered from a great weakness. Unlike many foreign-based anti-imperialist national groups elsewhere there was no logical center, such as London or Paris often served for Africans, Middle Easterners and Southeast Asians. Shanghai remained an important center of anti-Japanese activity and the home for the Korean Provisional Government established in 1919 and initially headed by Yi Sŭng-man, better known to Americans as Syngman Rhee. But only a small fraction of the exiles were based there and the Korean Provisional Government was weak and ineffective. Other exiles were based in Manchuria, Tokyo, Hawaii, mainland USA and elsewhere. Overall, exiled groups played only a marginal role in the nationalist movement before 1945 but became extremely important when Japanese rule ended.

The Communist Movement(s) in Korea

North Korea today has reinterpreted history so that there is a linear progression from the anti-imperialist movements that emerged in the late nineteenth century to the anti-Japanese struggle and the single line of socialism formulated and fostered by Kim Il Sung. In reality, however, the Korean communist movement had multiple origins. It was characterized by several features. First, from its birth it was a geographically fragmented and varied movement lacking a single leader or base of operation. It fact, it is better to use the plural – movements. Second, except for a handful of cadres trained in the Soviet Union and a few intellectuals who seriously studied Marx, most Korean communists did not have a very sophisticated understanding of Marxism-Leninism. And third, the Korean communist movements were above all, nationalist, anti-imperialist movements seeking a means to achieve a Korea free of foreign control.

While few Koreans understood the finer points of Marxism-Leninism they took what they needed: the essence of their country was the Korean people or "masses" (Korean *minjung*); and the Korean people had been victimized by a parasitic feudal class of *yangban* aristocrats that kept the country in a backward state and who now collaborated with the Japanese. The struggle for the liberation of both the people and the nation was thus the same struggle; and it was a struggle not only against a foreign occupier but against both the landholding class and its feudal culture and values associated with Confucianism, and against the emerging capitalist class who cooperated with the Japanese. The masses, however, not being educated, needed leadership from dedicated revolutionaries who could organize them for the inevitably victorious struggle against the Japanese and their collaborators. With history on their side, they would establish a new progressive, rich and strong, independent Korea. This was the thinking that inspired those Koreans who became communists including Kim Il Sung and the other future leaders of North Korea.

The first communist organizations appeared in Siberia which was home to several hundred thousand Koreans who had emigrated there after 1860. Yet by and large, this population of Soviet-Koreans were not directly involved in the Korean nationalist movements. They had their own tragic history when, in the late 1930s, Stalin, fearing the loyalty of so many Koreans living near the border of the expanding Japanese empire, relocated the entire population to Central Asia. It is estimated that one-third of all Soviet-Koreans may have perished owing to this clumsy and ruthless resettlement. This was accompanied by purges of Soviet-Koreans in the Bolshevik Party and in the military. As a result, by 1945, the Soviet-Koreans were isolated from Korea, and Moscow lost a potential cadre of Korean-speaking party and military personnel that could have assisted them in their postwar occupation of northern Korea. Instead the Soviets had to find Korean speakers among the scattered surviving Soviet-Koreans to supply them with translators and to aid in the occupation and construction of the socialist regime. These "Soviet-Koreans" would form one of the major groups among the North Korean leadership during the first decade after World War II.

Another group of communists that would prove important in the early history of North Korea was the "domestic communists" who had their origins in the communist movement within Korea. This movement began when Korean students studying in Japan became familiar with Marxism and brought communist ideas back with them. In its early years this domestic communism remained largely confined to small circles of students and intellectuals in Seoul. On April 17, 1925, two leftist organizations – the Tuesday Society and the North Wind Society – comprising mostly young intellectuals merged to form the Korean Communist Party (Chosŏn Kongsandang).[5] Later that year the colonial authorities arrested most of the small band of young people. A second Korean Communist Party was organized in 1926 but, as before, its leaders were soon arrested. When a third party was organized in December 1926 most of its members too were arrested in January 1928. Still another, fourth attempt to create a party in February 1928 led to another wave of arrests in August.[6] Dismayed by these repeated failures in December 1928 the Communist International (Comintern) issued what became known as the December Theses, analyzing the reasons for the Korean communists' failures. The Korean Communists were criticized for consisting of only intellectuals and students, for letting factionalism weaken them, for their lack of a firm grasp of Marxist-Leninist principles and for their failure to attract industrial workers and poor peasants.

The constant police surveillance and efficient repression made it difficult to organize a major and successful communist movement within Korea. However, a number of communists remained active, some trained in the Soviet Union and associated with the Comintern. Several of these attempted to organize industrial workers and peasants. One example was the Moscow-trained O Ki-sŏp, who was active in the northeastern province of Hamgyŏng in the 1930s, a center of labor and peasant activism. People like O spread egalitarian ideals, preparing the way for the North Korean communist regime, but they were mostly marginalized or purged shortly after liberation. There were Red Peasant Unions (*chosaek nongmin chohap*) in the 1930s, mainly in northern Korea, that managed to survive Japanese suppression.[7] They formed as a response to the unrest in the countryside where the conditions of most peasants had worsened under Japanese colonial rule. Landownership declined as local landlords took advantage of legal reforms and the commercialization of agriculture to consolidate and expand their holdings at the expense of impoverished farmers who went from owner-cultivators to landless or land-poor tenants. The most active center of the domestic communist movement remained in Seoul where most of the intellectual community was concentrated.

When arrested the Japanese would place enormous pressure on them to renounce communism. Many activists under duress while imprisoned did so, were released and left the movement. Others perished in prisons. But some survived, including Pak Hŏn-yŏng (1900–1955) who served as the leader of the underground Communist Party in Korea during World War II, apparently undetected by the colonial authorities. A founding member of the first Communist Party in 1925, Pak was arrested by the

Japanese and then released after faking mental illness. He was later rearrested, served six years and released in 1939. Under the guise of an itinerant bricklayer he traveled around the country in an effort to re-establish a national party.[8] But in 1945 he and other domestic Korean communists lacked an effective organization, were to a great extent cut off from contact with Korean communists in exile, and had limited contacts with Moscow and the international communist movement.

A third important group were the "Yanan communists." With Japanese repression too severe in Korea and the Soviets too suspicious of the loyalty of their Korean community, China became the most important base for the Communist movement. Many Korean activists traveled to China where Shanghai became the center for exiled patriots. Nationalists of all hues – rightists, anarchists, socialists – gathered there, many associated with the Korean Provisional Government, the then-exiled government established in 1919. Many of these Koreans started working with the Chinese Communist Party not long after it was founded in 1921. Among them were Kim Chŏng, better known by his revolutionary name Mu Chŏng, who made the 1934–1935 Long March with Mao and the other Chinese communists to their new base at Yanan. He was joined by Kim Tu-bong who became one of the leaders of these "Yanan Koreans" as they are often called.[9] Kim was born in a poor fishing village, taught in middle school and, following his participation in anti-Japanese activities, fled to Shanghai in 1919. He became a distinguished linguist and was one of the many exiled intellectuals. Another "Yanan Korean" was Ch'oe Ch'ang-ik, also of humble background, who spent six years in prison for anti-Japanese activities before fleeing to China in 1936. When war broke out between China and Japan in 1937 Koreans joined the anti-Japanese struggle, with some fighting alongside the Guomindang and hundreds of others joining the fight alongside the Chinese Communists. In 1942 Yanan Koreans formed the Korean Independence League headed by Kim Tu-bong and Ch'oe Ch'ang-ik. A military wing, the Korean Voluntary Army, was headed by Mu Chŏng, with Pak Il-u, another prominent leader, as his deputy. It fought in battles against the Japanese in northern China and engaged in anti-Japanese propaganda work. Eventually Koreans working for and fighting alongside the Chinese Communist Party numbered in the thousands.[10] Ch'oe Ch'ang-ik, Kim Tu-bong,

Pak Il-u and many other Yanan communists would play an important role in the early years of the North Korean state.

The group of communists that would dominate and eventually almost completely shape North Korea were the Manchurian guerillas who were active in the mountains near the Korean border. The Manchurian border region with Korea was a frontier-like area and a hotbed of guerilla activities in the 1920s and 1930s. There were 400,000 Korean in Manchuria in 1920 and 900,000 by 1931. About two-thirds of them lived in the Jiandao (Kando) region of Manchuria bordering northeast Korea.[11] Most who settled in the region came from the adjacent northern provinces of Korea to escape poverty and seek opportunities in this climatically harsh but less populated region. Some were fleeing Japanese rule for political reasons. Most worked as farmers. When the Japanese took over Manchuria in 1931–1932 the Korean residents found themselves once again within the boundaries of an expanding Japanese empire. In the 1930s many of these Korean settlers fought in guerilla groups against the Japanese, the most famous being Kim Il Sung. It was a rough and sometimes lawless area with widespread banditry, but with its rugged terrain it was ideal for guerillas to operate in.

The Young Kim Il Sung

Perhaps no one has so shaped the society he ruled as Kim Il Sung did. In modern world history a few comparisons come to mind: Ataturk the founder of modern Turkey or perhaps Mao Zedong. But Ataturk could not erase Islam from its hold over the Turkish people and much of Mao's legacy was rejected or ignored almost immediately after his death. Neither so entirely remolded their society or so successfully arranged for their succession. The story of North Korea is to an unparalleled extent bound up with that of its founder. Who was Kim Il Sung? His official biographies, which in Orwellian fashion are periodically rewritten, are so far removed from historical reality that it is easy to dismiss them. Misinformation, sometimes spread in the past by South Korean intelligence, also complicates our understanding of his early career. Still, by working with Japanese police records and some Soviet documents, and by carefully analyzing published accounts in North Korea, scholars have been able to piece together a fair amount of detail about his early background.

Kim Il Sung was born Kim Sŏng-ju on April 15, 1912, the day the *Titanic* sank, in the village of Mangyŏngdae outside of Pyongyang. Around 1935 he adopted the name Kim Il Sung which means "sun-star." He was the eldest of three sons. His father, Kim Hyŏng-jik (1894–1926), was married to Kang Pan-sŏk (1892–1932). As with many Koreans he traced his family back many generations – in his case to twelve generations and to Chŏlla Pukto in the rich rice-growing region of the southwest. From there they emigrated to the north. Kim Il Sung's background was a favorable one for producing an active nationalist since his family was Christian and exposed to modern ideas, and already active in the nationalist movement. His father attended Sungshil School established by American missionaries in Pyongyang. He did not appear to have worked as a farmer but taught elementary school. Kim Il Sung's mother, Kang Pan-sŏk, was from a Christian family; her father, Kang Ton-uk, was a Presbyterian elder.[12] Kang Pan-sŏk's family was from the nearby village of Ch'ilgol. Several members of her clan later rose to prominent if not top-tier positions in North Korea where they were known as the Ch'ilgol faction.[13]

The young Kim grew up just outside Pyongyang, a city that was undergoing rapid modernization. It was a provincial city since everything – political, economic, cultural and intellectual life – was centered in Seoul. It was nonetheless one of the larger and more prosperous and intellectually active cities in Korea. It was a major center for Christianity, and sometimes called the "Jerusalem of the East" owing to the large Protestant community and the large number of Christian mission schools. Official biographies fail to mention Kim Il Sung's Christian background while highlighting and inflating his nationalist activities.[14] But both were linked since Christians were disproportionately represented in nationalist organizations. P'yŏng'an province, where the city was located, was also the center of the indigenous Ch'ŏndogyo religious movement which had many adherents among the peasantry. In 1923 the religious sect formed the Young Friends' Party (Ch'ŏng'udang) as its political wing which advocated for agricultural reform.[15] Its members, like Christians, were also active in nationalist movements.

Later biographers created a long revolutionary pedigree for Kim Il Sung. His great-grandfather, Kim Ŭng-u, moved to Mangyŏngdae and according to the official histories was a leading participant in the fight against the *General Sherman*. Thus, he was present and a key player in the birth of the modern anti-imperialist movement. Whether or not the role of Kim's great-grandfather in this incident has any basis in fact, his family does seem to have been politically active. According to official histories his father, Kim Hyŏng-jik, while attending Sungsil Academy, became filled with patriotic outrage when the Americans began using students as slave laborers and led a student strike against them.[16] Mostly likely this is a later fabrication to reinforce the family tradition of anti-American imperialism. More credibly he is said to have taken part in the creation of an organization called the Korean National Association. In 1917 he was arrested by the Japanese and released the following year. Kim Il Sung later described visiting his father in prison as a major turning point in his life when he became aware of the evils of Japanese imperialism.[17] One of Kim Hyŏng-jik's two brothers was arrested in South Hamgyŏng after a skirmish with police. He was interned in Seoul where he died while still imprisoned in 1936.[18]

The young Kim Il Sung did not spend much of his early life in Korea. In fact, he spent almost his entire formative years from seven until he was thirty-three outside of Korea. At the age of seven his family moved to Manchuria, apparently after his father's release by the Japanese authorities. They joined thousands of other Koreans, mostly from the north who crossed into Manchuria, a frontier area that only opened to massive Chinese settlement after 1860. Despite the harsh winters Manchuria had ample fertile land, but most Koreans settled in the hilly or mountainous areas adjacent to Korea. Some were escaping Japanese rule, others were simply escaping poverty. His father worked in Manchuria as a Chinese herbal medicine doctor. There Kim Il Sung attended Hwasŏng Middle School but then transferred to the Chinese Yuwen Middle School. Again it is interesting to note that most of his secondary education was in a Chinese not a Korean school, and, furthermore, that he was fluent in the language and is even said to have been fond of reading classic Chinese novels in later years.[19] It is not certain why he went to a Chinese rather than Korean school, but his Chinese education is left out of official biographies.

As a youth Kim Il Sung returned to Korea only once from 1923 to 1924. Supposedly at his father's suggestion he walked several hundred miles to learn about the oppression in Korea. More likely, his father sent him there to study in Pyongyang at a school where Kang Ton-uk, his mother's father, was the vice principal. Later this return to Korea at the age of eleven was celebrated in North Korea as the "One Thousand *Ri* Journey for Learning" (*Paeum ŭi ch'ŏlli kil*). The following year he returned to Manchuria in what North Koreans call the "One Thousand *Ri* Journey for Liberation" (*Kwangbok ŭi ch'ŏlli kil*).[20] At this point, North Koreans are taught, the young Kim "knew the reality of his homeland, marched across the snowy mountains, [and] on [his] way back across the Amok River made a resolve to liberate his county at any cost."[21] Now fully aware of the situation in his homeland, he began his lifelong quest to liberate it from the Japanese and build a great, independent nation.

Kim Il Sung left middle school in 1927 just before completing the eighth grade. His father died the year before but it is not clear why he left before graduating. The school was in Jilin, a major provincial city and a center of political activism. And he was politically active. North Koreans learn that he formed the "Down-With-Imperialism League" in 1926, an organization that prepared the way for the emergence of the communist movement in Korea. It is also when he formulated the ideological foundations of the North Korean revolution – a remarkable achievement for a 14-year-old. The official biographers have him busy educating the peasants and teaching *Das Kapital* to fourth graders.[22] These ludicrous claims aside, Kim Il Sung was, like so many youths in Jilin at that time, involved in political movements at an early age. In May 1929 the 17-year-old Kim Il Sung joined a small short-lived student group organized by members of the South Manchurian Communist Youth Organization. They were quickly arrested and Kim Il Sung spend a few months in jail. Later North Korean sources claimed he organized this group but since he was one of the youngest and least-educated members this was unlikely.[23] Sometime in the early 1930s he joined the Chinese communist-led anti-Japanese guerillas, possibly around 1932 about the time his mother died. From then on his life became inseparable from that of the Manchurian guerillas.

The Manchurian Guerillas

In North Korea the experience of Kim Il Sung and his fellow Manchu-rian guerillas in their conflict with the Japanese has provided the main background for plays, movies, songs, operas, children stories and every other conceivable form of entertainment. It provides examples and met-aphors for all forms of economic, political and social activity. People are constantly being taught to learn from the examples of their great leader and his heroic comrades. Perhaps, more importantly, it has shaped the way the country's leadership interprets and understands the world. Yet, as large as it looms in North Korea and for all its importance in under-standing that state's history, the Manchurian partisan campaign was a rather small-scale one. The Korean guerillas were tiny in number and the area of their activity was largely confined to remote peripheral areas in the mountainous countryside just north of the Korean border. Despite their aim of liberating Korea they rarely penetrated the well-protected border of the colony. Overall, the guerilla attacks on the Japanese imperialists were little more than a nuisance.

Kim Il Sung began his days as a guerilla fighter in an area near the border town of Antu with the National Salvation Army. North Korean official accounts have Kim establishing the Korean People's Revolution-ary Army on April 25, 1932, a date still celebrated. Yet there is no record of such an organization, which appears to be a later fabrication to dis-guise the fact that he fought under the Chinese Communists. Only in 1992, shortly before his death, did Kim admit he was a member of the Chinese Communist Party.[24] In fact, there was no Korean communist guerilla organization in Manchuria. Following Comintern instructions that there should be one communist party for each country, the Korean communists came under the authority of the Chinese Communist Party. Koreans fighters became absorbed into the Northeast Anti-Japanese United Army (NEAJUA), an offshoot of the Northeast People's Revolu-tionary Army that had been founded by the Chinese partisan Yang Jingyu in September 1933. It was based primarily in southern Manchuria. The NEAJUA was divided into three "Route Armies" which were subdivided into small units or corps, confusingly also sometimes labeled "armies." Yang Jingyu served as commander-in-chief of the First Route Army. Its second corps was consisted mainly of Koreans included the Third Division commanded by Kim Il Sung. Other prominent commanders in the NEUAJA included Ch'oe Hyŏn, Ch'oe Yong-gŏn and Kim Ch'aek who all later held prominent positions in the DPRK.[25] Although working under the Chinese Communist Party leadership, ethnic Koreans made up the majority of fighters in the border area of Jilin Province, where Kim Il Sung was active.[26]

The label "armies" was rather grandiose for what were modest-sized units rarely numbering more than several hundred fighters. Although most of the Chinese Communist Party guerilla fighters in eastern Manchuria were ethnic Koreans they served under the Chinese and Chinese was the operational language.[27] This led to tensions between the two ethnic groups which were aggravated by Chinese fears, often well founded, that many of the Koreans were agents working for the Japanese. In 1934 the Chinese Communist Party carried out a massive purge arresting and executing hundreds of Korean communists. Kim Il Sung was among those arrested but was released after a short time. The purge and its ethnically directed target provided Kim with an early example of how Koreans and he personally could be victims of comrades from a major communist power.[28]

With the Japanese firmly in control of major cities and towns, the guerilla movement was largely rural, consisting of small scattered groups supporting themselves by plundering wealthier farmers and "taxing" peasant villages. The Manchurian partisans established some self-governing bases. These were very small but are historically significant because they provided Kim Il Sung and his guerilla comrades with their earliest experiences of governance. About 20,000 people lived under these People's Revolutionary Governments. Later, historians gave credit to Kim for having organized them but they were actually organized by the Chinese communists.[29] The emphasis was on land redistribution. Land was expropriated from landlords and "Japanese puppets" and redistributed to impoverished peasants, including women. Leftover land belonged to the revolutionary government. As historian Charles Armstrong points out the guerillas in Manchuria often resorted to forcing young Koreans into serving in the resistance armies, levied unwelcome taxes on local peasants and raised money by kidnapping wealthy farmers for ransom.[30] These were hardly measures to win popular support. In the late 1930s the Japanese, by a variety of methods, were able to destroy these revolutionary bases. And in a final effort they then launched a successful new campaign to wipe out guerilla resistance during 1939 and 1940, killing Yang Jingyu and most of the guerilla leaders. During 1940–1941 the surviving Manchurians guerillas withdrew to the Soviet Union.

Kim Il Sung was one of these surviving guerillas. So wildly exaggerated are his exploits that many Western and South Korean critics have dismissed his anti-Japanese activities altogether. Yet his record is impressive if on a modest scale. He must have been an able young commander, for at the age of 24 he was in charge of a division of the NEAJUA, a unit of perhaps 200–300 men.[31] While he was only one of many guerilla leaders, and probably never commanded more men than that, he did secure notoriety with his raid on the Korean town of Poch'ŏnbo (known as Pojŏn prior to 1945) on June 4, 1937. This amounted to no more than killing seven Japanese policemen, destroying the police post and other Japanese buildings, and then occupying the town for several hours. Kim Il Sung gave a speech, handed out some leaflets and left. According to Japanese police reports only about 80 guerillas were involved. Although it was a rather minor affair it was one of the few successful raids across the heavily patrolled border at that time and was reported in the Japanese and Korean press.[32] Even before the incident the Japanese-controlled press in Korea had reported on Kim Il Sung's "banditry" but it was the "battle" of Poch'ŏnbo that received the most publicity and laid the foundations for his later reputation. North Koreans would later celebrate this as a great turning point in the anti-Japanese struggle. According to an official account, "the significance was not in the fact that we killed a few Japanese but in the fact that the Poch'ŏnbo battle threw revolutionary rays of hope inspiring confidence to the Korean people that they were alive and could beat Japanese imperialism if they fought against it."[33] In reality it was far less significant. Still it was alarming enough to the Japanese that they created a special unit to try to hunt Kim down. For 110 days in the winter of 1937–1938 he fled from his pursuers with his little band, an incident later heralded as the "Arduous March" (*konan ŭi haenggun*).[34] Interestingly the Japanese unit hunting Kim included several Koreans who were to hold important positions in the South Korean military during the Korean War including Paek Sŏn-yŏp the army chief of staff.[35]

Assisting Kim when he was in Manchuria were socialist activists from northern Korea who crossed over to the Kapsan region where Kim's group was active and formed the Kapsan Operations Committee (*Kapsan kongjak wiwŏnhoe*) to coordinate anti-Japanese activities. The Kapsan Operations Committee was rather short-lived, destroyed by Japanese counterinsurgency forces in 1938. For a while its veterans, known as the Kapsan group, held many high-ranking posts in North Korea, although they never enjoyed quite the prestige or power of the actual guerilla fighters.[36] Kim Il Sung continued to fight on and led an attack on Musan, another border town, in May 1939 that was also well publicized. When Japanese forces carried out their determined and effective campaign in 1939–1940 to rid Manchuria of guerilla activities his was one of the last partisan bands to retreat to Siberia.[37] There he sat out World War II. In a report written in Chinese in 1942 Kim Il Sung analyzed the failures of the guerilla movement. They had failed to work with other anti-Japanese groups, had attacked the enemy too soon before building up their forces and their numbers had been too few to be a match for the Japanese.[38] It was a realistic appraisal by a young but experienced fighter.

Official biographies have Kim Il Sung heroically directing the anti-Japanese struggle from his mountain retreats in northern Korea. In fact, from 1940 to 1945 he was based outside the Siberian city of Khabarovsk. In the summer of 1942 the Soviets formed a special unit: the 88th Special Reconnaissance Brigade of the Soviet 25th Army made up of Chinese and Korean ex-Manchurian guerilla fighters. It was commanded by a prominent Chinese guerilla leader, Zhou Baozhong, and had between 1,000 and 1,700 men including 200 to 300 Soviets attached. About 140 to 180 Koreans served in a battalion under the command of Kim Il Sung, most of whom had previously served with him in the 1930s.[39] The brigade was to carry out intelligence and sabotage work and some members did so, but Kim Il Sung himself does not appear to have been involved in any such activities. Instead these years seems to have been uneventful, although it is not entirely clear how he spent his time other than that he became a father. His first wife, Kim Hyo-sun, was captured by the Japanese in 1940. He then married a fellow partisan, Kim Chŏng-suk. The daughter of a farmer, her mother and brother were killed by the Japanese and she joined the guerillas at the age of 16. Kim also lost a brother in the 1930s; Kim Ch'ŏl-ju, one of his two younger brothers, was killed while fighting the Japanese.[40] While in Siberia Kim Chŏng-suk gave birth to their son, Kim Jong Il (Kim Chŏng-il).[41] North Koreans are taught that Kim Jong Il was born at his father's secret guerilla headquarters on Paektu Mountain in northern Korea, but this too was a later fabrication. After her death in the late 1940s Kim Chŏng-suk, as the mother of Kim Jong Il, became part of the Kim family pantheon and an object of national veneration.

While only a minor figure in the independence movement whose guerilla exploits were later enormously inflated, Kim Il Sung was not a totally obscure figure. Many Koreans, as a result of newspaper accounts, had heard of him. To say he was famous would be overstating it, but nonetheless, he was far from an unknown figure when he returned to a Soviet-occupied northern Korea in 1945. Eventually almost the entire leadership of North Korea was drawn from these survivors of the Manchurian guerilla campaign. Many of the Koreans in the 88th Special Reconnaissance Brigade would emerge with prominent positions in the North Korean party and government. It is a remarkable and extremely important fact about North Korea that a handful of poorly educated, rural-based resistance fighters, living just beyond the borders of their homeland, most of whom had never been to a Korean city, came to entirely dominate their country. Their military exploits, though extremely modest in scale, grew into a legendary, heroic struggle, the basis for the legitimacy of the regime and the inspiration and guide for almost every endeavor it undertook.

When World War II came to a sudden end with the surrender of Japan on August 15, 1945, the Korean communist movement consisted of several thousand personnel fighting and serving with Mao Zedong in the interior of China, the remnants of the Manchurian-based guerillas now mostly living in the Soviet Far East, some serving in the Red Army, and a barely surviving underground movement within Korea. There were also a number of ex-Communist Party members and communist-leaning leftists in Korea who were in jail or no longer active; in fact, many were ostensibly supporting the Japanese war effort. A few Comintern members were in the Soviet Union. These groups had little contact with each other or in many cases may not have been aware of each other's existence. There was no coordinated communist movement and no obvious leadership. In this they resembled the other Korean nationalist groups: small isolated exiled groups in China and the USA, and domestic nationalists most of whom had been pressured to serve the Japanese and who also lacked any effective organization or widely recognized leadership. Thus, with the collapse of imperial Japan, Korea was a political vacuum.

Notes

1   Most of this section and the following two sections are based on the author's *A Concise History of Korea: From Antiquity to the Present*. Lanham, MD: Rowman & Littlefield, 2016.

2   Ki-baik Lee, *A New History of Korea*, translated by Edward W. Wagner with Edward J. Shultz. Cambridge, MA: Harvard University Press, 1984, p. 266.

3   Frank Baldwin, "Participatory Anti-Imperialism: The 1919 Independence Movement," *Journal of Korean Studies* 1, no. 1 (1979): 123–162.

4   Michael Robinson, *Cultural Nationalism in Colonial Korea, 1920–25*. Seattle, WA: University of Washington Press, 1988.

5   Chong-sik Lee, *The Korean Workers' Party: A Short History*. Stanford, CA: Stanford University, Hoover Institution Press, 1978, pp. 19–20.

6   Lee, pp. 20–29.

7   Gi-wook Shin, *Peasant Protest and Social change in Colonial Korea*. Seattle, WA: University of Washington, Press, 2014, pp. 75–91.

8   Dae-Sook Suh, *Kim Il Sung: the North Korean Leader*. New York: Columbia University Press, 1988, p. 127.

9   Lee, pp. 61–62.

10 Koon Woo Nam, *The North Korean Communist Leadership, 1945–1965: A Study of Factionalism and Political Consolidation*. Tuscaloosa, AL: University of Alabama Press, 1974, p. 45; Shen, Zhihua and Danhui Li, *After Leaning to Once Side: China and Its Allies in the Cold War*. Stanford, CA: Stanford University Press, 2011, pp. 52–53.

11 Charles K. Armstrong, *The North Korean Revolution, 1945–1950*. Ithaca, NY: Cornell University Press, 2003, p. 18.

12 Lim Jae-Cheon, *Kim Jong Il's Leadership of North Korea*. London: Routledge, 2009, p. 14.
13 Kim Hakjoon, *Dynasty: The Hereditary Succession Politics of North Korea*. Stanford, CA: Stanford University Press, 2015, p. 27.
14 Yong-ho Choe, "Christian Background in the Early Life of Kim Il-song," *Asian Survey* 26 (October 1986): 1088.
15 Armstrong, pp. 14–15.
16 Choe, Yong-ho, "Christian Background in the Early Life of Kim Il-song," *Asian Survey* 26, no. 10 (1986): 1082–1091.
17 Kim Hakjoon, 2015, p. 28.
18 Dae-Sook Suh, *Kim Il Sung: The North Korean Leader*. New York: Columbia University Press, 1988, p. 5.
19 Andrei Lankov, *From Stalin to Kim Il Sung: The Formation of North Korea, 1945–1960*. New Brunswick, NJ: Rutgers University Press, 2002, p. 51.
20 Jae-Cheon Lim, *Leader Symbols and Personality Cult in North Korea*. London: Routledge, 2015, p. 57.
21 "1,000-ri Journey of National Liberation," *Korea Today*, 306 (March 1982): 37.
22 Suh, p. 7.
23 Suh, pp. 7–8.
24 Kim Hakjoon, 2015, p. 31.
25 Kim Hakjoon, 2015, pp. 32–33.
26 Hongkoo Han, "Colonial Origins of Juche: The Minsaengdan Incident of the 1930s and the Birth of the North Korea-China Relationship," in Suh, Jae-Jung editor, *Origins of North Korea's Juche*. Latham, MD: Lexington Books, 2012, pp. 33–62.
27 Armstrong, *The North Korean Revolution*, p. 29.
28 Han, "Colonial Origins of Juche."
29 Lim, *Leader Symbols and Personality Cult in North Korea*, p. 62.
30 Armstrong, *The North Korean Revolution*, pp. 33–34.
31 Lankov, p. 53.
32 Lankov, p. 53; Suh, p. 36.
33 *Korea Today*, no. 173 (January 1971), p. 8.
34 Kim Kwang-un, *Pukhan Chŏngch'i yŏn'gu* 1 [Studies of North Korean Political History Vol 1.]. Seoul: Seonin, 2003, pp. 106–107.
35 Kim Hakjoon, 2015, p. 34.
36 Armstrong, *The North Korean Revolution*, p. 23.
37 Kim Kwang-un, p. 109.

38 Armstrong, Charles, "Centering the Periphery: Manchurian Exile(s) and the North Korean State," *Korean Studies* 19 (1995): 1–16.
39 Lankov, pp. 56–57.
40 Lim, 2009, p. 38
41 Lim, 2009, p. 11.

2

Birth of the DPRK and Failed Reunification, 1945–1953

North Korea was a product of two tragic events in Korean history: the division of the country by the USA and the Soviet Union at the end of World War II, and the Korean War. The first quickly led to the creation of two separate regimes in the peninsula, each seeing itself as the legitimate heir of the country's struggle for independence and national renewal; the second made the division permanent. Under the Soviet occupation from 1945 to 1948 the foundations of the North Korean regime were established and its leaders under Russian tutelage carried out a sweeping revolution. But like all good Korean nationalists the division was unacceptable to them. Furthermore, from the perspective of the North Korean leadership the revolution could not be completed until all of Korea was liberated. Thus, two years after the Democratic People's Republic of Korea was proclaimed in 1948, the leaders of the new socialist state attempted to carry out reunification by military means. But the USA's intervention led to the disastrous failure of North Korea's effort at unification and to China's entry into the conflict to ensure the new state's survival. After the armistice in 1953, the northern regime focused on rebuilding and remolding its society without losing sight of its long-term goal of creating a strong, progressive united Korean state.

Division

The division of Korea was a totally unexpected development for Koreans of all orientations. One could imagine the conflicting strains of the nationalist movement in Korea creating some sort of domestic power struggle or even civil conflict; but the division of the country into two halves was solely the result of the intervention of the USA and the Soviet Union. The organizationally fragmented, geographically scattered and ideologically divided nationalist movements, whether communist or non-communist, had little initial influence on events.

What actually happened at the end of the war was largely unanticipated by anyone. On August 8, 1945, just two days after the USA dropped an atomic bomb on Hiroshima, the Soviet Union declared war on Japan. The Soviets immediately began an offensive along Japan's northern frontier in Sakhalin, Manchuria, and along the extreme northeast corner of Korea that borders Siberia. The next day reports arrived in Washington of Soviet landings on the Korean peninsula. With the surrender of Japan imminent, Americans quickly began seeing Korea much as Tokyo had, as a strategic bridgehead into Japan. While Soviet forces were already entering the northeast of Korea, the closest American forces were six hundred miles away in Okinawa and would not be able to reach Korea for several weeks. It was therefore urgent that the USA work out an agreement to prevent the entire peninsula from falling into Soviet hands. On the night of August 10–11 the State-War-Navy Coordinating Committee assigned Colonel Dean Rusk and Charles Bonesteel the task of drawing up a line for the occupation of Korea by Soviet and American forces that would keep Moscow from occupying the entire country.[1] Rusk and Bonesteel chose the 38th parallel since it split the country into roughly equal halves but kept Seoul in the southern half. In reality, the southern half was more populous; the area north of the 38th parallel contained only 9.3 million people out of Korea's total population of 28 million, and of this, 8 million people were rural-dwelling while only 1.3 million lived in urban areas.[2] With President Truman's approval the proposal was sent to Moscow, and Stalin sent back his agreement the next day. It is not clear why he did so when his forces could have easily marched all the way to Pusan; Stalin may have hoped that by agreeing to a joint military occupation the door would be left open for a Soviet role in the occupation of Japan and perhaps Europe as well. Recent research suggests he also wanted to avoid a potential conflict with the USA in Korea.[3] No Koreans were consulted or even knew of these decisions until days after their implementation had begun.

The 38th parallel was not based on any historical or geographical boundaries; it cut across the two provinces of Kyŏnggi and Kangwŏn, and split counties and valleys. It simply divided the country into roughly two equally sized zones. As George M. McCune, chief of the Korean section in the Office of Far Eastern Affairs in the US State Department wrote, it was "an arbitrary line, chosen by staff officers for military purposes without political or other considerations."[4] It became a central axiom of North Koreans – indeed of all Koreans – that the division of their country was unnatural and unacceptable.

Korea in 1945

When the Japanese emperor announced Japan's surrender over the radio on August 15, 1945 most Koreans were taken by surprise. So carefully censored was the news in colonial Korea that the extent of Imperial Japan's reverses was not fully understood, at least not by most Koreans. So when, on Sunday, August 15, they were instructed to listen to an important radio announcement by the emperor the majority were stunned. Then, almost immediately, they broke out into both celebration and an orgy of destruction of the symbols of Japanese authority, such as the Shinto shrines which were set ablaze across the country. Unaware of Allied plans for a trusteeship they began to make immediate preparations for the creation of a new government. In Seoul and in other communities people of all political persuasions met to plan for independence in what appear to have been spontaneous gatherings. In retrospect it is hard to look back without a sense of sadness at the contrast between this brief moment of shared joy, with its promise of the rebirth of the Korean state as a new modern, autonomous nation, and the reality of occupation, division and war that was to come. Meanwhile, as Koreans celebrated their coming liberation, Washington and Moscow began to deploy forces for an occupation that neither had prepared for.

Soviet Occupation

North Korea, as a country and as a regime, had its birth in the Soviet occupation. On August 11 the Soviet Union's 25th Army crossed the border to enter northeast Korea. Two weeks later, on August 26, Soviet forces entered Pyongyang; soon after all of North Korea was under Soviet occupation. They were considerably ahead of US forces who did not begin to land in the South until September 8, 1945. The Soviet forces in Korea were commanded by General Chistiakov. But he was concerned with the military aspects of the occupation; the task of administration was left to Major-General Andrei Alekseevich Romanenko and Colonel-General Terentii Shtykov. Shtykov, the Political Commissar during the three-year occupation, was a party functionary not a military man. He appeared to be the most important figure among the Soviets in shaping the occupation from 1945 to 1948, and continued to serve as the first Soviet ambassador to the new state after 1948. According to Lankov, Shtykov "was the real supreme ruler of North Korea" during the three-year Soviet occupation.[5]

While the US government believed that Moscow had a clear blueprint for the takeover of their zone, most historians who have examined the Soviets' actions and the evidence from the Russian archives that has been made accessible to them find little support for this idea.[6] Historian Andrei Lankov, who carried out an extensive study of the Soviet documents from this time and interviewed some of the Russian participants in the Soviet occupations, has argued that Moscow saw North Korea as a military problem to be handled by its generals. In fact, it is surprising just how unprepared the Soviets were. Not only did they lack Korean experts to help with the military occupation, but they lacked interpreters.[7] In this way they resembled the American forces under General Hodge who had only Japanese-speaking interpreters. As with the Americans the Soviet military came to fight the Japanese not govern Koreans. As was also the case with the Americans, the Soviets entered without any contacts within Korea, and with little knowledge of the internal affairs of the country. In both cases the military appeared to be almost desperately searching for local Koreans they could work with. For the Soviets, this lack of expertise was in part due to the purge of Korean ethnic military and intelligence offices during the period 1936–1938. It was also due to the isolation of the domestic communists in Korea who, under intensive and effective Japanese repression, were unable to establish regular contact with Moscow. Other Korean communists were based in remote regions of China working for the Chinese Communist Party and had virtually no communication with the Soviet Union.

Despite many cases of looting and rape during the initial arrival of Red Army forces, the Soviets soon showed more skill at establishing order and working with local Koreans than did the Americans. In both the North and South, Korean people's committees began to fill the vacuum, maintaining internal order, avoiding clashes between Koreans and the Japanese, and securing food stocks. The main Korean organization to coordinate order and to prepare for the independence that most Koreans expected to happen soon was the Committee for Preparation of Korean Independence (*Chosŏn kŏn'guk chunbi wiwonhoe*) based in Seoul and with 143 branches throughout the country.[8] The Americans were suspicious of this organization and refused to recognize or work with it. They feared it was dominated by leftists and perhaps communists with links to Moscow. In reality, left-leaning nationalists played important roles in the organization, but there is little evidence that communists dominated either the central committee in Seoul or more than a very small number of the provincial branches. Local people's committees were grassroots organizations that sprang up with little planning as prominent citizens responded to the sudden collapse of Japanese rule. By November 20, 1945 people's committees had been formed in all seven provinces north of the 38th parallel, in 9 cities, 70 counties and 20 townships.[9] In contrast to the Americans, the Soviets utilized the committees that had sprung up across the country and turned them into instruments of support for their occupation. Upon entering Pyongyang the Soviets replaced the Japanese local governing authority with the South P'yŏngan Provisional People's Political Committee.[10] Again this was in contrast to the Americans' actions, as they initially kept the Japanese authorities in office.

The Soviets did not create a full-blown military occupation but worked through various Korean-led organizations. On October 3, the Soviets set up the Civil Administration to function alongside the various people's committees. The next month they created the Five Provinces

Administrative Bureau (*Odo haengjŏngguk*) with ten departments to carry out much of the administration, each headed by a Korean but with a Soviet advisor to assist. Although to a considerable extent they directed the events in North Korea, the Soviets preferred to give the appearance that Koreans were initiating change. And to some extent this was the case since when the Soviets found Korean communists that they were comfortable working with they let them implement policies.

Finding Suitable Partners

The Soviets needed to find reliable Korean partners. As in Eastern Europe their method was to form broad coalitions between communist and non-communist nationalists while gradually giving greater control over to the communists and removing uncooperative elements. The Soviets, however, had to deal with the fact that most of the non-communist nationalists had cooperated with the Japanese and therefore had tarnished nationalist credentials. An even greater problem was that the local communist movement was structurally weak, centered in the US-occupied South and few of its members were known to Moscow. Unlike the case of Eastern Europe there were no appreciable numbers of communist exiles in the Soviet Union.

In the North the most prominent Korean was the Christian leader Cho Man-sik, the head of the Pyongyang People's Committee. The 63-year-old Cho had compromised his nationalist credentials when he called upon students during World War II to volunteer and fight for Japan.[11] Nonetheless, he remained the best-known nationalist in the North and his prestige made him useful to the Soviets who made him head of the Five Provinces Administrative Bureau in November. Cho and other conservatives formed the Democratic Party (Minjudang) in November. They were a collection of landlords, prominent professionals and members of North Korea's significant Christian community. Although comprising less than 5 percent of the population, Christians tended to be better educated, better represented in the small middle class and active in disproportionate numbers in the nationalist movements. They were strongest in the urban areas, especially in Pyongyang. It is useful to recall that Kim Il Sung came from a Protestant Christian family in the area. Christians were more open to Western ideas, more active in progressive movements and often saw themselves as agents for modernization and national renewal. They were, therefore, influential beyond their modest numbers. The province where Pyongyang is located, P'yŏng'an, was also a center for Ch'ŏndogyo (Heavenly Way) an indigenous religious group that had its roots in the Tonghak movement in the late nineteenth century. Their concern with land reform was especially attractive to the communists who shared this part of their agenda. With Soviet approval the Ch'ŏndogyo organized a political party in early 1946 with the old name Ch'ŏng'udang. Christians and Ch'ŏndogyo members were the most organized non-communist groups in North Korea and the main coalition partners with the communists in the early days of the occupation.

North Korea's Communists

It is fair to say the Kim Il Sung was selected and promoted by the Soviets to be the communist leader in the North. But the process by which this happened was not carefully planned and was somewhat difficult to untangle. When surviving domestic communists did emerge from hiding or from jail they were centered in Seoul. This presented an awkward situation. The leader of the Communist Party of Korea in August 1945 was Pak Hŏn-yŏng. But Pak, like most of the other domestic communists, was largely unfamiliar to the Soviets and, of course, was operating out of the American occupation zone. On August 17, in the first days of liberation, the Communist Party in Seoul sent Hyŏn Chun-hyŏk to Pyongyang to help organize the party there. Hyŏn, a native of the city, was the de facto leader in the North but in reality he had limited authority over other local communists in the industrial and port cities of Ch'ŏngju, Sinŭiju, Haeju, Hŭngnam, Hamhŭng and Wŏnsan. Most of these were industrial towns in the northeast where communist labor movements had been fairly strong.[12] Hyŏn Chun-hyŏk does not seem to have impressed the Soviets. The domestic communists with a few exceptions had worked in isolation, had few contacts with the Soviet Union or communists elsewhere and were not trusted by Moscow. And they were little known among their countrymen. Needing Korean speakers the Soviets conducted a search for Soviet-Koreans. Some survivors of the 1930s purges were found and they began to arrive to assist with the occupation. However, they were Soviet citizens with only distant or indeed no connections with Korea so organizing a reliable and effective local communist group that could serve as loyal allies of the Soviets was not an easy task.

This was the situation that awaited Manchurian veterans of the 88th Brigade when they entered the country. They arrived in Korea on September 19 landing by boat in the port of Wŏnsan. Captain Kim Il Sung became the leader of this small band of about 60 former Manchurian guerillas, or partisans as they are often called. It is not clear how or why he became the leader of this group. There were several other captains and one major, and some of the other ex-guerillas were older and had as much if not more guerilla experience. At 33 he was younger than two-thirds of the group, although most were around his age.[13] Perhaps the Soviets for some reason were impressed with him and arranged this. Or he may have been selected by his peers out of their respect for his record as a fighter. These former partisans, many able to speak Russian and already familiar with working with the Red Army, were extremely useful in assisting with the occupation. The Soviet military, they were dispersed to various parts of the country. Some were strategically placed in security organs. For example, O Chin-u, who later became the highest ranking military person in the regime, was made police chief of Pyongyang. Since the Soviets made Pyongyang their occupation headquarters they sent Kim Il Sung there, assigning him to the commandant as deputy chief garrison officer.[14]

Thus, almost from the moment of his return to Korea, the first time since he was 12, Kim Il Sung rose to a key position in the occupation. This rise was aided by the vacuum in the communist leadership in the North which came about shortly after Kim Il Sung was assigned to Pyongyang: Hyŏn Chun-hyŏk, the highest ranking domestic Korean, returning with Cho Man-sik from a meeting with the Soviet occupation authorities, was assassinated on September 28. Two weeks later Kim Il Sung made his public debut when he was selected to address the crowd at a publicly organized rally to welcome the Soviet forces. This was a major public event, and the selection of Kim as the key speaker immediately placed him at the forefront of the communist leaders. This large ceremony organized by the Soviets took place on October 14, 1945; 300,000 people attended. Kim Il Sung, dressed in a Western-style suit and wearing Soviet medals, led it. Many who attended were surprised at his youth, aged only 33. Kim Il Sung later described this as the biggest day in his life. Why did the Soviets single out Kim Il Sung? There are many explanations, including the story that he had a secret meeting with Stalin before leaving the Soviet Union. This story is unlikely. More likely was that he was the best known of the communists largely owing to the publicity given to the Poch'ŏnbo raid in 1937. He appeared disciplined, worked well with Soviet officers and happened to be in the right place at the right time. And, of course, there was the shortage of other suitable candidates. The decision to promote Kim Il Sung was probably not a carefully planned one by the Soviets. According to Lankov, a study of the Soviet documents suggests that the "process of choosing a future leader was chaotic and spontaneous."[15]

Kim Il Sung's public appearance coincided with the organization of a North Korean communist party. On September 20, 1945 Stalin ordered that the Soviets should "support all of northern Korea's anti-Japanese democratic parties and organizations in order to establish to establish a proletariat democratic power."[16] From October 5 to 8, 1945, a conference of Korean Communist Party leaders of the five provinces met. Apparently, this meeting established the foundation for what would become the ruling party of North Korea. On October 12, 1945 the Soviet occupation authorities issued a proclamation allowing Koreans to organize political parties provided they were anti-Japanese and democratic.[17] The following day local communists created a North Korea Branch Bureau of the Korean Communist Party (*Chosŏn kongsandang Puk Chosŏn punguk*), officially announced on October 20, 1945.[18] This was technically a branch of the Seoul-based party and it recognized Pak Hŏn-yŏng in Seoul as head of the Korean Communist Party. It was organized, however, at the initiative of the Soviets, not by the main party in Seoul. Following two name changes it is still the ruling party of North Korea to this day. Oddly enough, in 1958 the North Koreans, rewriting history, changed the date of the founding of the party to October 10, which has since become an important day of commemoration. Why this was done is not clear but then North Korea has constantly changed important dates in its history, sometimes for obscure reasons. Kim Il Sung was not its chairman. Rather the post went to Kim Yong-bŏm, a rather minor cadre. It is not known why or how he was selected other than the fact he was the husband of Pak Chŏng-ae, an active Korean communist who had spent much time in the Soviet Union. Kim Il Sung only took over the chairmanship on December 17 or 18 after Kim Yong-bŏm died of a stomach tumor.[19] At that time the northern branch party was growing but still very small, with only 4,530 members.[20]

Just as Kim Il Sung began to emerge as the leader among the North Korean communists another group of communists began to trickle into the country. During the fall of 1945 members of the Yanan faction began returning to Korea. In January 1946 they formed their own Sinmindang (New Democratic Party) with Kim Tu-bong as its chair. It had no sharp ideological differences with the Branch Bureau. In June 1946 the Branch Bureau detached itself from the Seoul-based main Korean Communist Party. Renamed the Workers' Party of North Korea, it merged with the Sinmindang. The Workers' Party of North Korea held its first party congress on August 28–30, 1946. Kim Tu-bong was named chair and Kim Il Sung one of two vice chairs. Despite Kim Tu-bong's position as chair, it appeared that the real leader of the party was Kim Il Sung. Since many of the Yanan communists were a generation older, better educated and had longer records as communists and independence fighters their acceptance of Kim Il Sung's leadership must have been difficult but they had little real choice as the Soviets were supporting him. Most of the members of the Central Committee were also older than him, with Kim Tu-bong, aged 56, being the oldest member.[21] Moscow instructed leftists in South Korea to form a similar coalition in November 1946 known as the South Korean Workers' Party. Three years later, after most of the communists in the South had fled to the North or were forced underground, the two parties merged or rather the southern party was absorbed to form the Korean Workers' Party (Chosŏn Rodong-dang) (KWP) which has remained the name of North Korea's ruling party. Kim Il Sung was its chair.

At first the Soviet occupation was through a broad coalition of Korean nationalists, at least in theory. The Soviets then orchestrated the political domination by the communists in steps. When Cho Man-sik and his conservative colleagues organized the Democratic Party in November the Soviets pressured them to include some communist members. Ch'oe Yong-gŏn was made deputy chair of the party. Ch'oe had once worked with Cho Man-sik but later joined the guerillas in Manchuria and became a comrade of Kim Il Sung. Later he served as North Korea's head of state. Kim Ch'aek, another partisan, headed the Democratic Party's secretariat. When in early 1946 Cho opposed the Soviet–US plan for a trusteeship he was removed as party chair and placed under house arrest. Ch'oe Yong-gŏn was made the new Democratic Party chair. On July 22, 1946, also under the apparent direction of the Soviets, all legal parties formed the United Democratic National Front (*Puk Chosŏn minjujuŭi t'ongil chŏnsŏn*) under the leadership of the communists.[22] By this time most of the landlords, who formed an important base for the Democratic Party, had left for the South. Thus, the chief moderate nationalist party became a mere puppet organization of the communists.

The American and Soviet occupation zones were meant to be temporary arrangements under the trusteeship that had been discussed and agreed upon during the war. When the allied powers met at the Moscow Conference on December 27, 1945, to discuss the postwar settlement they agreed to carry out the four- to five-year four-power trusteeship of the USA, the Soviet Union, China and Britain. This was a considerable reduction from the earlier 20–30 years agreed at Yalta but it was still too long for most Koreans, who wanted immediate independence. Koreans, in general, were still unaware of the trusteeship agreement and reaction to the public announcement by the powers was universal outrage. Massive demonstrations took place in the South. In the North the Soviets demanded all parties were to support the trusteeship; Cho Man-sik's removal and house arrest when he refused to do so made this policy clear. At the conference Washington and Moscow created an American–Soviet Joint Commission which met in March 1946 to work out the terms of the trusteeship. Preliminary talks between the two powers were held prior to the commission in Seoul. The Americans wanted guarantees that there would be no interruption to the electricity supply to the South, most of which came from the Soviet zone. They also wanted freedom of movement across the 38th parallel where the Soviets had begun to establish roadblocks.

Birth of the North Korean State

While evidence suggests that Moscow initially had no clear plan when they occupied the area north of the 38th parallel, the outlines of the North Korean state emerged very quickly. In February 1946 the Soviets organized a North Korean Provisional People's Committee (NKPPC) with Kim Il Sung as chairman and Kim Tu-bong as vice-chairman. One could argue that with this, the North Korean communist regime began, just six months after liberation. The NKPPC acted quickly to carry out sweeping reforms; the most important being the land reform (see the section "A North Korean Revolution" below). Many other sweeping measures were carried out by the Provisional Committee. It established a new educational system, opened a new university and carried out adult literacy campaigns. Labor laws established the eight-hour day, and other laws established the legal equality of women, made divorce easier and ended the legal basis of the old patriarchal family system. The impact of these actions was profound and transformed North Korean society. Furthermore, in August of 1946 all major industries were nationalized.

Meanwhile, step by step, a new North Korean state was being consolidated. In November 1946 the Soviets carried out carefully managed elections to regional, provincial and city people's committees. In February 1947 the delegates from these people's committees met in the First Congress of the People's Committees.[23] They, in turn, created the North Korean People's Committee. Once again Kim Il Sung was named chair and the former partisan Kim Ch'aek vice chair. The deletion of the word "provisional" in this new governing organ is significant, for North Korea in 1947 was already becoming in reality a separate state. Gradually, a North Korean military was formed. This was done under the careful supervision of the Soviets. First, in 1946, the Soviets established a police force as well as railway defense units. A key figure in developing the security forces was Pang Hak-se, a former Soviet police officer who was sent to the Korea along with other Soviet-Koreans to assist the occupation.[24] Another important figure was the Manchurian partisan Kim Ch'aek who headed the Pyongyang Institute founded in November 1945 to train military officers and political cadres. A Central Security Officers' Training School was established and its first class graduated in the fall of 1947.[25] In

February 1948 the Korean People's Army (KPA) was officially organized, although in fact, the Soviets had begun forming the army in 1947. The Soviets played a big role in the training of KPA forces, attaching at least three Soviet advisors to each regiment.[26] In 1948 the KPA had 40,000 troops; the following year it had 60,000.

Contrast with the South

These orderly but revolutionary developments in North Korea contrasted with the South. There the Americans were far slower in working out a plan for a viable state, as they floundered while looking for partners to work with. Their occupation was also more violent and chaotic. The People's Republic of Korea, which was created prior to the arrival of the Americans, was ignored and all power was transferred to the United States Military Government in Korea (USAMGIK). The Americans created a Korean Advisory Council which was dominated by conservative landowners, and later that year an Interim Legislative Assembly, but unlike the Soviets in the North, the Americans ruled directly as a military occupation and were far less effective in creating the façade of local authority. And in contrast to the North there was no land reform. Rather the emerging institutions of the South Korean state were often dominated by the members of the landowning class. In general, the South underwent a turbulent occupation. Meanwhile, a kaleidoscope of political groups emerged and quarreled. Political assassinations were frequent; and labor, teacher and student strikes and demonstrations, many directed at the American support for trusteeship, were common.

In the fall of 1946 there was a bloody uprising in the southeastern part of the country that American forces and the Korean police put down at the cost of several thousand lives. The Americans blamed the communists for much of the disorder, banned the party and forced much of the leadership to flee to the North. Restlessness continued and a peasant insurrection on the island of Cheju in 1948 saw thousands more killed. Nonetheless, by late 1947 the Americans had created a South Korean national police force, and a political leadership of largely conservative anti-communists led by the American-educated nationalist hero Syngman Rhee emerged. Yet there was a serious problem for this emerging South Korean state. Except for Rhee, most of the leadership in the South lacked the untarnished nationalist credentials of the emerging communist regime in the north. Most of those that served in the government, officered the constabulary and directed the police had served and prospered under Japanese rule. For example, paralleling developments in the North, the Americans created a National Constabulary, eventually a military academy and then a formal military. However, the Americans relied on Koreans who had served in the Japanese colonial police force for their constabulary and on those who had attended a Japanese military academy for the officer corps of the army. The North Korean military and police were drawn from those who had no such compromising backgrounds. All this reinforced the beliefs of the emerging North Korean leadership that they were the true bearers of Korean nationalism and would eventually establish control over the conflicted and collaborationist-dominated South.

Independence

After the failure of the second meeting of the American–Soviet Joint Committee in the summer of 1947 the Americans who had become eager to disengage from Korea turned the issue of the country's future to the United Nations (UN). The international body set up the UN Temporary Committee on Korea (UNTCOK) to supervise the move toward independence. Elections, according to the UN plan, were to be held throughout Korea for a unified National Assembly no later than March 1948. Power would be transferred to this new political body, Korea would become a fully sovereign state and the Soviet and American forces would withdraw. This plan ignored the reality that two political systems were already taking shape on the peninsula. Furthermore, the USA had turned the process over to the UN without securing the Soviet Union's support. Without this support or Moscow's recognition of UNTCOK's authority there was no way the organization could sponsor elections in the North. The UN therefore decided, on February 26, to hold elections in "accessible" areas, in other words in the South. Many southern Koreans also opposed this process since they feared it would create a separate government in the South, a prospect they found appalling. Their objections were ignored and when UNTCOK carried out elections on May 10 for a 200-member National Assembly, many South Koreans boycotted it. The newly elected National Assembly adopted a constitution on July 17 and three days later elected Syngman Rhee as president. On August 15, 1948, the Republic of Korea (*Taehan Min'guk*) was proclaimed. On December 12, the UN General Assembly accepted the UNTCOK report that the elections were "a valid expression of the free will of the electorate" of that part of the country where they could be monitored; and it declared that the Republic of Korea (ROK) was the only "lawful" government and "the only such government in Korea."

By early 1947 the Soviets had established the basic skeleton of what was in effect a separate state in the North. When it was clear that the USA, through its working majority of sympathetic and allied states in the UN, was set to establish an independent Korean state on its terms, the Soviet Union began the final process of preparing North Korea for independence. In late 1947 the People's Assembly formed a commission to begin drafting a constitution headed by Kim Tu-bong. A draft roughly modeled on the 1936 Soviet constitution was sent to Moscow. At an April 24, 1948 meeting with Stalin, Soviet Foreign Minister Molotov and other high-ranking officials approved the draft constitution after it had been amended. Interestingly, the document, closely patterned on that of the 1936 Soviet constitution, was first written in Russian and then translated into Korean.[27] The Soviets were careful to avoid seeing this as creating a separate Korean state but instead as the true legitimate state representing all the Korean people. Seoul, for example, was still recognized in the constitution as the capital; a Korea without Seoul was like a France without Paris. And the new government was to be created by a peninsula-wide election process. To carry out the elections in the South, secret and illegal (from a UN or South Korean perspective) elections were held in each region to select representatives who met in Haeju just north of the 38th parallel. On September 2, 572 deputies, 360 for the South and 212 from the North, met and on September 8 unanimously approved the constitution.[28] The next day, September 9, the Democratic People's Republic of Korea (DPRK) (*Chosŏn Minjujuŭi Inmin konghwaguk*) was proclaimed. To distinguish itself it adopted a new flag in July, the *ingonggi* (or People's Republic flag) to replace the old national flag of Korea that the ROK was using, the *t'aegukki* whose yin–yang and trigram symbols were denounced as "feudalistic" and "imported from China."[29] A new national anthem was also adopted.

This was an outcome that few if any really wanted – the creation of two separate states. It is unlikely that the majority of leaders in either the North or the South saw this as more than a temporary measure until national unification could be achieved.

A North Korean Revolution

The changes that took place in North Korea from 1945 to 1950 can only be labeled as "revolutionary." Sweeping reforms were carried out in what Kim Il Sung referred to as the "people's democratic revolution," adopting the label given to similar reforms being carried out in other Soviet-occupied countries.[30] In just a few years the Korean communists and the Soviets, often with the assistance of ordinary men and women, created a new society. The Soviets provided the broad outlines of the revolution and worked closely with their Korean counterparts, but it would be wrong to see it as completely imposed from above. Although there is some disagreement among scholars over the extent to which this revolution was orchestrated by the Soviets, as Charles Armstrong and Suzy Kim have persuasively argued in their studies of captured documents it was carried out enthusiastically by the Korean communists. Nor were the farmers, workers and intellectuals passive participants but rather many eagerly embraced the new reforms and helped shape it.

No reform measure had a more immediate impact on society than the land reform. Three out of four Koreans were peasants. They were mostly poor and burdened by rents. In 1945, 75 percent of all land was worked by tenants; and half of all Korean farmers owned no land at all. Another one-third of farmers rented part of the land they farmed since their own personal holdings were insufficient to support a family. Tenants commonly paid rents up to half of the crop and sometimes up to 60 percent. There was a powerful demand for land reform and for limitations on rents in kind. The first major action by the new communist-dominated

NKPPC was a comprehensive measure issued on March 5, 1946, for redistributing land. All farmland owned by Japanese, by national traitors and by landlords who owned more than five *chŏngbo* (a *chŏngbo* was approximately two and a half acres) was confiscated and redistributed.[31] As Kim Seongbo (Kim Sŏng-bo) points out, this was "one of the most rapid and radical land reforms in world history."[32] The land reform was carried out with great speed, and largely completed in time for spring planting. Few actions by the communists could have done more to establish their support among the majority. And it served as a rebuke to the American zone where the landlords were still entrenched. There was some resistance to the reforms but they were generally rolled out smoothly.[33]

Yet, as popular as the measure was, it did not bring that much relief to farmers. Peasants got their land but their burden was still heavy. Taxes were set at 25 percent of the crop. While this was in theory considerably lighter than previous rents of up to half the crop, it was in reality not necessarily all that much lighter. The 25 percent tax was often based on overly optimistic projections so that the real figure was greater. In addition, special requisitions meant that the actual tax was often much higher than even these figures. Farmers also had to supply their best grain, and surpluses were to be sold to state-run markets that bought the produce at low prices.[34] And the land reform did little to solve North Korea's problem of limited cultivable land. The problem of food shortages would bedevil the country in the following decades.

Land reform was not just an economic measure but part of the radical restructuring of society. The old landholding *yangban* class vanished as their properties were confiscated, and most fled to the South. In contrast to traditional hierarchical society, with its many levels of deference in speech and honorifics, all workers were encouraged to address each other as comrade (*tongmu*) no matter what their position or age.[35] Nearly everyone was enrolled in a state-sponsored organization. A North Korean Democratic Women's League (*Pukchosŏn minju yŏsŏng tongmaeng*) was created in early 1946 and had over 1 million members by the end of the year.[36] Young people in their early teens to late twenties were organized into the North Korean Democratic Youth League (*Puk Chosŏn minju ch'ŏngnyŏn tongmaeng*). There was a North Korean Federation of Trade Unions and all workers were incorporated into it. These were not only means of mobilizing and controlling the population, but means to promote a new sense of identity. The emerging North Korean state rapidly expanded school enrollment and conducted mass literacy campaigns facilitated by the decision to switch from a mixed script of Chinese characters to the exclusive use of the Korean alphabet *han'gŭl*. It created a new educational system with Kim Il Sung University established in October 1946 at its apex.

One of the biggest breaks with the past was the insistence on gender equality. Women were to have equal pay, benefits and treatment in the workplace. In January 1947 the North Korean People's Committee passed the Law to Eradicate Remnants of Feudal Practices, which outlawed dowry exchange, child marriage and polygamy and legally guaranteed free choice in marriage.[37] When leftists in Seoul organized a nationwide women's movement in August 1946, the North Koreans objected to the use of the term *puin* for women, a word that also meant wife and had the connotation of subservience to men. Although this was the common term among Koreans the new regime preferred the term *yŏsŏng* (female) without such connotations.[38]

Yet for all the emphasis on equality a new hierarchy replaced the old. Those at the bottom of society – poor peasants and workers – were now, at least in theory, at the top of society. Those branded landowners, rich peasants, capitalists and former officials in the colonial regime were placed at the bottom rungs of the social hierarchy. Inherited status, which had always existed in Korean society, still mattered and priority in education and jobs was given on the basis of *ch'ulsin* (or origins – in essence, one's family background). But now it was those who had humble backgrounds that were favored.

Under the emerging North Korean regime artists and writers served the revolution. Although the Korean cultural center had been Seoul, a number of left-wing intellectuals and artists arrived in the North, both to flee the right-wing political order that was forming in the South and to eagerly help build a new socialist society. Some initially played prominent roles in North Korea, including the writer Yi Ki-yŏng, historians Paek Nam-un and Pak Si-hyŏn, and the dancer Ch'oe Sŭng-hŭi.[39] Kim Wŏn-ju, a female writer and intellectual, arrived from Japan to become editor of the party newspaper *Rodong sinmun*.[40] The composer Kim Wŏn-gyun wrote the national anthem of the DPRK and the "Song of General Kim Il Sung."[41] But free-thinking intellectuals, even those sympathetic to the regime, did not fare well in the DPRK, and most fell out of favor in the 1950s and 1960s.

Most North Koreans lived in the countryside where life was improving. Rural electrification campaigns doubled the amount of farm households that had electricity from one in six in 1945 to one in three in 1948.[42] Tiled roofs replaced thatched ones. This much-desired improvement in rural housing was not achieved in South Korea until the early 1970s. While the standard of living was low, and life difficult for most, it was no worse off than in the South and for the majority it was getting better. Landless tenant farmers received land, workers got an eight-hour day as well as accident and health insurance, and women gained equal pay. The expansion of schooling provided greater opportunity for ordinary people to get an education for their children, and literacy campaigns enabled many unschooled adults to read. North Korea was experiencing a true social revolution. The revolution was creating a more equitable society where the poor were probably better off materially, and where marginal groups – women, laborers and peasants – enjoyed an improvement in their social status that was almost inconceivable before 1945.

North Korea followed the Soviet economic model with its highly centralized planning, its emphasis on industrialization and its early nationalization of much of industry. Nationalization was aided by the fact that most industry had been owned by the Japanese, and much of the rest by "national traitors." Economic planning began in early 1947 with a National Economic Rehabilitation Plan intended to promote rapid industrialization. A second one-year economic plan was implemented for 1948 and a two-year plan launched for 1949–1950. In general, North Korea's economic recovery from the initial chaos and destruction in 1945 proceeded rather rapidly. Abundant supplies of hydroelectric power contributed to the rapid increase in electrification. Economic development was carried out with assistance from the Soviet Union. This was not overly generous and some of the aid provided was paid in mineral wealth including uranium. Moscow sought to integrate North Korea's economy into the Soviet Union's, although not a lot of progress was made in this period toward that end. Its chief interest was in the land's rich mineral resources.

By the late 1940s many of the features of North Korean society were already appearing, such as the use of mass mobilization campaigns to achieve economic targets. Perhaps the most salient aspect of North Korean society is the all-pervasive glorification of the leader. This too appeared early. Once the Soviets had settled on Kim Il Sung they began to fashion his cult of personality in Stalinist fashion. During 1946, his portrait appeared alongside Stalin's in almost every public place. Songs about him were sung, and in October 1946 the new national university was named after him. He held the position as the head of the government, but even at the founding of the North Korean Workers' Party, he was praised as "the leader of all the Korean people," the "hero of the nation" and the "great leader" despite officially being only one of two vice chairmen along with Chu Nyŏng-ha.[43] The adulation of the leader started almost with the inception of the new state. An early biography described him as a great general "winning every battle."[44]

There was nothing unusual about this. Throughout the Soviet bloc the "little Stalins" carried out their own cults of personality alongside that of Stalin himself – a development encouraged by Moscow. However, there were some distinctive characteristics of the cult that emerged in the late 1940s. Some of the language and symbolism appeared to reflect the influence of the intense emperor worship of the colonial period. For example, as early as 1946 the writer Han Sŏr-ya referred to Kim Il Sung as "our sun" (*uri ŭi t'aeyang*), consciously or unconsciously using the same sun metaphor that had been associated with the Japanese emperor.[45] Another distinctive North Korean feature was the legend of the Manchurian guerillas. This legend would grow to wildly exaggerated proportions in later years but even as early as 1946 the "Song of General Kim Il Sung," composed by Kim Wŏn-gyun and played at public occasions, spoke of "the snowy winds of Manchuria / the long, long nights of the forest / who is the timeless partisan, the peerless patriot / the beneficent liberator of the working masses / Great Sun of democratic new Korea?"[46] No other feature of the North Korean leadership cult so differed from Stalinism as the glorification of Kim Il Sung's family. Most of this developed later but even before the start of the Korean War, Kim's "revolutionary family heritage" (*hyŏngmyŏngjŏk kagye*) appeared in a textbook.[47]

The consolidation of the regime was not accompanied by violent class warfare. Partly this was due to the fact that most of the landlord and business class fled to the South after 1945. But even if the creation of North Korean society was not characterized by the levels of violence that had accompanied the creation of the Soviet Union and the People's Republic of China, there was still opposition. As early as November 1945 protests in the city of Sinuiju were violently repressed. Student-led protests took place in Hamhŭng in March 1946 calling for the Soviet troops to leave.[48] On March 1, 1946, the date commemorating the great national uprising against the Japanese in 1919, public protests directed at the occupation and its communist allies took place. Most anti-communist protests were carried out by Christians and often led by church groups. They were quickly suppressed and participants arrested. Many Christians and other dissenters fled to the South.[49] Thousands of opponents were sent to Siberia, a practice that continued until North Korea established its own system of political prison camps.

The Leadership of the New North Korean State

The new North Korean state was theoretically a coalition government but in fact the North Korean Workers' Party was the unchallenged ruling institution. It differed from most other communist parties in that a majority of its members were peasants rather than workers. Therefore, few had any training or much knowledge of Marxism-Leninism. Under Soviet advice, six-month ideological training sessions were conducted for a select elite at the Central Party School, and an even smaller number were sent to the Soviet Union for further ideological training.[50]

At the Second Party Congress in March 1948 Kim Il Sung assumed the role as party chair. Kim Il Sung, although the preeminent leader of North Korea and already the subject of a personality cult, was still first among equals. His fellow partisans held key posts but were far from dominating the party. Nor did Kim's partisans dominate the administration. Only three partisans held cabinet positions: Kim Il Sung as premier, Kim Ch'aek as minister of industry and Ch'oe Yong-gŏn as minister of defense. The partisans, while holding only a minority of the top positions in the party and the government, were over-represented in the security organs and the military. Many key positions where held by the Yanan and Soviet-Koreans but domestic communists from the South held the most cabinet posts. Subject to relentless persecution by the US occupation authorities and their South Korean allies most of the communists in the South had fled to the North by 1948. Most prominent was Pak Hŏn-yŏng, the leader of the South Korean Workers' Party. Pak was vice premier and also the foreign minister and was considered the number two ranking figure in the regime. In contrast to the importance of South Korean communists, few local communists from the North held important posts. Despite, their local roots and knowledge they had the least support from the Soviets and were the early losers in the competition for power. Almost all were eliminated from even minor leadership positions. As a result, the leadership of North Korea came entirely from people who had largely lived their adult lives in Manchuria, China, South Korea or the Soviet Union; and in most cases they had never lived in what became the DPRK at all until after liberation.

The North Koreans were still very much dependent upon the Soviet Union for economic and military assistance and advice. Soviet troops withdrew in 1948 but many advisors stayed behind, including General Shtykov who now served as ambassador. Moscow's continued tutelage is evidenced in a document given to Pyongyang on foreign policy in October 7, 1948. Issued by the Politburo and signed by Stalin it instructed the North Koreans to establish diplomatic relations with other people's democracies with the exceptions of Mongolia and Albania.[51] The proclamation of the People's Republic of China in October 1949 provided another neighboring ally that would eventually prove useful as a counterweight to the Soviet Union but until 1950 the leadership of North Korea remained under Moscow's wing.

An Unstable Division and Kim Il Sung's Plans for Reunification

North Korean leadership saw reunification as their main task. From their point of view the liberation of the South, with its government beholden to the USA, was a continuation of the nationalist anti-imperialist struggle. Furthermore, the liberation of the South from its domination by the old "feudal" landlord class and their comprador bourgeois allies in power was also a continuation of the socialist revolution. There was no question about the need for reunification. Even the constitution of 1948 stated that Seoul was the capital of the Democratic People's Republic of Korea; Pyongyang was simply a temporary seat of government. Kim Il Sung, in his first public statement as premier of the DPRK on September 10, 1948, declared that unification of the fatherland was to be a top priority in his government's eight-point agenda. Pyongyang's drive to reunify the country, reflected not just the ambitions of its leaders but the aspirations of most Koreans, North and South, who regarded both the division of the country as unacceptable and the unification as inevitable.

The option, if not a definite plan, for armed intervention to liberate South Korea was part of the regime's thinking from 1948.[52] To that end the DPRK built up its military. Moscow assisted in this effort by providing training and equipment. Officers in the KPA began training in Soviet Union. Pyongyang, also benefited from the influx of Koreans who fought with the People's Liberation Army during the civil war in China. At North Korea's request about 35,000 experienced fighters returned to join the KPA from the summer of 1949 to the end of the year. About 14,000 returned in early 1950.[53] After 2–4 months' retraining they were then integrated into the KPA.[54] They provided combat-experienced soldiers and established links and goodwill between the People's Liberation Army of China and the KPA. Having so many experienced soldiers was a great advantage for the North.

A key part of the regime's strategy for the invasion and liberation of the South was to promote internal uprisings. Pak Hŏn-yŏng and other southern communists were optimistic about the prospects for widespread uprisings that would assist any invasion. There were grounds for this optimism. In many ways the Rhee regime seemed rather shaky. Peasants were disappointed with the failure to enact land reform. Political strikes by workers and students were common. The politics of the country was contentious and divisive. In May 1948 protests against holding separate elections led to a full-scale insurrection on the island province of Cheju. On October 13, 1948, just one month after the USA transferred command of the ROK forces to the Korean officers, troops who had been sent to the southern city of Yŏsu on their way to put down the Cheju rebellion mutinied, taking over the town and setting up people's courts. When more loyal forces regained control and quashed the rebellion many of the rebels fled into nearby mountains and joined local partisans in guerilla resistance.

Pak and his fellow communists from the South had already been involved in peasant and worker revolts against the US occupation, especially in late 1946, and were fully aware of just how deep the discontent was. They sent more than 3,000 guerillas to the South, including 600 cadres trained at the Kangdong Institute, to promote pro-communist uprisings. They included two important experienced communists, Kim Sam-yŏng and Yi Chu-ha. Many of these cadres were sent to fight in the Odae Mountain region of South Korea and another group to the T'aebaek Mountain area.[55] However, the ROK conducted successful counterinsurgency campaigns against the guerillas in 1948–1949 and 1949–1950, including the setting up of strategic hamlets and the carrying out of frightful reprisals against rebel supporters. And, in March 1950, prospects for a successful guerilla campaign were dimmed when both Kim Sam-yŏng and Yi Chu-ha were captured.[56] But the North Koreans appear to have believed resistance to the ROK would be rekindled by a northern invasion. Meanwhile, the situation along the border was tense with frequent military clashes, some initiated by South Korean forces.

Besides the perceived weakness of the ROK, the somewhat ambiguous American position in South Korea was also encouraging. The USA supported the state and wanted to prevent communism from spreading closer to Japan, which all in Washington agreed was vital to US interests; however, the American political leaders in the Truman administration and in Congress did not want to invest too much in a land that remained of peripheral concern. The USA began withdrawing its forces in September 1948, with the last troops leaving the following year. It allocated funding for the establishment of a 65,000-man ROK army and left behind a 500-member Korean Military Advisory Group to help train the new South Korean army. The USA also provided generous economic aid to Seoul. But this generosity soon waned; the US Congress considerably reduced economic aid for 1950 and limited funding for the South Korean army. Americans were particularly wary of President Rhee's strident nationalism and were concerned over reports of ROK raids along the northern border, as they wanted to avoid the risk of conflict on the peninsula. They provided only small arms for the ROK forces and no significant aircraft. Even in small arms, the ROK army had a mere 15-day supply in June 1950.[57] The USA was unclear about the extent of its commitment; the most famous example of this was Secretary of State Dean Acheson's January 12, 1950 press conference in which he excluded South Korea from the USA's defensive perimeter. Not only did all this point to the South's vulnerability, but the winds of change seemed favorable to Pyongyang. The People's Liberation Army had defeated the US-backed Guomindang in China in 1949, and a triumphant Mao Zedong proclaimed the People's Republic of China on October 1. By the spring of 1950 the Guomindang held only the island of Taiwan. Its erstwhile ally, the USA, appeared resigned to the imminent fall of that last non-communist stronghold.

Politically unstable, with a restive population, a weak military, a foreign patron that seemed less than fully committed to its defense, and thousands of sympathizers ready to rise up in support of the KPA (or so Pyongyang may have believed), South Korea seemed ripe for a quick conquest. By June 1950 the KPA had 150,000 men under arms compared to less than 100,000 in the ROK. It had more experienced troops than South Korea's military; and it was better equipped, including tanks and planes which the ROK lacked. For Pyongyang an invasion seemed likely to result in a swift victory and the completion of the struggle for national liberation and reunification.

From 1948 the DPRK prepared for war while Kim Il Sung and Pak Hŏn-yŏng sought Soviet permission and support for an invasion. On March 1949 Kim Il Sung met with Stalin to ask for assistance for the two-year economic plan. He also requested Stalin's approval and support for a military invasion of the South. Kim Il Sung is reported to have told him:

> Comrade Stalin, we believe the situation makes it necessary and possible to liberate the whole country through military means. The reactionary forces of the South will never agree on a peaceful unification and will perpetuate the division of the country until they feel themselves strong enough to attack the North.

Furthermore, he went on, "Our people are very anxious to be together again to cast off the yoke of the reactionary regime and their American masters."[58] With some US troops still in the South and the civil war in China unresolved Stalin was unwilling to support an invasion. However, Stalin then seems to have changed his mind. On January 30, 1950, he telegrammed Ambassador Shtykov to tell Kim Il Sung "that I am ready to help in this matter." He explained that he understood Kim Il Sung's impatience but "he must understand that such a large matter … such as he wants to undertake needs large preparation" and "the matter must be organized so that there would not be too great a risk."[59] The next day Shtykov reported that Kim Il Sung received the news that Stalin would support his invasion plans "with great satisfaction."[60] At Stalin's invitation Kim Il Sung and Pak Hŏn-yŏng went to Moscow in April and met with him and other leaders. Kim Il Sung told Stalin: "The attack will be swift and the war will be won in three days: the guerilla movement in the South has grown stronger and a major uprising is expected."[61] It is not clear why the Soviet Union decided to back the plan. Typically, the Soviets focused on Europe and took a more cautious stand in Asia. Mao's victory in China and the end of the civil war there, and the USA's abandoning of its Guomindang allies, may have been a factor. Perhaps Secretary of State Acheson's comments of January 12 persuaded Stalin that the USA was unlikely to intervene. Perhaps, the Soviets became persuaded by Kim and Pak's arguments that the war would be a swift and easy victory.

In May, Kim and Pak went to Beijing to gain Mao's support. Initially Mao had not been in favor of the plan and warned of possible Japanese and American intervention, but he reluctantly agreed to back the North Koreans after Moscow assured him of its likely success. However, he made clear that Chinese forces would not assist if the Americans intervened unless they crossed the 38th parallel.[62] A team of Soviet advisors drew up plans and the Soviet Union began supplying more tanks, artillery and other weapons. In late spring Soviet advisors completed their "Preemptive Strike Operational Plan." By the end of May the Soviet ambassador reported that the KPA infantry was nearly ready for combat and that Kim Il Sung wanted to carry out the "attack" in late June before the rainy season began in July.[63]

Reunification Failed

On June 25 the DPRK launched predawn artillery barrages along the Ongjin Peninsula, the scene of frequent clashes. Within hours it had become a full-scale offensive along the border. The next day, on June 26, in a broadcast to his people, Kim Il Sung announced that the ROK forces had attacked but that the KPA had successfully counterattacked.[64] North Korea's plan was to quickly capture Seoul, to strike a crippling blow to the ROK army and then to advance further south as the South Korean state collapsed. ROK forces defended Seoul for two days and then, as Pyongyang had anticipated, they began to crumble. On the third day of fighting Seoul fell to the KPA amid horrendous scenes of thousands of panicked, fleeing civilians. Symbolic of the chaos and horror was the Han River Bridge incident. The South Korean military prematurely blew up the only bridge over the river that separated the capital from the country to the south, killing hundreds of civilians as they tried to escape the city.

Initially everything went as Kim and Pak had planned but very soon that changed. Pyongyang, as hoped, caught the USA and the ROK completely by surprise. However, after some initial confusion over whether or not this was a full-scale invasion was cleared up President Truman acted swiftly. On June 27, as Seoul was falling to the KPA, he ordered General MacArthur in Japan to use available US air and naval forces to support the South Korean army. Partly because he was uncertain of support from a Republican-dominated Congress and partly to give an international legitimacy as well as gain allied support Truman went directly to the UN and called for a resolution to give the USA authority to intervene. At the time the Soviet Union was boycotting the UN in protest of its refusal to allow the new communist regime in Beijing to take China's seat, which was still held by the nationalist government now headquartered on Taiwan. With Moscow absent the Security Council swiftly passed a resolution that demanded the withdrawal of DPRK forces and called for UN members to assist the ROK. On July 7, the UN Security Council established a unified military command under the USA. The UN forces that North Korea now faced were at least nominally an international force with 16 nations contributing troops. By the spring of 1951, this international force included British, Canadian, Turkish and Filipino personnel. It was, however, largely an American operation with the USA supplying most of the troops, paying the costs and in command.

Even with the US intervention Kim Il Sung's forces were still in a strong position. Since it would take weeks to mobilize forces from the USA, Washington relied on the 100,000 troops it had in occupied Japan who began arriving on June 30. But these soldiers were mainly involved in administrative and clerical duties and had little combat readiness. The US armed forces had been downsizing since the end of World War II, from 12 million men and women in uniform in 1945 to 1.6 million in June 1950. There were fewer than 600,000 in the army and many of these were based in Europe. When the first American troops saw action at Osan south of Seoul on July 5, they were forced into retreat along with their accompanying ROK forces.

North Korean forces continued their offensive. The KPA captured Taejŏn over one hundred miles south of Seoul in early July, and then advanced toward Pusan in the southeast corner of the country where the South Korean government had fled. It was now imperative to complete the conquest before American troops could be fully ready. However, two things were going wrong for Pyongyang. Although, the ROK forces were overwhelmed by the KPA and Seoul fell in days, the retreating South Korean troops did not collapse as fast as the North Koreans had expected but often put up stubborn resistance. And there was no popular uprising in support of the liberators from the north. Although there was some communist guerilla activity in the southeastern mountains this was merely the work of the remnants of the partisan forces that had largely been wiped out in the 1949–1950 campaign. By June 1950, most leftists in the South had been killed, imprisoned or had fled to the North. For the most part, the South Korean population fled or acquiesced to the North Koreans, but with some minor exceptions they did not rise up in arms against their own government. So Kim's expectation that the war would be over in a matter of days was wrong. Yet his forces continued to advance southward. By early August, they had reduced the ROK-controlled territory to a small area in the southeast corner of the country around Pusan, the so-called Pusan perimeter. Nearly 90 percent of the country was in the hands of the communist forces. But by that time enough US forces had arrived to halt the KPA's offensive and the war temporarily stalemated.

By early August, the Chinese were already becoming concerned, and Mao had decided to send Chinese volunteers to assist Pyongyang if US forces were to reverse the tide of war and advance toward his border. And soon the war did turn against the DPRK when UN forces commander General Douglas MacArthur came up with a daring plan to launch a surprise landing at Inchon (Inch'ŏn), entirely outflanking and trapping the KPA. Ignoring the objections of many military officials in Washington who feared it was too risky, MacArthur brought 75,000 marines and 260 ships to Inchon, negotiating the treacherous tides and sandbars to land. Despite Soviet and Chinese warnings that the Americans might land on the west coast Kim Il Sung focused on the Pusan perimeter. As a result he was caught unprepared. His forces were quickly overwhelmed as UN and ROK forces fought their way back into Seoul. By the end of September most of the KPA was in near total disarray, although some troops managed to retreat intact up the east coast. North Korean forces had been defeated with the loss of an estimated 50,000 killed, captured or missing. The attempt by Kim Il Sung and the rest of the KWP to unify the country under their leadership had failed disastrously.[65]

A panicky Kim Il Sung wrote to Stalin about the situation. Addressing him as "the liberator of the Korean people and the leader of the working peoples of the entire world," he explained the situation. "The adversary suffering one defeat after another, was cornered into a tiny piece of land at the southern-most tip of South Korea and we had a great chance of winning a victory," but the USA, in order to "restore its prestige and to implement by any means its long-held plans of conquering Korea and transforming its militarily strategic bridgehead," launched the attack on Inchon. The military situation, he reported, had now become "extremely grave." Street fighting is going on in Seoul, units in the south are cut off without communication with each other. Korea was in danger of becoming "a colony and a military springboard of the U.S. imperialists." Only direct assistance from the Soviet Union or "international volunteer units in China and other countries of people's democracy," he implored, would be able to prevent that from happening.[66] If the USA had been willing to accept the prewar status quo hostilities might have ended soon. But Kim was correct about the plans to invade the North. Both MacArthur and Syngman Rhee were determined to "rollback" the North Koreans. The UN resolution had only authorized that the North Korean invasion be repelled. Some in the USA and some allies, especially Britain, were wary about widening the war fearing Chinese or even Soviet intervention. But MacArthur wanted the complete destruction of the DPRK and the South Korean leaders wanted reunification, which now seemed so close.

China, which maintained no diplomatic relations with the America, sent a warning in early October through India's ambassador in Beijing that it would not tolerate a US presence on its border, but Washington ignored this. On September 30, ROK forces crossed the 38th parallel in pursuit of the KPA troops. Perhaps overconfident after the success of Inchon, Washington now gave MacArthur permission to destroy all KPA forces and, on October 7, the UN passed a vaguely worded resolution that approved the use of UN troops to cross the 38th parallel to establish a unified government. On October 9, UN forces moved north of the parallel. On October 10, the provincial capital of Wŏnsan fell to ROK forces as Kim Il Sung in a radio broadcast urged the KPA to "fight to the last drop of blood."[67] Throughout October, UN and ROK forces which were under UN authority, swept across North Korea capturing Pyongyang and other major cities while Kim Il Sung and the other DPRK leaders fled to the mountainous strongholds near the Manchurian border. On October 20, a triumphant President Rhee visited Pyongyang. Within a few weeks about 90 percent of North Korea was occupied by UN and ROK forces.

The UN/ROK occupation of the North was just as brief as the KPA occupation of the South had been. Just as Korea appeared to become reunified under the leadership the South, China came to the North Koreans' rescue and saved the regime, however, not before Stalin indicated a willingness to abandon the regime in October.[68] The fact that at this crucial moment Moscow was ready to abandon him, could not but have had a profound impact on Kim Il Sung who would seek to no longer be reliant on his former patron.

By late November the DPRK had been reduced to a few mountainous regions in the North, mostly near the Chinese border. Then, on November 27, the Chinese forces calling themselves the Chinese People's Volunteers and led by veteran commander Peng Dehuai counterattacked. From this point on the Chinese effectively took over control of military operations from the North Korea leadership. Overextended and overconfident UN troops were forced into a full retreat. Chinese forces advanced as swiftly as the UN and ROK forces had done weeks earlier. They retook Pyongyang on December 6 and within two weeks had forced the withdrawal of UN and ROK troops out of most of North Korea. Making the same error as the USA had done, the Chinese then advanced southward, crossing the 38th parallel and retaking Seoul on January 4 and continuing to the 37th parallel. But by late January their offensive was losing momentum. UN forces regrouped and stopped the Chinese. Beijing conducted a new offensive in February which was repelled with enormous Chinese losses. Despite the use of massive assaults, the so-called "human wave" tactic designed to compensate for China's inferior firepower, the UN forces were able to retake Seoul on March 15. It was the fourth time the city changed hands in nine months.

The conflict was now carried out mainly between China and the USA, with the DPRK and ROK leadership on the sidelines. With the two sides now arrayed roughly around the 38th parallel, the Truman administration was willing to negotiate a truce. By Spring, Mao too was ready to accept a stalemate with the peninsula divided approximately where it had been before the outbreak of the conflict. With Stalin's approval Mao signaled his willingness to begin armistice talks. On July 10, 1951 formal negotiations began as representatives of the Chinese People's Volunteers, the KPA and the UN command met. They came to an understanding that the boundary between the two would be roughly similar to but not exactly the same as the 38th parallel, instead extending a little below it to the west and above it to the east and separated by a demilitarized zone (DMZ). They also agreed to the creation of a Military Armistice Commission. Then progress slowed down. The conflict continued for two years after negotiations began.

Wartime Occupations

North Korea attempted to bring its revolution to the areas of the South that came under its control. Kim II Sung in his June 26 radio speech announced that South Korea was being liberated from Japanese and US imperialism, and called for the reinstatement of the people's committees that had sprung up in the days after liberation, calling them the "real organs of the people."[69] During the two to three months that KPA forces occupied Seoul and other major cities they attempted to carry out the same revolutionary changes as in the North. They set up people's committees as the local governing bodies. DPRK officials confiscated the property of the ROK government, its officials and "monopoly capitalists," and drew up plans to redistribute land in the countryside, completing the partial land reform that had begun under the US occupation. They released political prisoners from the jails, many of whom sought the opportunity to take revenge on the police and others who had persecuted them.

To what must have been a great disappointment to the North Korean leaders few South Koreans showed much enthusiasm for their liberators. Instead of embracing the communists, hundreds of thousands fled. Pusan, which became the wartime capital of the ROK, and other southern cites swelled with refugees. Some moderates joined the committees and the new North Korean liberators enjoyed some enthusiastic support from students and labor activists, but overall most South Koreans were wary of the new regime at best. The brief occupation served instead to create hostility toward the northern regime when it impressed thousands of young men into the KPA and carried out executions and confiscations. The worst atrocities were committed by the North Koreans during their hasty retreat. Many "traitors" were executed and others were taken with them as the North Korean forces retreated. It was a brief and, ultimately, bloody occupation.[70]

The occupation of the North was just as violent. Although nominally under the command of General MacArthur, ROK forces and intelligence officials often acted without much supervision. They carried out bloody reprisals. Any member of the Korean Workers' Party was subject to arrest or abuse. Since this was a mass party that included a sizeable proportion of the entire North Korean population, these punishments were unrealistic. North Korea, in a 26-volume official history of the conflict published in 1981, claimed 15,000 people were murdered in Pyongyang and tens of thousands elsewhere by the occupation forces. While exaggerated, ROK military and civilian officials did in fact execute thousands of civilians.[71] Farmers were required to return land to their former landlords. And when the ROK forces retreated they too took tens of thousands of North Koreans with them, most of whom were young men who had been forcibly conscripted. As with most civil wars, this was a vicious, unpleasant conflict. The brutality on both sides probably did little to win over support but rather left a legacy of fear and bitterness on both sides of the 38th parallel. Nonetheless, for all their heavy-handed methods few ordinary North Koreans put up much resistance to their southern "liberators" and their UN allies, and many seemed to have willingly cooperated with them. Their failure to actively resist was alarming to Kim Il Sung and his government. His response to this after the war was to make every effort to indoctrinate his people in the goals of the revolution and instill in them unquestioned loyalty to the regime.

Bringing the War to an End

Chinese intervention saved the North Korean regime but it also resulted in its loss of control over the war. Once the Chinese intervened actively in the fighting in November 1950 they assumed operational command. Mao, who blamed Kim for his failure to prepare for the defense of Inchon, confined him and the KPA to a subordinate role in the fighting for the rest of the war. In essence, the two main opponents in the war became the USA and China. From the summer of 1951 to the summer of 1953 the two powers were at a stalemate, with conventional fighting largely confined to a narrow strip of land. Kim Il Sung spent most of the war in a bunker in Chagang province near the Manchurian border.[72] On July 16, 1952, his weariness and concerns over the continual American bombing were expressed in a letter to Stalin requesting air defense. He wrote: "the enemy almost without suffering any kind of losses constantly inflicts on us huge losses in manpower and material values." And about the bombing campaign he reported that: "In only one 24 hour period of barbaric bombing, of only one city of Pyongyang (on July 11 and the night of July 12) more than 6,000 peaceful inhabitants were killed or wounded."[73]

Eventually all parties became weary of war. Shortly after his November 1952 election, Eisenhower, who had promised to end the conflict, visited Korea and made it his intention to bring the conflict to a close soon. The Soviet Union, however, may not have minded its continuation. The Soviets were careful not to become directly involved in the conflict. They supplied equipment to the North Koreans and Chinese, and flew some reconnaissance aircraft, but did not commit troops. This was in good part because Stalin was not eager to get into a conflict and did not want to take forces away from Europe which was the area of confrontation with the West that mattered most to the Soviet Union. The war from the Soviet point of view tied the US forces down in the east, lifted pressure from Europe, drained American resources but cost the Soviets little since it was fought by the Chinese and North Koreans. Mao may have found the cost of the conflict bearable as there were many troops no longer needed for the civil war, there was no shortage of cannon fodder and the war was a useful rallying support for his new regime. Furthermore, having fought the Americans to a stalemate added to his prestige. Yet as the war dragged on indications were that Mao was willing to bring it to an end. Stalin's death in March removed an obstacle to peace as his successors showed little interest in continuing the conflict. In the spring of 1953, the USA carried out the most extensive bombing of the war, raining horrific destruction upon the civilian population of North Korea as well as on the Chinese People's Volunteers and KPA forces. North Korea needed a respite from the constant American bombing; its hope of reunifying Korea was clearly dashed, at least for the near future. So in the spring of 1953 all parties were ready to bring the war to an end.

Talks were delayed over the issue of repatriation of prisoners since many of the Chinese and North Koreans held by the UN did not want to go home, but Beijing and Pyongyang insisted that all be returned. South Korea's President Rhee, still hoping for a victory that would reunite the country on his terms, did not want to end the conflict and tried to sabotage the talks by releasing many of the prisoners. When an agreement for a ceasefire was arrived at, he refused to sign it. The North Koreans, on the other hand, had little incentive to prolong the war, whose continuation only brought about more destruction from US bombing raids. Whatever his sentiments, Kim Il Sung probably had only a modest input in the negotiations. The UN, North Korea and China signed an armistice on July 27, 1953. Kim Il Sung's attempt to reunify the Korean peninsula had failed. But the DPRK survived and the war was not over.

Impact of the War on North Korea

North Korea's revolutionary regime may have survived but its losses in the conflict were appallingly high. Three years of conflict left a terrible toll. No one knows for certain the extent of losses. In fact, estimates vary wildly since there was so much confusion during the war as people fled and neither North Korea nor China has ever released figures. At least 2 million military personnel and civilians perished, and perhaps many more. These included 37,000 Americans and 4,000 UN allies killed and around 200,000 South Korean military casualties. Approximately 400,000 South Korean civilians may have died when all factors including starvation, disease and other causes related to dislocation are factored in. At least 200,000 from the Chinese People's Volunteers were killed; some estimates place this figure much higher, as many as 500,000. But it was North Korea that suffered the most. Out of a population in 1950 of about 9.6 million, at least 1 million most likely perished. These included around 200,000 North Korean troops and thousands of civilians, many as a result of US bombing campaigns. Altogether at least 10 percent of the population perished. In percentage terms this is far greater than German or Japanese losses in World War II, and possibly greater than Soviet losses in that conflict. In fact, it represents one of the highest rates of wartime death suffered by any country in the twentieth century.[74]

The sheer scale of destruction in North Korea was horrific. Few factories or public works escaped damage or destruction. A large proportion of the population were left homeless. Cities in the DPRK were totally destroyed, as was most of the infrastructure. Much of the destruction was the result of American bombing. The USA only intensified its air campaign against North Korea as the war dragged on. Civilians suffered especially when, on July 11, 1952, the Americans launched Operation *Pressure Pump* in which US planes undertook a massive bombing campaign of Pyongyang and 30 other cities.[75] Sŏng Hye-rang, a member of the North Korean elite, recalls that up to early 1952 Pyongyang streets were filled with people, and life still seemed vibrant.[76] But this attempt at normalcy ended with the mass bombing campaign. In May 1953 the USA carried out a bombing campaign directed at dams to destroy the rice crop.[77] The USA dropped 635,000 tons of bombs in Korea. This was 20 percent more than in the entire Pacific theater of World War II and slightly more than the Americans had dropped on Germany. Additionally, the Americans dropped 32,000 tons of napalm on North Koreans.[78] All this bombing was on a small country with less than 10 million people. North Korea's cities, even very small ones were devastated. Official US estimates were that between 50 and 90 percent of 18 of the 22 largest North Korean cities were destroyed, including 75 percent of Pyongyang, and 80 and 85 percent of Hamhŭng and Hŭngnam, the two largest industrial cities. This compares with an estimated 43 percent destruction of Japan's largest cities in World War II.[79] The North Korean regime never let its people forget the death and destruction the Americans inflicted upon them.

Although the war that Kim Il Sung was so eager to carry out was a disastrous failure, it had the effect of strengthening rather than weakening his hold on power. This may seem surprising. Yet when the Chinese took control of the military operations during the war they did not interfere with domestic political affairs. At the same time, as Andrei Lankov has stated, the war "untied the hands" of Kim Il Sung since it weakened the Soviet Union's influence. Militarily dependent upon China, North Korea achieved a greater measure of political independence from Moscow.[80] When the war went against him, Kim was quick to point the finger of blame at his rivals in the leadership. At a party meeting on December 21, 1950, Kim Il Sung carried out a purge of some party leaders.[81] Mu Chŏng, the veteran of Yanan, was dismissed in late 1950; he died shortly afterward. The communist leaders from the South were assigned special blame for the failure of the great guerilla uprising that had promised to appear. He also purged Hŏ Ka-i, a leader of the Soviet-Koreans and an expert on party organization. Hŏ had sought a balance between workers and peasants and wanted to restrict membership to a small vanguard based on the Soviet model, while Kim argued for a broad-based party whose membership ought to reflect the fact that 80 percent of all North Koreans were peasants. Finally, Kim Il Sung carried out the purge of those who had collaborated with the UN forces during their occupation of Pyongyang and much of the North.

Rather than unifying the peninsula the war hardened its division. The conflict solidified popular support for the South Korean state if not necessarily its leadership, and a generation of southerners developed a deep hostility toward the Kim Il Sung regime. The brutality of the North Korean occupiers during 1950–1951 alienated ordinary citizens who developed a deep antipathy toward the DPRK. Of course, the South, during its briefer occupation of the North, was also brutal and no doubt reinforced Pyongyang's propaganda about the nature of the southern regime, although it is hard to measure this. Furthermore, the USA was now fully committed to the defense of the ROK, which in the 1950s and early 1960s was one of the largest recipients of American aid. Seoul possessed and maintained an army of 600,000 troops equipped by the Americans. The USA maintained tens of thousands of troops stationed at a string of military bases in the South and patrolled the border along with ROK forces.

Kim Il Sung proclaimed the war a great victory since it defeated the attempt by the USA and ROK to invade and enslave the people of the North. A later official history declared it a "righteous fatherland liberation struggle" that fought and defeated the "U.S. and its puppets [who] launched an armed attack."[82] The conflict, however, was, in fact, a serious setback for the Kim Il Sung regime and its revolution. It was also a tragedy for Koreans who suffered so much yet failed to achieve the unity they all desired. Instead, the conflict drove the two Koreas bitterly apart and consolidated their separate systems. Fittingly, the Korean War ended in a ceasefire not a peace, for few Koreans regarded the settlement in 1953 as permanent. It was certainly not over for Kim Il Sung. For Kim, a battle had been lost but not the broader struggle. The DPRK would continue to pursue the goals that he and his comrades had decided upon years earlier: to liberate the country from imperialism, from its backward, feudal past, and to create a progressive, prosperous nation state free from foreign control, a nation that encompassed all Koreans.

Notes

1 Lee, Chong-sik, "Why Did Stalin Accept the 38th Parallel?," *Journal of Northeast Asian Studies* 4, no. 4 (Winter 1985): 67–74.
2 Kang Kwang-un, p. 95.
3 Jungsoo Lee, *The Partition of Korea After World War II: A Global History*. New York: Palgrave Macmillan, 2006, pp. 40–42.
4 Jungsoo Lee, p. 38.
5 Lankov, 2002, p. 2.
6 Armstrong, p. 41.
7 Lankov, 2002, p. 3.
8 Armstrong, 2003, p. 143.
9 Kim Sŏng-bo [Kim Seongbo], *Pukhan ŭi yŏksa Vol.1: Kŏn'guk kwa inminjujuŭi ŭi kyŏnghyŏm* [North Korean History Vol. 1: Establishment and Experience of the People's Democracy]. Seoul: Yŏksa Pip'yŏngsa, 2011, p. 31.
10 Kim Sŏng-bo, pp. 28–29.
11 Armstrong, 2003, p. 55.
12 Armstrong, 2003, p. 58.
13 Kim Kwang-un, pp. 116–121.
14 Lankov, 2002, p. 18.
15 Lankov, 2002, p. 18, n. 33.
16 Kim Kwang-un, p. 152.
17 Suh, p. 70.
18 Shin Jongdae, "North Korean State-Makin: Process and Characteristics," in Michael Seth (ed.), *The Routledge Handbook of Modern Korean History*. London: Routledge, 2016, pp. 197–210.
19 Suh, p. 71.
20 Armstrong, 2003, p. 59.
21 Kang Kwang-un, p. 372.
22 Lankov, 2002, p. 22.
23 Lankov, pp. 34–36.
24 Lankov, 2002, pp. 37–38.
25 Suh, p. 102.
26 Kang Kwang-un, p. 577.
27 Lankov, 2002, pp. 42–43.
28 Lankov, 2002, p. 47.
29 Armstrong, 2003, p. 220.
30 Miller, Owen, "North Korea's Hidden History," *International Socialism* 109 (2006): 153–166.

31 Kim Seong-bo [Kim Sŏng-bo], "The Decision-Making Process and Implementation of the North Korean Land Reform," in Pang Kie-Chung and Michael D. Shin, editors, *Landlords, Peasants and Intellectuals in Modern Korea*. Ithaca, NY: Cornell University Press, 2005, pp. 207–241.

32 Kim Seongbo, p. 207.

33 Kim Seongbo, pp. 232–234.

34 Armstrong, 2003, p. 147.

35 Armstrong, 2003, p. 91.

36 Suzy Kim, *Everyday Life in the North Korean Revolution, 1945–1950*. Ithaca NY: Cornell University Press, 2013, p. 119.

37 Suzy Kim, p. 175.

38 Armstrong, 2003, p. 94.

39 Lankov, 2002, pp. 38–39.

40 Sŏng,Hye-rang, *Tŭngnamu chip: Sŏng Hye-rang Chasŏjŏn* [*Wisteria House: The Autobiography of Song Hye-rang*]. Seoul: Chisiknara, 2000.

41 Kim Hakjoon, 2015, p. 49.

42 Armstrong, 2003, p. 148.

43 Armstrong, 2003, p. 134.

44 Jae-Cheon Lim. *Leader Symbols and Personality Cult in North Korea*, p. 79.

45 Armstrong, p. 223.

46 Armstrong, 2003, p. 228.

47 Kim Hakjoon, p. 42; Armstrong, 2003, p. 226.

48 Miller, Owen, "North Korea's Hidden History," *International Socialism* 109 (2006): 153–166.

49 Suzy Kim, pp. 121–122.

50 Hwang Chang-yŏp *Na nŭn yŏk-sa ŭi chilli rŭl poatta* [I saw the truth of history]. Seoul: Hanul, 1999.

51 Lankov, 2002, p. 47.

52 This follows the interpretation of the origins of the Korean War now supported by most scholars. For an alternative interpretation see the exhaustively researched Bruce Cumings, *Origins of the Korea War*, Vols I and 2. Princeton, NJ: Princeton University Press, 1981, 1990.

53 Shen Zhihua and Li Danhui, *After Leaning to Once Side: China and Its Allies in the Cold War*. Stanford, CA: Stanford University Press, 2011, p. 25.

54 Kim Kwang-un, p. 577.

55 Wada Haruki, *The Korean War: An International History*. Latham, MD: Rowman & Litttlefield, 2014, pp. 39–40.

56 Suh, p. 121.

57 Adrian Buzo, *The Guerilla Dynasty: Politics and Leadership in the DPRK 1945–1994*. Sydney: Allen & Unwin, 1999, p. 77.

58 Weathersby, Kathryn, "Korea, 1945–50, To Attack, or Not to Attack?: Stalin, Kim Il Sung, and the Prelude to War," *Cold War International History Project Bulletin* 5 (Spring 1995): 1–9.

59 Telegram from Stalin to Shtykov, January 30, 1950, *North Korean International Documentation Project*. Washington, DC: Wilson Center.

60 Shtykov to Stalin, January 31, 1950, *North Korean International Documentation Project*.

61 Lankov, 2013, p. 10.

62 Shen and Li, pp. 24, 32.

63 Shykov to Vishinsky, May 30, 1950, *North Korean International Documentation Project*.

64 Lankov, 2002, p. 61.

65 Wada, pp. 112–114.

66 Kim Il Sung and Pak Heonyeong to Stalin, September 29, 1950, *North Korea International Documentation Project*.

67 Wada, p. 127.

68 Alexandre Mansourov, "Stalin, Mao, Kim and China's Decision to Enter the Korean War," September 16–October 15, 1950.

69 Callum A. MacDonald, Callum, "So Terrible a 'Liberation': The U.N. Occupation of North Korea," *Bulletin of Concerned Asian Scholars*, 23, no. 2 (1991): 6–7, 17.

70 Armstrong, *Tyranny of the Weak*, pp. 25–27.

71 Kang Chŏng-gu, "Han'guk chŏnchange kwa pukhan sahoechuŭi kŏnsŏl," [The Korean War and the construction of North Korean Society] in Son Ho-ch'ŏl (eds), *Han'guk chŏnchaeng kwa nampukhan sahoe ŭi kuchojŏk pyŏnhwa* [The Korean War and Structural Change in North and South Korean Society]. Seoul: Kyŏngnam Taehakkyo kungnipdong munje yŏn'gyso, 1991, pp. 159–201, 170.

72 Suh, p. 138.

73 Kathryn Weathersby, "New Russian Documents on the Korean War," introduction and translations by Kathryn Weathersby. *CWHIP Bulletin*, no. 6/7 (Winter 1995/1996): 77.

74 Estimates of North Korean casualties vary considerably and there seems to be no consensus on the numbers.

75 Bruce Cumings, *The Korean War: A History*. New York: The Modern Library, 2010, p. 152.

76 Sŏng Hye-rang, p. 227.
77 Cuming, *The Korean War: A History*, p. 154.
78 Cumings, p. 159; Crane, *American Airpower Strategy in Korea, 1950–1953*. Lawrence, KS: University of Kansas Press, 2000, pp. 168–171.
79 Cumings, p. 160.
80 Lankov, 2002, p. 62.
81 Wada, p. 155.
82 Kang Chŏng-gu, p. 162.

3

Industrialization and Political Consolidation, 1953–1967

Following the disastrous failure at reunification North Korea underwent an impressive recovery. It then experienced one of the world's most rapid rates of industrialization, transforming itself from a predominately rural to an urban-industrial nation while completing the socialization of the entire economy. In view of the achievement of these years, there could be little doubt in the minds of the leaders of the regime or in those of many foreign observers that the country was becoming one the most industrialized, modern and developed states in Asia. Accompanying this economic progress was the political consolidation of Kim Il Sung and his guerilla partisans, as they eliminated real or potential rivals. All this was achieved as DPRK gained further political autonomy and avoided being a satellite of either Beijing or Moscow.

Reconstruction and Total Socialism

Reconstruction 1953–1956

Few nations in modern history were more devastated than North Korea at the end of the Korean War, and few recovered so quickly. In the summer of 1953 North Korea was in ruins. American bombing had destroyed much of the country's infrastructure. Many smaller plants had been repaired yet industrial production was at only 36 percent of its 1949 level.[1] In May 1953, during the last months of the conflict further bombing targeted the country's main irrigation dams disrupting agricultural production and contributing to severe food shortages. The country was poor, hungry and in desperate need of aid. Hwang Jang Yop (Hwang Chang-yŏp), later the regime's chief ideologist, returning from studying in Moscow described the shock at how bad conditions were. In Pyongyang few houses were standing. People were living in dugouts in the hillside, beggars filled the streets along with thieves desperate for food. Even as a new faculty member at the elite Kim Il Sung University food rations were limited; he recalls living on turnip soup. The wife of one his colleagues gave birth in the morning and was standing in line waiting for food rations in the afternoon.[2] The enormously high war casualties meant there was a shortage of younger men. Foreign observers were struck by this shortage of men and the fact that women were doing much of the work in construction and other fields.[3]

Yet North Korea, despite this, made a strong recovery. In just three years cities were rebuilt and factories were operating. By 1957 industrial production in most sectors had returned to their modest 1949 levels and the country was about to embark on a spurt of rapid economic growth.

North Koreans would later claim almost full credit for the recovery but foreign aid was crucial to the effort. There was a dire need for assistance and the regime wasted no time in asking for it. Within days of the armistice Kim Il Sung supplied the Soviets with a list of aid requirements. A month later, in September 1953, he led a delegation to the Soviet Union to meet with Stalin's successors and negotiate assistance. In November he journeyed to Beijing. Meanwhile, other North Korean officials traveled in the countries of Eastern Europe from June to November seeking aid. The Soviets and the Chinese agreed to new loans, and the Chinese canceled all previous debts.[4] Soviet and Eastern bloc countries sent thousands of advisors, mostly engineers and technicians, to assist. China also helped, not only with loans but also by using its Chinese People's Volunteers still stationed in the country to help with construction and thereby somewhat easing the labor shortage. With the help of this aid from its communist allies the regime launched a three-year economic plan for the period 1954–1956.

Pyongyang's allies helped rebuild some of the prewar infrastructure such as the chemical fertilizer complex from the colonial period at Hŭngnam.[5] Soviet aid projects were instrumental in the construction of the Sup'ing hydroelectric power plant (the largest in Asia), a large steel mill at Sŏngjin (the city was renamed Kim Ch'aek) in the northeast and in the rebuilding of the port of Namp'o. Each of the Soviet Union's allies contributed. The Czechs provided buses, Albania asphalt, Mongolia provided 10,000 horses and the East Germans sent a term of 350 engineers and technicians to supervise the rebuilding of the industrial city of Hamhŭng.[6] Eastern Europeans were especially active in rebuilding old and constructing new factories. Several hundred Soviet-Korean technicians and experts came and provided valuable expertise. Thousands of North Koreans went to the Soviet Union and Eastern Europe for training programs. It is difficult to measure this foreign assistance since aid was calculated in ways that did not reflect market prices. Some of it came in the form of materials which were sold at extremely low prices and loans with generous repayment terms. The Soviet Union and its Eastern European satellites financed 77 percent of imports from 1954 to 56. By one reckoning, aid accounted for 33 percent of state revenues in 1954.[7] Furthermore, the Soviets supplied military equipment and important resources such as oil as subsidized prices. But this assistance needs to be placed in perspective. While the Soviets and their Eastern European allies supplied technical help and material on a large scale, Soviet aid to North Korea was smaller proportionally than the assistance the USA provided to South Korea. Washington financed half the government budget of the ROK in the 1950s. It also was over a shorter period of time—South Korea remained heavily reliant on the USA until the mid-1960s, but by 1960 Soviet aid accounted for only 2.6 percent of the DPRK's revenues.[8] This massive aid injection was confined to just the first several years after the war.

Another contributing factor to the country's rapid recovery was the effective use of mass mobilization campaigns involving the entire population for reconstruction projects. Calling it "war by another means" Kim Il Sung organized reconstruction efforts as if they were military campaigns complete with "speed-battles" and "144-day campaigns" to reach targets. Immediately after the war, mass mobilization succeeded in clearing the destruction, rebuilding houses, schools, factories and other facilities. The population was called upon to make heroic sacrifices for the national effort; and this they did, working extremely long hours while living barely above the subsistence level. Nearly everyone, including students, were enlisted to work on building projects. Sŏng Hye-rang, recalled that during her four years as a student at Kim Il Sung University she spent only one year and eight months studying, with the rest of the time devoted to laboring on construction sites.[9]

A major effort in the reconstruction was to rebuild Pyongyang into a showcase city. Since the city had been so systematically bombed by the USA in 1951 there were few structures still standing; thus Kim was able to recreate an entirely new city. He personally supervised the rebuilding as chairman of the Pyongyang City Rehabilitation Committee. It became a city designed for display with great squares—the People's Army Square, Mao Zedong Square and the largest, the Kim Il Sung Square. It had impressive public buildings such as the National Theatre and Kim Il Sung University, and a Stalin Street lined with modern apartments.[10] Less visible were the more modest residential apartments along muddy streets. But while housing was terribly crowded by Western standards, with several families sharing a single bathroom, at least it provided adequate shelter.[11]

Collectivizing Agriculture and Total Socialism

The most important sector of the economy in private hands was agriculture. While some communist countries allowed for small-scale markets for private produce, Kim, following the Soviet command economy model, opted for total collectivization. Kim Il Sung had several reasons for pursing collectivization or "cooperativization" (hyŏpdonghwa) as he called it—North Korea never actually used the term collectivization. It seemed the most effective way to modernize agriculture without compromising the country's need to develop heavy industry. With his focus on was industrialization, Kim sought to extract the agricultural surpluses from the peasantry to supply the anticipated large urban workforce, much as Stalin had done in Russia. Geography and the labor shortage may have contributed to this decision. Food supplies were a problem in this mountainous region with its short growing season. Nor did the DPRK's allies have the large food surpluses to offer as aid, as the USA was able to give the ROK. Food shortages appeared early. Both in 1954 and in the early 1970s the state had forcibly requisitioned crops.[12] Agricultural problems were compounded by the Korean War, which resulted in a shortage of manpower and of draft animals. Kim and his planners saw the solution to these problems in consolidating small plots of land into large farms that could be worked by tractors and other mechanized equipment.

The original plan was for the collectivization of agriculture to be carried out as a gradual three-stage process, beginning the mutual aid teams called *p'umassi-ban* that would help each other in carrying out the work. This collective method drew from traditional practices of village cooperation in which farmers would share the use of oxen or help each other. In the second stage, members of a hamlet would go beyond mutual aid to pooling and sharing tools as well as labor. Finally, the third stage was carried out whereby farmers were simply allotted a share of the crop and supplied other goods in accordance with their work. At the Third Party Congress in April 1956 Kim Il Sung reiterated that the policy was to proceed slowly, and gradually move toward a more "voluntary" approach to collectivization. But later that year this policy changed and it was decided to accelerate the process. The decision may have been in emulation of Mao who in September 1955 decided to speed up collectivization. And indeed the pace of collectivization was similar. By the end of 1956, 80.9 percent of households joined a cooperative at a similar speed to that of China where the figure was 83 percent. By end of 1957, 95.6 percent of all farm families were part of agricultural collectives (according to a 1981 official census).[13]

In the summer of 1958 the state announced that collectivization had been completed. It had all proceeded swiftly and rather smoothly. There was none of the resistance and upheavals that characterized the Soviet Union's collectivization two decades earlier. Why this was so is not entirely clear but collectivization may have been aided by the disruptions of the Korean War which saw many farmers displaced.[14] Few changes impacted so many people. Several million farmers who had become small private landowners now became laborers for the state. One can imagine how the complete collectivization of agriculture must have been an unwelcome and unexpected outcome for the millions of peasants who had so enthusiastically embraced land reform only a few years earlier. In 1946 the peasants had attained ownership of the land they worked; a decade later they had lost this same right.

In 1957 cabinet decrees 96 and 102 prohibited the buying and selling of grain.[15] Basic commodities were collected and redistributed by the state, with no private markets. The few remaining private enterprises were taken over by the state. Eventually, as the system evolved, there was virtually no local or regional autonomy; all decision making came down to the basic allocation of food and clothing to each household through the public distribution system directed from the center. As was the case in the Soviet Union from 1928, Kim focused on developing heavy industry that would increase the industrial base of the economy and could support a strong military rather than a focus on consumer goods. All private ownership was prohibited and private markets were all but eliminated. By the late 1950s North Korea had gone beyond most Soviet bloc states in creating an entirely state-directed socialist economy.

The Political Consolidation of Kim Il Sung and His Manchurian Guerilla Comrades

During the first few years after the Korean War Kim Il Sung established his personal autocracy and eliminated from power all but his Manchurian guerilla comrades. He had begun the process of removing non-partisans from power during the Korean War as he rebuilt the party. During the war, while often powerless to decide military policies, he was free to conduct party business. Kim blamed Mu Chŏng, the experienced and respected military commander from the Yanan group, for the military disasters of the early war and had him dismissed from his posts. The prominent Soviet-Korean Hŏ Ka-i was, as we have seen in the previous chapter, also purged. While consolidating his hold on the Korean Workers' Party (KWP) he also appeared to strengthen his power over the Korean People's Army

(KPA). In December 1952 he appointed himself marshal of the army, outranking all his military officers.[16] But it was only after the conflict ended that the major purges began.

First, Kim Il Sung eliminated the domestic communist leadership—those communists who had remained in Korea working underground during the colonial period. This first major purge took place on August 3, 1953, only a week after the armistice when the DPRK conducted its first Stalinist show trial. Twelve domestic communists were indicted and convicted during the three-day affair. The most prominent was Yi Sŭng-yŏn (1905–1953).[17] Yi had been active in the Korean Communist Party almost since its inception, when he had joined at the age of 20. Arrested many times he worked under Pak Hŏn-yŏng and enjoyed a prominent career in the Korean Communist Party, including serving as editor of the party newspaper *Haebang ilbo* after liberation.[18] The charges against him and others were absurd. They were accused of spying for the USA, of deliberately working with it to destroy the Communist Party in the South and of trying to overthrow the DPRK government. The defendants confessed to all charges and were executed. They also admitted to attempting to replace Kim Il Sung with Pak Hŏn-yŏng. Pak, perhaps owing to his prominence, was arrested but only expelled from the party. His one-day trial took place in December 1955. He was sentenced to death after he admitted to all charges, including being the chief spy for the USA and having worked for the Americans since 1939.[19]

With all the prominent domestic communists eliminated, Kim Il Sung turned to the removal of members of the Soviet and Yanan groups. His decision to eliminate Soviet and Yanan Koreans was not only intended to consolidate power and remove potential rivals but also part of his effort to establish the DPRK's autonomy and protect himself from the de-Stalinization policies of the Soviet Union after 1953. The North Korean revolution he led was, at heart, a nationalist, anti-imperialist movement, one that sought to regain the country's full sovereignty. Soviet help was crucial in the beginning but Kim had no desire for North Korea to be a Soviet tributary state. Certainly, as Armstrong and others have argued, the North Korean revolution had strong indigenous routes, with the leadership in Pyongyang being important actors in shaping events.

Yet Moscow and its deputies in North Korea held ultimate authority during the years immediately after liberation from Japan. Even after independence in 1948 North Korean leaders, dependent on Soviet aid and military support, consulted with Moscow before making important decisions. This changed with Chinese intervention in the Korean War. From November 1950 to July 1953 it was the Chinese, not the North Koreans or Moscow, that had operational control over the war. When Beijing took over direction for the war from the North Korean leadership this also weakened Moscow's political control. After the conflict the DPRK remained heavily dependent on Soviet aid but the period of tutelage was over. Kim Il Sung sought to ensure that the Soviets did not try to re-establish control over his country and make it a satellite of Moscow.

At the same time the de-Stalinization efforts taking place in the Soviet Union were as much a threat to Kim Il Sung as they were to other "little Stalins" in Eastern Europe. Kim, who had patterned his leadership after Stalin, could only be alarmed by the changes. So the purges of the late 1950s were an assertion of the autonomy North Korea had gained from the Soviet Union during the Korean War, a resurgence of Korean nationalism, a resistance to the contagion of de-Stalinization and consolidated Kim Il Sung's personal power by removing those who were not closely associated with him, especially those with links to the outside powers—the Soviet Union or China.

In early 1955 Kim removed the Yanan faction member Pak Il-u. Pak had served as a liaison between the Chinese People's Volunteers and the KWP during the Korean War and was known as "Mao's man" because of his close ties with the Chinese leader.[20] On December 28 that year, at a meeting of KWP Central Committee Members, Kim criticized Pak Ch'ang-ok the most prominent of the Soviet Koreans for excessively copying the Soviet Union. Calling for more Korean themes in art and literature Kim introduced the term *juche* (or *chuch'e*, often translated as "self-reliance"). This was the first public mention of the term that would later evolve into the official state ideology. The following month Pak Ch'ang-ok was removed from his position as Chair of the State Planning Committee. Then came new policies in Moscow. During February 1956, in a closed session of the 20th Congress of the Soviet Communist

Party, Khrushchev launched his attack on Stalin, denouncing his many crimes and cult of personality. Since Kim Il Sung's own cult of personality was modeled on Stalin's and since Stalin himself was still revered in the DPRK this was threatening. Furthermore, the new Soviet leadership's call for greater emphasis on consumer goods and light industry also ran counter to Kim's own plans to focus on heavy industry.

Initially Kim seemed to deflect the potential challenges to his own power by the new Soviet currents. When the Third Party Congress of the KWP met in April 1956, he used the new criticism of personality cults as a means for justifying his purge of domestic communists. He criticized the personality cult that had been built around the now disgraced and recently executed Pak Hŏn-yŏng.[21] Yet trouble for Kim came while he was overseas from June 1 to July 19 on an extended trip to the Soviet Union and Eastern Europe. While absent, members of the Soviet-Korean and Yanan groups, possibly with Soviet encouragement, plotted for change. Later official accounts made accusations that Pak Ch'ang-ok sought to become party chair with Ch'oe Ch'ang-ik of the Yanan faction serving as premier, but the truth of what took place is not clear. Returning from his trip Kim Il Sung seems to have become aware of the pending challenge to his leadership and appeared ready to face his critics at a Central Committee meeting held in August. Although the details of what went on are rather uncertain, Pak Ch'ang-ok, Ch'oe Ch'ang-ik and apparently others criticized Kim's policies, including placing too much emphasis on heavy industry and the recent appointment of his guerilla comrade Ch'oe Yong-gŏn to a top leadership post.[22] Kim maintained control at the meeting and if—and this is not certain—the real aim of his opponents was to remove him from the top party post it failed. Pak and Ch'oe were arrested and six other high-ranking officials fled to Manchuria. Some members of the party issued a declaration critical of Kim Il Sung but were quickly arrested.[23] In general, the opposition to Kim seemed unorganized and largely ineffective.

Alarmed at the prospect of a Stalinist-type purge, Anastas Mikoyan, a Soviet Politburo member; and Peng Dehuai, the Chinese military commander during the Korean War, arrived in North Korea in September and jointly called on Kim for restraint. Under pressure Kim halted his attempted purge. This intervention by Moscow and Beijing appears, from later documents, to have been a bitter experience for Kim Il Sung, highlighting the very situation that he was so determined to avoid—his country's subservience to outside foreign powers. Its effect seemed to have made him even more determined to achieve as much freedom of action for himself and autonomy for his country as possible. In fact, it may be one of the truly defining events of his regime, reinforcing all his fears. For his opponents the Soviet and Chinese appeals bought them only a few months. After the crisis cooled Kim launched a full-scale purge in 1957.

The Great Purge

A major purge began in 1957. This time it was not confined to a few top leaders but was part of a thorough investigation of all citizens—the sorting of people according to degrees of loyalty to the regime. Kim Il Sung was determined to rid himself of opponents, a determination that was most likely reinforced by the Soviet intervention in political upheavals and the Soviet invasion of Hungary in October 1956.[24] The prelude to the purges was a party investigation into the background of members which began toward the end of 1956. Initially the North Koreans explained to their allies that this was being carried out to replace deteriorated party membership cards, to rehabilitate former rank-and-file party members, and to educate them.[25] The following year saw the removal of almost all Soviet-Koreans and then Yanan group members. In 1957 Kim Tu-bong was replaced as president of the Supreme People's Assembly and titular head of state by Ch'oe Yong-gŏn. Many, if not most, of the Soviet-Koreans, including Pak Ch'ang-ok, fled to the Soviet Union and some of the Yanan faction members, including Ch'oe Ch'ang-ik, went to China. The scope of the purge widened in the summer of 1957, perhaps influenced by the anti-rightist campaign that Mao had launched against his critics in June of that year.[26]

But even before this, the Standing Committee issued on May 30, 1957 a directive "On Transforming the Struggle against Counterrevolutionary Elements into an All-Party, All-People's Movement" which called for a thorough investigation of all party members.[27] The backgrounds of all were scrutinized and everyone was placed into three general categories (*kyech'ŭng*): those deemed "loyal" or the core (*haeksim*), those classified as "wavering"(*t'ongyo*) and those considered "hostile" (*choktae*). The loyal or core class members were known as tomatoes—red through and through; the "wavering" members as apples (red on the outside only); and the "hostile" members were called grapes. This consolidated and refined one of the most distinctive features of North Korean society: its rigid social structure. Each category became what amounted to a hereditary caste whose status was passed on from parents to children. Later this system was further elaborated with the creation of subcategories. In the late 1950s this new class system served as a means of conducting a thorough purge of party members. Accompanying this purge the North Korean Cabinet issued Decree No. 149, which prohibited people belonging to "hostile forces" from living near the border, the seacoast, within 50 km of Pyongyang or Kaesong (Kaesŏng), or within 20 km of any other big city. As a result, according to Lankov, some 70,000 people are believed to have been relocated to remote areas in the mountainous regions of the north.[28] In the summer of 1957 the state introduced another measure: the *oho tamdangje* (five households-in-charge system) of neighborhood collective security. This revived an old East Asian custom by which families were lumped together into neighborhood units and held accountable for the actions of their unit members. Under this system citizens were encouraged to spy and report on each other.

More than 100,000 citizens fell victim to arrests during 1957–1959, some 2,500 were executed, some publicly. This was a number equal to all those previously punished since 1945 and proportionately on a scale not far short of the Soviet Union's Great Purges of 1937–1938.[29] Show trials took place for those accused of being South Korean agents, of being saboteurs and of cooperating with the South Korean and American forces during their occupation of the North in the fall of 1950.[30] Meanwhile, the themes and subjects of art, literature and textbooks became more Korean. In 1956 the state ordered an end to all performances of Soviet plays in Korean theaters.[31] As this Koreanization continued streets named after foreign allies were renamed, pictures of Soviet leaders disappeared and references to the Soviet role in the liberation of the country were removed from the history books.

When the Fourth Congress of the KWP met in 1961, Kim Il Sung's control over the party and its domination by his fellow ex-guerillas were near complete. At the party congress in 1956 there was a higher percentage of ex-guerillas in the Central Committee than in the past, five of the eleven members of the Standing Committee (Politburo) were former guerillas versus only two out of seven in 1948.[32] But they were still a minority sharing posts with Yanan and Soviet comrades. In 1961, by contrast, ex-guerillas completely dominated the upper echelon of the party. Of the eleven members of the Standing Committee, the highest body of the party, all were partisans with the exception of Nam Il, a Soviet-Korean, and Kim Ch'ang-man from the Yanan faction. Nam Il was an early and loyal supporter of Kim Il Sung. Kim Ch'ang-man was an interesting case. Throughout the 1950s he enthusiastically championed the party leader. Outdoing others in proving his loyalty he had first denounced the domestic communists as traitors and collaborators with the enemy and then attacked the leaders of the Yanan faction, including Pak Ch'ang-ok and Kim Tu-bong, accusing them of being American spies. But self-serving demonstrations of total loyalty did not save him from being dropped from the leadership only a few years later.[33] Of the 85 members of the Central Committee only 28 returned. All but one of his partisans (who had died) retained their posts; almost all non-partisans were demoted or purged. There were now 37 ex-guerillas, only two Soviet-Korean and three Yanan members and only one member of South Korea's domestic faction, historian Paek Nam-un. Almost all the rest were clients of guerillas.[34] A few with no partisan background owed their positions to family ties to the partisans, including Kim Yŏng-ju, Kim Il Sung's younger brother.[35] Kim Il Sung's partisans were in full control of the party.

Kim Il Sung's removal from power of all but his fellow Manchurian guerillas had a profound impact on North Korea's development. The entire society became molded by the guerilla culture. Party propaganda constantly extolled the deeds of the Manchurian fighters. The Poch'ŏnbo Museum was opened to commemorate Kim's great military achievement, and in 1957 its 20th anniversary was publicly celebrated.[36] In 1958 the Research Center for the History of the KWP began a program of elaborating on the myths of Kim and his guerilla comrades. In 1959 it published the first part of the four-volume *Memoirs of the Anti-Japanese*

Guerillas.[37] This would soon be a must-read for all citizens.[38] The Manchurian guerillas not only featured as the heroes in exaggerated stories, memoirs, fiction, films and songs but became the only legitimate bearers of the Korean communist and national liberation tradition. In their study of the North Korean political culture, Hoenik Kwon and Byung-ho Chung remarked that the anti-colonial armed resistance of Kim Il Sung's partisans in Manchuria became "the single most important, most sacred, all-encompassing saga of the nation's modern history."[39] But the feats of the partisans were more than just a source to legitimize the regime and form a basis for national pride; they became the model to be emulated in almost every endeavor. This was accompanied by a general decline in the intellectual level of society, resulting from the purge of many of the best educated people. According to Hwang Jang Yop, the North Korean scholars who survived the purges were less academically trained and compensated by demonstrating greater loyalty.[40] This intellectual decline was reinforced further by the country's increasing isolationism, as contact with even its East European allies, already restricted, became more so and North Koreans married to foreigners were required to divorce them.[41]

Kim's purges eliminated most of the more educated and broadly experienced members of the leadership. With power firmly in the hands of the Manchurian partisans and their clients, fewer and fewer positions of responsibility were held by people with any exposure to the outside world other than the Manchurian mountain villages near the Korean border. The leadership had become largely restricted to an extremely narrow segment of the communist and nationalist movements. And they were the least educated. The party itself was a mass party with over a million members, the largest in proportion to the size of its population of any communist country. It also differed from most other communist regimes in that almost all party members had been recruited since 1945. They were for the most part poorly educated, had no foreign experience and knew of no other leader than Kim Il Sung. Fewer than a quarter of the party cell secretaries had a secondary education and many had no formal education at all.[42] Perhaps in no other modern society was power so effectively monopolized by people with so little education and so little exposure to the larger world.

North Korea's Great Leap Forward

North Korea's great purges coincided with its economic great leap forward, an initiative to quickly transform the country into an industrial nation. In 1957, with the economy restored to its prewar level and agricultural collectivization being accelerated to near completion, North Korea spelled out in its Five-Year Plan (1957–1961) as part of its great push for industrial transformation. It would be the only five-year plan until 2016. The focus shifted from recovery to an emphasis on rapid industrialization. The term "Great Leap Forward" was not actually used by North Korea but the policy did resemble Mao Zedong's own drive to transform a poor, agrarian society into an industrial state by setting wildly ambitious targets and employing mass mobilization to make up for a shortage in technology. This was not coincidental, as Kim Il Sung was indeed influenced by Mao. When Mao inaugurated the Great Leap Forward in China in the spring of 1958, Kim began accelerating his own targets, announcing later that year that the Five-Year Plan would in fact be completed in just three and a half years.[43] Mao boasted that China would soon surpass Britain in steel production; in 1959 Kim proclaimed that in ten years North Korea would surpass Japan in per capita industrial output.[44]

The symbol of North Korea's great leap was the *Ch'ŏllima* movement, so called after a mythical Korean horse capable of galloping a thousand *li* (several hundred miles) a day. The Ch'ŏllima movement had its reputed origins in December 1956 just before the Five-Year Plan was rolled out and when Kim Il Sung visited the Kangsŏn steel mill to personally direct the work. The plant had a capacity for 60,000 tons but was producing only 40,000. Needing more steel Kim Il Sung ordered that the plant increase its production by at least 10,000 tons. When the plant managers said this was impossible Kim went to the plant and took matters into his own hands. Discussing problems of production with the workers he spurred them on to exceed the production quotas assigned to them and to come up with their own solutions for overcoming production problems and developing more efficient methods. As a result, production at the mill not only met the target but exceeded it, with an output of 90,000 tons of steel; this increased even more the following year to 120,000 tons.[45]

The steel mill success became a legendary event, cited for decades by party propaganda organs and learned by all North Koreans as a story of inspiration and emulation. "The creative power of our working class and our people is really inexhaustible," Kim declared; and he tested this proposition in endless campaigns.[46] Using the Kangsŏn steel works as a model Kim Il Sung inaugurated the Ch'ŏllima movement at a party plenum in September 1958. In a radio broadcast that month he urged North Koreans to "rush forward like a flying horse" and fulfill the Five-Year Plan in three and a half years.[47] Fired up with enthusiasm, a plant worker, Chin Ŭng-wŏn, was reported to have created the first Ch'ŏllima Work Team, a group of workers tasked with exceeding their quotas. The media presented reports of workers accomplishing extraordinary feats of production by working extra hours and putting in near superhuman efforts. Construction projects were completed ahead of schedule and factories exceeded their targets through these efforts.[48] Propaganda organs carried out endless exhortations to increase production, seeking to grind out more output from the people. There was a "Movement to See the Early Morning Stars" to make workers and farmers get up and go to work very early, and a "Movement Not to Have Soup" which originated in textile factories to minimize the time lost on bathroom breaks.[49] In 1959 students were sent to construction sites under the slogan "One Stretch After One Thousand Shovels."[50]

Kim's big push for rapid economic modernization resembled Mao's Great Leap Forward in two other ways: the development of local-based industries and the consolidation of collectives into larger units. At a June 1958 KWP meeting a new plan was announced to develop each of the 209 counties into largely self-sufficient units for the production of consumer goods.[51] Kim Il Sung, like Mao, sought to make each local government unit self-sufficient in basic necessities—with their own facilities for clothing, footwear, food processing and so on. This was partly to enable central government to devote its resources and attention to heavy industry. Kim, again like Mao, also decided to consolidate the newly created agricultural cooperatives into larger units. In November 1958 the state announced that the nation's 13,309 cooperatives, which averaged 79 households, were to be merged into 3,880 large units or around 300 households each. The state's aim was to create economies of scale that would improve grain production.[52] Meanwhile, official reports claimed enormous success, with grain production increasing from 320,000 metric tons in 1957 to 483,000 tons in 1961.[53]

The attraction of the Chinese model for the North Korean leadership was irresistibly strong. China in the late 1950s was arguing that its Great Leap Forward was a special road for China and other Asian societies to follow and one that relied on a voluntarist approach and mass mobilization to compensate for the shortage of capital and technical expertise. As Kim distanced himself from Moscow he may have found in Beijing a more compatible model for development. He and many others in the party leadership spoke Chinese and felt culturally closer to their giant neighbor. However, Kim was not simply emulating Mao Zedong. Both policies were driven by incessant needs. Even before 1958 Kim had displayed a concern for local self-sufficiency, perhaps deriving his experiences from the guerilla base areas in Manchuria. The lessons from the Korean War were also still fresh in Korean memory and there was a concern to ensure local self-sufficiency in the event of another invasion. And the consolidation of farms was an attempt to increase efficiency and free labor for industrial needs. Kim did not imitate all aspects of Mao's Great Leap Forward. The collective farms were consolidated but not on the scale of China's. There were no communal kitchens or backyard steel furnaces; nor were they ever called communes but remained "cooperatives."[54] As one Eastern European reported in 1960, the "Korean comrades have never tried to copy the Chinese experiences." The idea of introducing Chinese-style communes "was firmly rejected."[55] Overall the effort was nothing as extreme as the disastrous policies of Mao which led to mass famine.

Kim Il Sung, also differed from Mao by showing greater flexibility. It did not take long before the problems in pursuing these wildly ambitious targets became apparent. By the end of 1959 he decided to slow down his efforts. Kim admitted that the fast pace of economic development was creating many "defects," including shortages in manpower and industrial raw materials, housing and food.[56] The year 1960 was declared a "buffer year," a period of adjustments. He moderated some of his more extreme demands for production increases and admitted to some shortcomings. Still, when he began a new Seven-Year Plan (1961–1967) its ambitious targets reflected all the optimism of the early years, and considering the success of the Three-Year and Five-Year Plans this was not entirely unreasonable.

While he began to modify some of his economic policies somewhat in 1959 and 1960 Kim never abandoned his dedication to the idea of working with and learning from the people. He continued in his efforts to seek to overcome bureaucratic inertia, to avoid party officials being cut off from the masses and to tap the creative energies of the people. To achieve this he developed two new economic policies: Ch'ŏngsan-ri method (*Ch'ŏngsan-ri munbŏp*), to spur production on the farm, and the Taean work system, to increase production at the factory. The Ch'ŏngsan-ri method began when Kim Il Sung visited a collective farm not far from Pyongyang in February 1960. As at the Kangsŏn steel mill he closely supervised the work, giving instructions on major tasks such as when to plant and on minor details including when to schedule soccer games so that they did not interfere with work. He initially spent 14 days at Ch'ŏngsan-ri and subsequently between February and October 1960 he made another 38 trips to the farm. It was reported that "He was so kind and unceremonious that the people could tell him their minds without any cautions." He was thus able to listen and learn from the people.[57] Kim's intention was to set an example for all party cadres to follow. Like Mao he worried that the new officialdom had become divorced from the people. Based on his "on-the-spot guidance system" (*hyŏnji chido*) he had high-ranking officials of the KWP visit and work with the farmers. This too had Maoist echoes, resembling the similar *xiafang* (downward to the village) efforts in China in 1956.[58] Farmers were encouraged to present their grievances and their suggestions for improving production, and to be active participants in the management of the enterprise. Bonuses, financial incentives as well as awards and titles were also used as incentives to get farmers to increase output. The Ch'ŏngsan-ri method became the standard model involving party officials in direct intervention, participation and interaction with farmers for the next 50 years.

The following year Kim Il Sung launched the Taean work system (*Taeanŭi saŏpch'ekye*). Again it commenced with Kim Il Sung carrying out on-the-spot guidance to workers at the Taean electric machine plant in December 1961. This brought the management of factories under the control of KWP committees consisting of managers, engineers, plant workers and party officials. The idea was to establish direct worker participation in the management of plants while preventing arbitrary control of decision making by local managers and bureaucrats. While the initiative was designed to draw upon the wisdom and creativity of the workers by having them actively involved in decision making, the reality was usually quite different. Production sites were dominated by the factory's party chair and other cadres rather than by trained managers or engineers, while the lines of responsibility for decision making became unclear.[59] Again the influence of Mao can be detected with his mass-line method of sending party cadres to learn from the people. It paralleled the Ch'ŏngsan-ri method in that it encouraged interaction between party officials and workers. In their efforts to seek greater worker input both methods can be seen as attempts to provide a more rational system of economic production and avoid the arbitrary directives issued during the Five-Year Plan which had often proved inefficient. But they did little to change the fundamental features of North Korea's economy—its relentless demands on the workers and farmers with little in the way of material incentives.

North Korea's great leap forward may not have been as extreme or as immediately disastrous as China's, but unlike Mao's failed experiment it was never abandoned. All of its elements—the Ch'ŏngsan-ri method, the Taean industrial system, the Ch'ŏllima movements—and various campaigns to exceed economic targets remained permanent features of the DPRK. Kim Il Sung and his successors continued their on-the-spot guidance, party officials were personally involved in production and renewed calls for local self-sufficiency in the production of basic consumer goods were issued periodically. Mass mobilization for militarized campaigns became an unchanging part of the lives of ordinary citizens. The exhortations, political indoctrination, endless campaigns and "speed battles" remained the prime means of boosting production. To a large extent these were features that appeared in the late 1940s. They were further elaborated on and given institutional permanence in the late 1950s and early 1960s. All are perfectly understandable efforts to achieve the goals of modernization using the Soviet and Chinese models, while drawing from the memories of imperial Japan's forced industrialization during the Second World War, and on the experiences of Kim Il Sung and his partisans. Initially they achieved impressive results. The tragedy for the country and its revolution was the failure to abandon them when they were no longer effective.

The great leap in industrialization was accompanied by an enormous expansion in education. In 1956 four years of primary school was made compulsory. By 1959, with almost all children receiving this basic education, compulsory schooling was extended to seven years. This was again extended after 1967 to nine years. By the 1970s at least ten years of formal schooling was becoming the norm for young people. The regime vigorously pursued adult literacy with two-year workers' schools *kŭlloja hakkyo* and adult education middle schools *kŭlloja chunghakkyo*. In 1967 workers' schools which taught basic literacy were so little needed that they were abolished, only the after-hours middle schools continued to function.[60] North Korea placed a great emphasis of developing practical work schools. As of March 1959 all students in middle school and above were required to work eight to ten weeks in factories, mines or on other projects.[61]

From the standpoint of the early 1960s North Korea's economic development can only be regarded as a success. Industrial production increased more than three-fold from 1956 to 1960, admittedly starting from a very low base.[62] The limitations of its methods of modernization, that is forcing people to constantly toil on focused economic and infrastructural targets, were not yet apparent.

Militarization and Foreign Policy Shifts

The Fourth Party Congress

When the Fourth Congress of the KWP assembled in September 1961 Kim Il Sung had much to be satisfied with. He had secured his personal power. The country had recovered from the devastation of the Korean War and for all its problems had made enormous strides toward building an industrial society. North Korea was now completely socialized, all agriculture was carried out in state-owned cooperatives, and all business and industry from the smallest retail shop upwards was now state-owned. Industrial production was well above prewar and war levels. The country was becoming more industrialized than it had been under Japanese rule. In 1957 the first tractor rolled out of a DPRK plant to much fanfare. There is a famous story about this event. Supposedly the reversed-engineered tractor would only go in reverse.[63] Whether or not that is true, what is clear is that the domestic production of tractors, soon to be followed by trucks, cars and military vehicles, was a symbolically significant achievement. Living standards were spartan and chronic shortages in food and housing were a problem; still, even in these areas there was much improvement. Universal primary education had been achieved and secondary and higher education greatly expanded. Most adults were now literate owing to successful campaigns to teach the Korean alphabet. A major point of business at the congress was inaugurating the new Seven-Year Plan. It was ambitious with a target of 12.8 percent annual growth rate. Industrial production was to increase 3.2 times and agricultural production, which was lagging behind the country's other economic sectors, was to increase 2.4 times.[64] Two developments, however, were soon to hamper the efforts to realize these goals. First was North Korea's decision to place greater emphasis on military build-up. The second was the country's involvement in the Sino-Soviet dispute.

Equal Emphasis and Militarization

The DPRK remained in a state of war with the South. Yet in the first decade after the Korean War priority for scarce resources went to economic development. This changed in late 1962. The sea change came about at the Fifth Plenum of the Fourth Congress of the KWP which met in December 1962. At this meeting, under the slogan "with a hammer and sickle in one hand and arms in the other," it adopted the "equal emphasis" (*pyŏngjin*) policy of placing the same emphasis on economic development as on military build-up. The new effort in enhancing the nation's military preparedness consisted of four parts, or four lines (*sa nosŏn*): arming the entire population, intensifying training for its armed forces, turning the entire country into an impregnable fortress and providing modern equipment for its armed forces. The policy was put into effect immediately, although it was only officially implemented by name at the Second Party Conference in 1966.[65] To coordinate this military build-up a Military Committee (*kunsa wiwŏnhoe*) was reconstituted at the December 1962 meeting. This was a body that had been established by the Supreme People's Assembly shortly after the start of the Korean War and abolished at its end. Its revival now suggested the extent to which the nation would be on a permanent war footing. The Committee's membership was not publicized but Party by-laws issued in 1970 stated it operated under the direction of the Central Committee and functioned as a military policy making body that directed both the armed forces and the defense industries.[66]

Not all of this was new. With the slogan *chŏnmin mujanghwa*, "arming the whole people," in 1959, after the withdrawal of the Chinese People's Volunteers, the regime created a civilian militia, the Worker-Peasant Red Guards (*Nonong chŏkwidae*). This was now expanded until all able-bodied men between 18 and 45 and single women between 18 and 35 were required to join. Members of a hamlet formed a squad, a village a battalion and they were organized into regiments at the county level and corps at the provincial level. Men and women were required to attend training sessions after work and farmers during the quieter season.[67] Intensifying training for the military included further political indoctrination to ensure high morale and a sense of purpose. This too had already begun earlier when Kim ordered more ideological training programs for troops in January 1961 but was now intensified.[68] The size of the army was a problem—only 400,000 were under arms compared to 600,000 in South Korea. Ideological training would, the leadership hoped, partly compensate for this. At the same time the size of the military forces was continually increased until they matched and eventually greatly exceeded that of the South despite having only half the population. This was achieved by lengthening the period of military service. In the 1970s and 1980s the ROK had a three-year conscription while the DPRK's averaged at over eight years. Young men who did not enter higher education began military service after completing secondary school around the age of 16. Later some of the men served until the age of 28. Thus North Korea had the most onerous military service in the world.

The country was made "an impregnable fortress." As Kim Il Sung stated in 1963:

> We have to fortify our entire country. By doing so, we can defeat those who have atomic weapons even though we do not possess them ourselves. … We have to dig underground tunnels. We have to fortify not only the front line, but also the second and third defense area as well as strengthen anti-aircraft and coast-line defenses. We have to build many factories under the ground … when we fortify the whole country, not even the strongest enemy, not even the Americans will be able to invade us.[69]

Accordingly shelters were constructed throughout the country, including the Pyongyang subway, which was designed as much as a deep underground shelter as a means of transportation. As during the Korean War underground factory and military installations were constructed around the country. The elaborate tunnels that hide so much of the country's military activity became permanent characteristics of North Korea to the dismay of later US intelligence analysts heavily reliant on satellite photos. Of no less importance was the fourth policy of developing modern weapons. The production of military hardware, especially from the 1970s, became a central focus of industrialization targets.

Although there was "an equal emphasis" on military and economic development, in practice the Seven-Year Plan's targets were scaled back. There was a sharp increase in the amount of resources devoted to the military, beginning a policy that was never really reversed. Of course, North Korea had always maintained a large military; it was technically in a state of war and remained, in theory at least, ready to resume the conflict. After 1962, however, there was a vast increase in military and military-related industrial development. According to the researcher Joseph Chung, defense spending was 8 percent of the state budget in 1954 and fell to 3.7 percent in 1959; after 1962 it rose to 18 percent, peaking at 30 percent between 1967 and 1972. By the late 1970s it had fallen somewhat but would remain among the highest, if not the highest, of any country.[70]

It is not entirely clear what brought about this change in policy. Kim Il Sung himself later cited the US increased military involvement in Vietnam after the Tonkin Resolution as a factor, but this took place in 1964 nearly two years after the equal emphasis policy was adopted. He may have been concerned about the new threat of the newly formed South Korean government of General Park Chung Hee which came to power in May 1961. What seems to have precipitated the shift to military development was the Cuban Missile Crisis in October 1962. Kim Il Sung could hardly have been pleased when the Soviet Union agreed under US pressure to withdraw missiles from Cuba. It called into question just how reliable Moscow would be in a crisis when US forces were stationed on his border, and seemed to confirm Kim's worst suspicions about Khrushchev. That the Soviets largely ignored their small ally in their negotiations with the USA could hardly be comforting. The Soviet Union's abandoning of its ally Cuba and conceding to the USA only appeared to demonstrate that the DPRK would have to rely on its own military prowess.

Troubled Relations with Its Patrons

The equal emphasis hampered the country's breakneck pace of economic development. Another obstacle to rapid economic growth was the DPRK's involvement in the Sino-Soviet dispute. The DPRK initially remained neutral amid the growing Sino-Soviet tensions. For all the difficulties associated with Khrushchev's reforms, Pyongyang was careful to maintain proper relations with both Moscow and Beijing even as the two powers began to be at odds. From 1956 to 1961 Kim Il Sung made five visits to the Soviet Union, attending three congresses of the Communist Party of the USSR. He visited China in 1958 and 1959.[71] And he visited both countries in July 1961 shortly before the Fourth Congress of the KWP, concluding negotiations with a Treaty of Friendship, Cooperation and Mutual Assistance with each of the two powers, with the separate treaties between North Korea and China and North Korea and the Soviet Union respectively signed just one day apart. But North Korea's sympathies were clearly with China. Kim Il sung remained uncomfortable with the direction Khrushchev was taking: de-Stalinization and the idea of peaceful coexistence with the USA and its allies. The first threatened to undermine Kim's own legitimacy and the second was highly unacceptable so long as American forces were stationed along his border and the task of national unification was still uncompleted. Kim Il Sung attended the 22nd Congress of the Communist Party of the USSR in the fall of 1961 where he heard Khrushchev renew his attack on Stalin and criticize the independent stance of Albania and its Stalinist dictator Enver Hoxha. Khrushchev's attacks on Albania were indirectly aimed at the small country's ally, the PRC, but they must have sounded alarming to Kim whose personality cult, economic policies and independent stance in the communist movement were quite similar. Pyongyang, ignoring Moscow's criticisms of the small European state, reaffirmed its ties with Albania signing, in March 1962, an agreement on cultural cooperation.[72]

The Soviet Union and North Korea continued to conduct economic exchanges and send congratulatory messages to each other on appropriate occasions but there was no high-ranking visits between the two states, and no increases in Soviet aid. This contrasted with increased exchanges at all levels with China. During the October 1962 border war between India and China, North Korea wholeheartedly backed China in contrast to the neutral stance taken by Moscow. Meanwhile, Kim Il Sung resisted efforts to join with Mongolia and become a member of Comecon, the economic partnership between Moscow and its Eastern European allies. North Korea sought economic aid but opposed Khrushchev's idea of an integrated socialist economy with a division of labor among individual countries. Still, Kim maintained an open stance of friendship toward Moscow.

Yet this changed in late 1962 as relations with the Soviet Union deteriorated and North Korea began to lean toward China. The North Korean press became openly critical of Soviet policies and began taking an openly pro-Beijing line. In response the Soviet Union greatly reduced economic and technical aid. North Korea sided with China when it refused to sign the Nuclear Test Ban Treaty of July 1963.[73] The first sharp attack on the Soviet Union came in an article by three historians at Kim Il Sung University in September 1963, which criticized a Soviet world history published in 1955. They accused the Soviet historical interpretation of having "many distortions, falsifications and fabrications which came from the prejudice and ignorance of the authors with regard to the history of Korea."[74] The Soviets, they charged, were basing their history on Japanese imperialist accounts. The article continued by claiming the Soviet publication had shortchanged Korean history by placing the first

Korean state in the second century BCE when a state existed centuries earlier, by maligning the nationalist and progressive credentials of the late nineteenth-century political leader Kim Ok-kyun and other bourgeois reformers, and by minimizing the impact of the Bolshevik Revolution on the March First Uprising.[75] The following month the *Rodong sinmun* responded to Khrushchev's attempt to call a world conference of communist parties to expel China with the editorial "Let Us Defend the Socialist Camp." It criticized the idea of excluding China and went on to scold the Soviet Union for trying to interfere with the internal affairs of the DPRK as well as other countries. The Soviet Union was attacked for not supporting Pyongyang's emphasis on heavy industry and a self-supporting economy. It went on to criticize Moscow for "trying to force the anti-personality cult" campaign on other socialist countries, and called Soviet policy "imperialism."[76] Thus the editorial made explicit the fears and concerns Kim Il Sung had about the Soviet Union.

Moscow responded to these attacks with the suspension of both aid and purchases of minerals. This was a sharp blow to the North Korean economy. The equal emphasis policy diverted resources away from economic development and now the pace of industrial growth was slowed by the loss of Soviet aid. China may have stepped in somewhat with increased aid and trade, although this is unclear, but if so, it was insufficient to compensate for the economic sanctions.

Relations never came to a complete break. Kim Il Sung himself restrained from publicly criticizing Moscow; in fact, he rarely made any public statements on foreign affairs at all during this period. Moscow too was careful not to personally attack Kim Il Sung, responding to further attacks with silence. The fall of Khrushchev in October 1964 provided the opportunity to mend fences. Soviet Premier Alexis Kosygin paid a visit in 1965, relations improved and aid and economic exchanges were renewed. Like it or not, North Korea was dependent on Soviet aid and technical assistance if it was too carry out its industrialization and military build-up. On this Kim was pragmatic and realistic. He may have also been put at ease by Moscow's support for the Vietnamese as US involvement in the conflict grew. The dispute with the Soviet Union proved to be a severe economic blow to the state as economic and military aid was reduced or suspended for several years. Until the end of the Soviet Union, relations between the two powers became strained at times but after 1965 Pyongyang was careful not to alienate its primary economic patron too much. Moscow, for its part, found it useful to maintain influence in the strategically located DPRK.

Improvements with relations with the Soviet Union, so vital to the economic well-being of North Korea, were accompanied by worsening relations with China. North Korean leaders were always more comfortable with the Chinese, their fellow Asians with whom they share many cultural links. Mao's mass line, his emphasis on voluntarist efforts in overcoming a backward state and China's championship of national liberation wars also resonated with the North Koreans. Additionally the Korean War had forged some strong bonds between the two nations including their militaries. But when in 1966 Mao plunged his country into the Great Proletariat Cultural Revolution tensions between the two nations appeared. The extremist antics of his youthful Red Guards and their backers in the party made the leadership in Pyongyang uncomfortable. Although as mentioned in the next chapter, North Koreans had their own version of the Cultural Revolution they were less than sympathetic to Mao's. According to the Cuban ambassador to Pyongyang, officials made jokes about Mao being senile. Kim, according to the East German reports, told Brezhnev in a secret meeting in December 1966 that it was "massive idiocy."[77] And the Cultural Revolution soon turned on him. In 1967 a poster signed by veterans of the Korean War accused Kim Il Sung of being "revisionist and a disciple of Khrushchev." Other reports issued by Red Guard publications accused Kim of living like a millionaire and of showing concern for traditional filial piety by making his mother and father revolutionary saints.[78] At one point a train arrived in North Korea from China with the dead bodies of murdered China-based Koreans with a warning to the leadership that they should expect the same fate.[79]

More serious was a border dispute. The Sino-Korean border was demarked in 1712 with a few modifications made in the early twentieth century by the Japanese. In dispute was Paektu Mountain, the highest point in Korea, a place regarded in Korean tradition as sacred and the home of the legendary founder of the nation Tan'gun. This paralleled simultaneous border disputes China was having with the Soviet Union. But this dispute appeared to have been resolved in 1970 as the Cultural

Revolution began winding down. Premier Zhou Enlai's visit that year marked a return to normal relations. At the Second Party Conference in 1966 Kim Il Sung ended a long silence on Sino-Soviet dispute by stating that the country maintained an independent position in the international communist movement. The country took no further sides in the dispute among the two major communist powers but would for the most part skillfully maintain correct relations with both, using this as a means for receiving aid while achieving political autonomy.

Fostering the Three Revolutionary Forces

North Korea's foreign policy often seemed unpredictable and even irrational to outsiders but it adhered closely to one goal: the unification of Korea. The North Korean revolution with its aim of creating a strong, progressive, independent Korean nation could only be completed when that happened. From the leadership's point of view the Korean War was only a temporary setback toward the goal of reunification, not a defeat. It is likely that Kim Il Sung never doubted the inevitability of liberating the South, at least not until the last years of his nearly half-century in power. And this goal of unification followed a clearly articulated three-fold strategy based on promoting the "three revolutionary forces" given its official formulation in a speech Kim Il Sung delivered at a party meeting on February 27, 1964– "Let Us Strengthen in Every Way Revolutionary Forces for the Realization of the Great Task of Fatherland Unification."[80] There were three revolutionary forces, he explained, those at home, those in the South and international, and all had to be strengthened to complete the liberation of Korea. Thus there were three parts to the process of reunification. First, in the North not only must the nation be strong but the people must realize their full revolutionary potential. In other words, North Korea had to be made economically, militarily and ideologically strong. Second, the revolutionary forces in the South were hindered by the people's ignorance of their own degree of suppression by their "puppet" government and their subjection by the American imperialists. This had to be corrected so that, unlike 1950, the people would rise up against their government in support of the DPRK. Third, strengthening the "international revolutionary forces" necessitated promoting ties with Third World nations as well as socialist ones and exploiting the weaknesses and divisions among the imperialists. The main aim here was to force the USA to withdraw its forces from the South.

Kim Il Sung had made clear from the mid-1950s that the unification project would be a long-term one. In a meeting with Chinese Premier Zhou Enlai in 1958 he explained that if "we can successfully finish our [long-term] construction plan" then "it is possible to unite Korea, peacefully."[81] Not only did the North need to build up its industrial and military forces but the process of fostering the revolutionary forces would take time. Yet they were essential to the task. All this suggested that rather than invade and expect the people to rise up, the idea was to wait for the people of the South to rise up first and then join forces with them—what can be called the "South Korean Revolution first and then unification policy."

To promote the South Korean revolution Pyongyang established the Department of External Intelligence Inquires (*Taeoe chŏngbo chosabu*) often known as the "35th office" in April 1963. It trained agents to work in the South. This worked with two other institutions: the South Korean Liaison Bureau (*Taenam yŏllakpu*) and the Department of Culture (*Munhwabu*). The Liaison Bureau was a channel linking the KWP with the communists below the DMZ. It originally was staffed by communists from the South. When the domestic communists were purged in the early 1950s, they were replaced by partisans who had little experience or knowledge of the South.[82] The Department of Culture was founded in 1956 as a propaganda organ aimed at South Koreans and Koreans living in Japan.[83] In 1964 North Korean agents were able to contact a few sympathetic southerners and create the Revolutionary Party for Reunification (*T'ongil hyŏngmyŏng tang*). This underground communist organization was headed by Kim Chong-t'ae, a high-school teacher and store owner. It remained small, ineffective and was discovered by the South Korean intelligence officials in 1968. Kim Chong-t'ae was executed and 158 others arrested.[84] Although the Revolutionary Party for Reunification ceased to exist, North Korea insisted otherwise and sponsored radio broadcasts and other propaganda in its name. Pyongyang also used the two non-communist parties, the Democratic Party and Ch'ŏngudang, which, of course, existed only as instruments of the regime, to issue appeals to their South Korean compatriots.[85]

Meanwhile, the DPRK pursued an opportunistic policy taking advantage of any seemingly favorable developments in the South or in the international situation. In 1960, for example, there was the political turmoil in the ROK. A student-led uprising in April of that year overthrew the authoritarian Syngman Rhee regime. This was followed by the creation of a parliamentary democracy, an experiment plagued by pent-up demands by labor, teachers, students and intellectuals that led to sometimes violently suppressed demonstrations. In August of that year Kim Il Sung, probing sentiment in the South, proposed a Confederal Republic of Koryo as an intermediate step toward unification. The name was chosen because of its neutrality. The other two common names for Korea already had associations, with *Han'guk* used by the South and *Chosŏn* by the North. Nothing came of the idea but Kim would revive it 20 years later. In the spring of 1961 Pyongyang proposed meetings with radical student groups who responded positively but this effort was cut short by the military coup of May 16, 1961. Kim sent Hwang Sŏng-t'aek, an official who had fled to the North in 1946, to meet one of the coup leaders, Kim Jong-p'il, but the new military government of Park Chung Hee which took a hard anti-communist line executed Hwang.[86]

Discouraged by the hard nationalist, anti-communist stance of the Park regime, the North Korean regime began to draw up possible plans for armed conflict on the peninsula. Initially these were based on a Vietnam-style guerilla campaign but were modified in 1964 as a more defensive "Flying Dragon" plan which would use both PRC and KPA forces. Another plan in 1965, the "Charging Bull," was based on a more aggressive response to liberate the peninsula.[87] In 1967 North Korea began to take a more provocative stance toward South Korea. North Korea had from time to time caused "incidents." And there were frequent seizures of southern fishing boats. Along the DMZ there were constant little crises ranging from failures to adhere to some agreed-upon protocol, such as having soldiers along the border wear the proper insignia, to exchanges of gunfire. In 1967 there was an eleven-fold increase in such incidents, keeping the American and South Korean forces in a constant state of tension. By the end of the year gunfire erupted almost daily across the border.[88] These included artillery shelling for the first time since the armistice. North Korea appeared to have decided to place pressure on South Korea to undermine the government and promote a revolution.

In 1968 North Korea carried out a series of highly aggressive measures. To carry them out the North began training a special Unit 124 in July of 1967. One was aimed at assassinating South Korean President Park Chung Hee. On January 18, 1968, this unit infiltrated into the South and three days later 31 commandos launched a night time attack on the presidential palace getting within 500 meters before being stopped by security forces. Twenty-nine were killed, one was captured and one escaped and fled to North Korea. Between October 30 and November 2, eight infiltration teams each with about fifteen commandos from the same 124th Army Unit landed on the east coast between Samchŏk and Uljin.[89] Villagers were rounded up and forced to hear speeches about the socialist paradise to the North. Most of the guerillas were quickly reported and killed or captured but only after 63 southerners were dead.[90] On the sea, 115 southern fishing boats were seized by the North that year.[91] South Korea responded by stepping up patrols of the coast line, tightening security and offering generous rewards for all reports. These efforts were successful enough to make the infiltrations increasingly difficult.

One of North Korea's most risky moves was the seizure of an American intelligence ship the USS *Pueblo* off the east coast near the port of Wonsan which took place the two days commandos stormed the presidential palace in Seoul. If the attacks on the South Korea may have had a purpose of trying to destabilize the country it is not clear what purpose the capture of the Pueblo served. It was perhaps a fortuitous event. North Korea claimed the ship was in its territorial waters which the USA denied. The 82-member crew was held captive for 11 months before being released in December. The Americans initially responding with a show of force sending the aircraft carrier the Enterprise into the waters off the east coast. However, rather than leading to military retaliation as Kim Il Sung might have feared, the USA negotiated for the release of the crew issuing an apology and the crew signed a confession. Americans were amused by the confession written by the crew. It contained many puns mocking the DPRK which the North Korean apparently didn't understand. However, the Pueblo Incident provided a useful lesson for the North. The failure of the USA to militarily respond to the seizure of its ship indicated to Pyongyang just how much the USA sought to avoid armed confrontation. This was reinforced the following year in April 1969 when North Korea shot down a US EC-121 spy plane, again with no serious retaliation from the Americans. Later North Korea would engage in aggressive acts and then seek to negotiate with the Americans, frequently winning both concessions and demonstrating its military prowess to its people.

As in the case of the Korean War North Koreans had an unrealistic idea of the support they had among their countrymen in the southern part of the peninsula. The activities of 1968 seemed senselessly reckless even to Pyongyang's closest allies. The Romanians, for example, described the Blue House attack as an "incredibly daring and narrow-minded" act that would only exacerbate tension.[92] As in the Korean War, Kim Il Sung turned on his generals for these failures and conducted a purge, most likely in early 1969. At least ten partisan generals were removed from top posts and replaced by more technocratic-minded officials, most ex-guerilla fighters who had been serving in civilian posts. By 1970 the North Korean leadership made a modest retreat from its extreme militaristic stance.

Just why they chose to be more aggressive at this time is not known for certain. One factor may have been America's military build-up in Vietnam and South Korea's military participation in the conflict, both troubling for the North Koreans. In July 1968 a new slogan appeared, "Cutting off the Limbs of US Imperialism Everywhere." It went, "Vietnam is breaking one leg of the American bandit, we are breaking the other one."[93] Especially worrisome was the treaty of normalization the Park government signed with Japan in 1965. This opened the way for Japanese trade and foreign investment but it also raised fears of the former colonial power reasserting its economic hegemony over the country. The normalization treaty between South Korea and Japan in 1965 was accompanied by huge and sometimes violent protest demonstrations by students and political opposition groups who saw it as a betrayal of national sovereignty. These demonstrations may have given Pyongyang the impression that there was enough hostility toward the government to form the basis for a general revolt. It is not clear how captive the leadership was to its own propaganda but there seems to have been a genuine belief that most South

Koreans viewed their government as the illegitimate heir of Japanese imperialism, a clique of former Japanese collaborators and now active collaborators of American imperialism; and that it was a regime with little popular support. According to this line of thinking, the situation was potentially favorable, therefore, for the revolutionary forces in the South. Internal politics may have been a factor. Following the purge of the Kapsan faction (see Chapter 4) Defense Minister Kim Ch'ang-bong and another military man, Hŏ Pong-hak, who may have sought to brandish their credentials through more aggressive measures, were in charge of South Korean operations.[94] Both were removed from their positions in 1969. Certainly the military provocations served to create a sense of a nation threatened by outsiders. Residents of Pyongyang were required to wear backpacks in case they had to evacuate and dig emergency shelters. Troops moved through the main streets, a sight likely to impress the urgency and preparedness on the populace.[95]

Whatever the motivations behind them, the raids were a failure. Whether or not they were the work of a small group of military men or the product of internal politics, they reflected the fact that Kim Il Sung and those around him appeared to have interpreted opposition to government policies as sympathy or potential sympathy to the DPRK. In fact, the situation was much less ripe for a communist revolution in the South than it had been. In the early 1950s land reforms had been carried out in the South. The countryside was now the home of often conservative, small, independent farmers. The North's invasion of the South had hardened anti-communist attitudes among many southerners, and in the 1960s the country was beginning to make real economic progress. While anti-Americanism was common enough among South Koreans, there was also a great reservoir of goodwill toward the USA as well as a growing number of people enamored with American culture. Furthermore, the stridently anti-communist regime of Park Chung Hee had developed extensive and effective intelligence services that made serious infiltration of the South and the organization of any large-scale communist organization extremely difficult. North Korea was also handicapped since it had purged most of the South Korean communists with knowledge and contacts, and placed the Liaison Office in the hands of partisans with little experience in the South.

Dialogue with the South and Confrontation

North Korea continued with its provocative acts, albeit not on the scale of 1968. On December 11, 1969, North Korean agents hijacked a YS-11 civilian airplane with 51 passengers, and on June 22, 1970, they detonated a bomb at South Korea's national cemetery in an attempted assassination of Park.[96] On January 23, 1971, they tried to hijack a Korean Airlines plane; and in April 1971, at a party meeting, Kim Il Sung gave a more militant than usual speech about the need for struggle against American imperialists, Japanese militarists, and their agents in the South.[97] Then the international situation began to change dramatically. The most startling event was the breakthrough in relations between the USA and China. First there was the announcement in 1971 that the two countries had been secretly holding diplomatic meetings and of the planned visit of President Nixon to Beijing. In February 1972 Nixon met with Mao Zedong and other Chinese leaders, starting a process toward normalization of relations. News of a thaw must have been disturbing to Kim Il Sung, suggesting Beijing might follow Moscow's earlier mellowing of its stance toward the USA. He reacted to this news of the coming visit by declaring "Nixon's visit to China will not be a march of a victor but a trip of the defeated, it fully reflects the destiny of U.S. imperialism which is like a sun sinking in the western sky."[98] Yet he must have known it called into question China's future support for his regime.

However, this geopolitical change, for all its disturbing implications, also suggested the possibility of an American withdrawal from South Korea, which prompted North Korea to open talks with the South. As early as April 1971 Foreign Minister Hŏ Tam presented an Eight-Point Plan for Addressing the Problem of Unification through Peaceful Negotiations.[99] In August 1971 the South Korean Red Cross proposed to its northern counterpart the exchange of information about and the possible reuniting of families separated by the DMZ. Several million South Koreans had family members or relatives in the North. Hundreds of thousands of siblings were separated from each other, parents from their children, even spouses. There was absolutely no communication, no postal service let alone telephone links between the two countries so they were entirely ignorant of the fate of their loved ones in the North. The issue of divided families was an emotional one in the South and a good starting point for any movement toward rapprochement between the two sides. The North responded favorably to the proposal, and on August 20 the two sides met for only four minutes but this was followed by secret visits by Yi Hu-rak, the chief of South Korea's Central Intelligence Agency to North Korea, and by Vice Premier Pak Sŏng-ch'ŏl to Seoul. After these secret talks North and South Korea issued a joint communiqué on July 4, 1972, stating three fundamental principles on unification. First, that unification must be carried out independently, without outside interference. Second, it must be achieved peacefully. Third, it must be implemented as a show of great national unity based on the homogeneity of the people first, with the differences in thinking, ideologies and systems worked out later.[100]

A North–South Coordinating Committee was formed that held three meetings: one in Seoul from November to December 1972, a second in Pyongyang in March 1973 and a third in Seoul three months later in June. But little progress was made at the meetings. South Korean officials wanted to proceed with gradual confidence-building measures. Family reunifications would be a good first step, and from there gradually work on bigger, more complex issues. The North proposed they discuss major issues across the board. DPRK representatives also insisted that South Korea's National Security laws, which gave the government broad powers to arrest communists or communist sympathizers, had to be repealed before any family reunions or other humanitarian issue could be pursued. They also insisted on the withdrawal of US troops from South Korea being a precondition for any further negotiations. South Korea insisted that the DPRK end its propaganda campaign for the Revolutionary Party for Reunification. In the face of these demands the talks deadlocked. After seven meetings between August 1972 to July 1973 the Red Cross talks came to an end.[101] The North–South Coordinating Committee ceased to meet after mid-1973. Mid-level meetings continued at Panmunjom from December 1973 to March 1975; with little promise of any breakthroughs these too fizzled out. The talks failed because Kim Il Sung lost interest when he realized that a withdrawal of US troops was not imminent and, in fact, would not be on the table for serious consideration. He also turned down a proposal by President Park in 1973 for dual admission to the United Nations. This would have meant a de facto mutual recognition of each other's regime. In the mid-1970s he returned to the rhetoric of military confrontation with the South. North Korean officials told Hungarian diplomats in 1976 that "Korea cannot be unified in a peaceful way."[102]

The 1972–1973 negotiations began a pattern that would be repeated for the next four decades. North Korea would initiate or respond to offers for talks. There would be some diplomatic or even cultural and economic exchanges. Optimism would rise over the prospect of a thaw in relations. Pyongyang would then set conditions that were difficult or unrealistic or that it knew the South would find unacceptable. Seoul would offer small confidence-building measures that would eventually be rejected with the DPRK insisting that major issues be discussed.[103] Talks would break down and Pyongyang would ratchet up the tension with its rival again.

A principal aim of the DPRK's foreign policy was the withdrawal of US troops in the ROK, whose presence it saw as perhaps the greatest obstacle to reunification on its terms. When the talks with Seoul proved unsuccessful the DPRK tried another tactic to get the USA to withdraw its forces from Korea: direct negotiations with Washington. It first called for direct talks in March 1973.[104] When the Nixon administration ignored this the Supreme People's Assembly in March 1974 issued an open letter to the US Congress calling for direct peace treaty negotiations.[105] The USA, however, remained adamantly opposed to bilateral talks.

For the rest of the 1970s North Korea resumed its policy of hostile acts against the South. On February 4, 1972, they kidnapped five fishing boats and wrecked one. Another fishing boat was captured on August 30, 1976.[106] Among the most menacing activities was its construction of tunnels under the DMZ. The DPRK constructed tunnels under the border capable of providing passage for substantial numbers of troops. The first was discovered in November 1974. It was 3.5 km long, ran 1.2 km under ROK territory, contained a narrow-gauge railroad and was capable of transporting a regiment an hour. Three more were found in 1975, 1978 and 1990. The second was even wider, capable of being driven through in small vehicles and transporting a division in an hour.[107] A particularly dramatic event, most likely orchestrated by Pyongyang, occurred on August 15, 1974, celebrated as liberation (from Japan) day in South Korea. An agent of a North Korean front organization in Japan made an attempt on President Park's life as he was making a televised speech. The assassin missed Park but fatally wounded his wife. Another act of aggression took place in August 1976 when North Korean soldiers attacked and killed two American officers who were trimming a tree in the area. The USA responded with a show of force but as with earlier incidents there was no military retaliation.

These provocative actions seemed irrational and reckless, creating in the minds of many outsiders an image of a dangerously unpredictable and relentlessly hostile regime. They were not intended to immediately foment a pro-North rebellion, since even Kim Il Sung must have understood by this point how limited his support was in the South; but they did have a rationale. First, they acted to probe the ROK's defenses. More importantly they were attempts to destabilize the South. Kim Il Sung held the firm conviction that he represented the will and the progressive forces of the Korean revolution and of Korean nationalism. Eventually the people of the South would rise up, eventually the Americans would withdraw and eventually the situation would be ripe for reunification. The terrorist attacks were intended to speed this process along. And continuing tensions with the South served a domestic purpose: sustaining a state of military alertness was useful for maintaining a high degree of control over the population, as well as making the country better prepared for war when it resumed.

Courting the Third World

A third part of North Korea's strategy for reunification was creating an international environment that would isolate South Korea, pressure the USA to withdraw its troops and win the support of progressive nations to its cause. For this purpose, Kim Il Sung began cultivating close relations with the Third World. "If the small countries jointly dismember him, the American bandit will be torn apart," a North Korean propaganda slogan proclaimed.[108] This also served to help the DPRK emerge from the shadow of its two patrons, the Soviet Union and China, and announce its presence as an independent state. Moving far beyond the days when he needed Stalin's approval to establish diplomatic relations with a short list of friendly socialist states, Kim Il Sung aimed at playing an active role in international affairs. In this he resembled leaders of South Korea who also sought to overcome their country's reputation as a dependent American client state. Additionally being a major world leader may have added to Kim's prestige at home as well as appealing to his vanity. This became even truer in the 1970s when Kim Il Sung began portraying the DPRK to his people as a shining example of progressive socialism admired around the world. Above all it was another front in his rivalry with the South. He wanted to demonstrate that the DPRK was the true representative of the Korean people and to isolate South Korea. As a result a competition began between the two Koreas as each sought to receive more diplomatic recognitions than the other.

North Korea initially had some success in gaining Third World support for its demand for the withdrawal of all foreign troops from Korea. At the Non-Aligned Movement (NAM) conference in Lima in August 1975 it became a full member. A committee of the General Assembly in 1975 passed a pro-North Korean resolution on the Korean Question that year which called for the withdrawal of all foreign troops from the peninsula. At another NAM conference in Colombo the member states endorsed Kim's stance on Korean unification. By the early 1980s the DPRK had established relations with 110 countries around the world. It had more missions abroad than its rival South Korea and its voice was heard louder in Third World forums. A constant stream of leaders from Africa and other Third World countries visited Pyongyang, where no matter how small their influence or of how little actual strategic or economic importance they might have had, they were sure to receive an enthusiastic welcome from the thousands of North Koreans who dutifully turned out on the streets to greet them. These visits also served a domestic purpose of highlighting the global recognition of the great leader and his achievements. In an outreach effort, North Korean performance troupes and exhibitions were sent around the world. These were given much publicity at home, also contributing to the official line that the DPRK, its culture, its socialist path and especially its leader were globally admired.

These often expensive efforts produced little in the way of practical benefits, and the goodwill and influence they developed were often undermined by the clumsy and ill-informed behavior of North Koreans. Much of this problem was based on the ignorance of North Koreans of the outside world as well as the general lack of experienced diplomats. NAM representatives soon tired of having North Korea use its meetings as forums for pushing its agendas. The crude use of bribery and bluster to try to get their way offended many governments. Many were becoming wary of the growing cult of Kim Il Sung, and some were also concerned over the country's acts of terrorism against its southern neighbor. North Korean prestige was also undermined by its abuse of diplomatic protocol. Its representatives abroad came into trouble for carrying out smuggling, drug dealing and other illegal activities. In the 1970s, for example, North Korean diplomats were expelled from several Scandinavian countries for drug smuggling. Nor did Pyongyang generate much of a popular following outside its borders. North Korea sponsored 200 pro-Pyongyang organizations in 50 countries, but these never generated much local support and remained dependent on DPRK funds.[109] In the long run, this stage of the three revolutionary forces strategy proved as unsuccessful as the other two: Kim Il Sung's effort to build up the DPRK as an economically powerful nation and unchallenged superior Korea, and to promote the revolutionary forces in the South.

Notes

1 Chin O Chung, *Pyongyang Between Peking and Moscow: North Korea's Involvement in the Sino-Soviet Dispute, 1958–1975*. Tuscaloosa, AL: University of Alabama Press, 1978, p. 23.
2 Hwang Chang-yŏp, p. 26.
3 Bazacs Szalontai, *Kim Il Sung in the Khrushchev Era: Soviet-DPRK Relations and the Roots of North Korean Despotism, 1953–1964*. Stanford, CA: Stanford University Press, 2006, p. 43.
4 Suh, p. 40.
5 Stephen Kotlin and Charles K. Armstrong, "A Socialist Regional Order in Northeast Asia After World War II," in Charles K. Armstrong, K. Gilbert Rozman, Samuel S. Kim, and Stephen Kotlin (eds). *Korea at the Center: Dynamics of Regionalism in Northeast Asia*. Armonk, NY: M.E. Sharpe, 2006, pp. 110–125.

6 Charles, K. Armstrong, "'Fraternal Socialism': The International Recon-struction of North Korea, 1953–62." *Cold War History* 5, no. 2 (May 2005): 161–187; Szalontai, 47.

7 Ginsburgs, George. "Soviet Development Grants and Aid to North Korea, 1945–1950," *Asia Pacific Community* 18 (Fall 1982): 42–63.

8 Kotlin and Armstrong, "A Socialist Regional Order in Northeast Asia after World War II," p. 121.

9 Sŏng Hye-rang, p. 258.

10 Armstrong, 2005, pp. 172–173.

11 Lankov, 2007, pp. 93–94.

12 Stephan Haggard and Marcus Noland, *Famine in North Korea: Markets, Aid, and Reform.* New York: Columbia University Press, 2007, p. 25.

13 Andrei Lankov, *Crisis in North Korea: The Failure of* De-Stalinization, *1956.* Honolulu, HI: University of Hawaii, 2005, p. 179.

14 Chong-sik Lee, "Land Reform, Collectivization and the Peasant in North Korea," in Robert A. Scalapino (ed.). *Korea Today.* New York: Praeger, 1963, pp. 65–81.

15 Yim, Sang-chŏl, *Pukhan nongŏp* [North Korean Agriculture]. Seoul: Tosŏ Ch'ulp'an Sŏil, 2000, p. 35.

16 Sŏ Tong-man, *Puk chosŏn yŏn'gu* [Studies on North Korea]. Paju: Han'guk wŏnsik, 2010, p. 126.

17 Kim Sŏng-bo, *Pukhan ŭi yŏksa* 1, pp. 154–155.

18 Nam, Koon Woo, "The Purge of the Southern Communists in North Korea: A Retrospective View," *Asian Forum* 5, no. 1 (1973): 43–54; Suh, p. 360.

19 Suh, pp. 132–134.

20 Shen and Li, p. 71; Lankov 2005, p. 17.

21 Lankov, 2005, pp. 62–63; Sŏ Tong-man, pp. 130–135.

22 Polish Embassy, October 16, 1957, *North Korean International Documenta-tion Project.*

23 Hwang Chang-yŏp, p. 109.

24 Balazs Szalontai, "You have No Political Line of Your Own': Kim Il Sung and the Soviets, 1953–1964," *Cold War International History Project Bulle-tin* no. 14–15 (Winter 2003/Spring 2004): 87–137.

25 Conversation with Comrade Samsonov First Secretary of the Soviet Embassy, Polish Embassy, December 24, 1956, *North Korean International Documentation Project.*

26 Nam, pp. 113–124.

27 Lankov, 2005, p. 181.

28 Lankov, 2007, p. 67.
29 Lankov, 2005, pp. 181–183; Lankov 2007, p. 68.
30 Lankov, 2005, p. 180.
31 Szalontai, p. 89.
32 Lankov, 2005, pp. 70–71.
33 Suh, p. 174.
34 Nam, pp. 121–122; Lankov 2005, p. 208.
35 Suh, pp. 171–172.
36 Lim, 2015, p. 65.
37 Lankov, 2005, p. 205.
38 Lim, 2015, p. 22.
39 Heonik Kwon and Byung-ho Chung. *North Korea: Beyond Charismatic Politics*. Lanham, MD: Rowman & Littlefield, 2012, p. 16.
40 Hwang Chang-yŏp, pp. 102–103.
41 Lankov, 2007, p. 279.
42 Lankov, 2005, p. 217.
43 Kim Sŏng-bo. *Pukhan ŭi yŏksa* 1, p. 212.
44 Robert Scalapino, "Korea the Politics of Change," *Asian Survey,* 3, no. 1 (January 1963): 31–40, 63.
45 "Kangson, Home of the Chollima," *Korea Today* 241 (September 1976): 25–32; Joan Robinson, "Korean Miracle," Monthly Review 16, no. 9 (January 1965): 541–549.
46 Lim, 2009, 30–31.
47 Chin O Chung, 33, no. 169.
48 Suh, p. 165.
49 Ilpyong J. Kim, *Historical Dictionary of North Korea*. Lanham, MD: The Scarecrow Press, 2003, p. 24.
50 Bon-Hak Koo. "Political Economy of Self-Reliance: Juche and Economic Development," in *North Korea, 1961–1990*. Seoul: Research Center for Peace and Unification of Korea, 1992, p. 85.
51 Hy-Sang Lee, *North Korea: A Strange Socialist Fortress*. Westport, CT: Praeger, 2001, p. 65.
52 Chin O Chung, no. 42, p. 170.
53 Sŏ Tong-man, *Puk chosŏn yŏn'gu* [Studies on North Korea]. Paju: Republic of Korea, Han'guk wŏnsik, 2010, pp. 167–168.
54 Chin O Chung, p. 36.
55 Report, Embassy of Hungary to Hungarian Foreign Ministry, July 2, 1960, *North Korean International Documentation Project*.
56 Chin O Chung, p. 36.

57 "Chongsan-ri A Historic Village," *Korea Today* 221 (January 1975): 46–48; Suh, p. 167.

58 Il-pyong Kim, p. 25.

59 Kim, Sung-chull. "Fluctuating Institutions of Enterprise Management in North Korea: Prospects for Local Enterprise Reform," *Harvard Asia Quarterly*: 10–33 (no volume number or date).

60 Mun Woong Lee, *Rural North Korea Under Communism: A Study of Sociological Change*. Houston, TX: Rice University Press, 1976, p. 100.

61 Kim, Yong Soon. "Language Reform as a Political Symbol in North Korea," pp. 216–235.

62 Lim, 2009, p. 91.

63 Martin, pp. 157–158.

64 Lim, 2009, pp. 91–92.

65 Han Monikka (2003) '1960 nyŏntae Pukhan-ŭi kyŏngche kukpang pyŏngchin nosŏn-ŭi ch'aet'aek-kwa taenam chŏngch'aek [North Korea's choice of the simultaneous economic-military strengthening strategy and its policy toward South Korea]', *Yŏksa-wa hyŏnsil* [History and Reality], 50, pp. 133–164.

66 Suh, p. 215.

67 Hy-Sang Lee, p. 54.

68 Sung-joo Han, "North Korea's Security Policy and Military Strategy," in Robert A. Scalapino and Jun-Yop Kim (eds). *North Korea Today*. Berkeley, CA: University of California Press, 1983, pp. 144–163, 155.

69 Sung-joo Han, p. 151.

70 Joseph S. Chung, "Economic Planning in North Korea," in Robert A. Scalapino and Jun-Yop Kim (eds). *North Korea Today*. Berkeley, CA: University of California Press, 1983, pp. 164–188, 180.

71 Suh, p. 178.

72 Chin O Chung, pp. 65–66.

73 Chin O Chung, p. 86.

74 Chin O Chung, p. 88.

75 Suh, pp. 182–183.

76 Chin O Chung, pp. 88–90.

77 Bernd Schaefer, *North Korean "Adventurism" and China's Long Shadow, 1966–1972*. Washington, DC: Woodrow Wilson International Center for Scholars, pp. 5, 9.

78 Suh, pp. 192–193.

79 Sheila Miyoshi Jaeger, *Brothers at War: The Unending Conflict in Korea*. New York: Norton, 2013, p. 376.

80 Byung Chul Koh, *The Foreign Policy Systems of North and South Korea*. Berkeley, CA: University of California Press, 1984, pp. 123–124.

81 Koh, p. 276.

82 Kim Sŏng-bo, *Pukhan ŭi yŏksa* 1, pp. 154–155.

83 Lim, 2009, p. 72.

84 Suh, pp. 234–236.

85 Andrei N. Lankov, "The Demise of Non-Communist Parties in North Korea (1945–1960)," *Journal of Cold War Studies* 3, no. 1 (Winter 2001): 103–125.

86 Kim Hakjoon, 2015, p. 60.

87 Han Monikka, pp. 142–143.

88 Mitchell Lerner, *"Mostly Propaganda in Nature:" Kim Il Sung, the Juche Ideology and the Second Korean War*. Washington, DC: Woodrow Wilson International Center for Scholars, 2011.

89 Michishita Narushige, "Calculated Adventurism: North Korea's Military-Diplomatic Campaigns," *Korea Journal of Defense Analysis* 16, no. 2 (Fall 2004): 188–197.

90 Lerner 2011, pp. 22–25; Suh, p. 232; Lankov, Andrew. *The Real North Korea: Life and Politics in the Failed Stalinist Utopia*. Oxford: Oxford University Press, 2013, p. 30.

91 Soon Sung Cho, "North and South Korea: Stepped-Up Aggression and the Search for New Security," *Asian Survey*, 9, no. 1 (January 1969): 29–32.

92 Romanian Embassy to Bucharest, January 26, 1968, *North Korean International Documentation Project*.

93 Bernd Schaefer, *North Korean "Adventurism" and China's Long Shadow, 1966–1972*. Washington, DC: Woodrow Wilson International Center for Scholars, October 2004, pp. 12–13. https://www.wilsoncenter.org/sites/default/files/Working_Paper_442.pdf, Accessed January 16, 2016.

94 Lim 2009, pp. 48–51.

95 Mitchell Lerner, *"Mostly Propaganda in Nature": Kim Il Sung, the Juche Ideology, and the Second Korean War*. Washington, DC: Woodrow Wilson International Center, 2010, https://www.wilsoncenter.org/publication/mostly-propaganda-nature-kim-il-sung-the-juche-ideology-and-the-second-korean-war, Accessed July 26, 2016.

96 Michishita, Narushige, "Calculated Adventurism: North Korea's Military-Diplomatic Campaigns," Korea *Journal of Defense Analysis* 16, no. 2 (Fall 2004): 188–197.

97 Suh, p. 254.

98 Robert R. Simmons, "North Korea: The Year of the Thaw," *Asian Survey* 12, no. 1 (January 1972): 245–231.

99   Kim Hae-wŏn, *Pukhan ŭi Nambukkhan chŏngch'I hyŏpsang yŏn'gu* [Research on North Korea's Political Negotiations with South Korea]. Seoul: Sŏnin Publications, 2012, p. 71.

100   Kim Hae-wŏn, pp. 71–72.

101   Suh, p. 256.

102   Memorandum Hungarian Embassy February 16, 1976, *North Korean International Documentation Project.*

103   Buzo, pp. 95–96.

104   Chong-sik Lee, "The Evolution of North-South Korean Relations," in Robert A. Scalapino and Hongkoo Lee (eds). *North Korea in a Regional and Global Context.* Berkeley, CA: University of California Press, 1986, pp. 115–132.

105   Koh, p. 286.

106   Yongho Kim, *North Korean Foreign Policy: Security Dilemma and Succession.* Lanham, MD, Lexington Books, 2011, p. 102.

107   Koh, p. 288.

108   Schaefer, pp. 12–13.

109   Suh, p. 267.

4

Creating a Monolithic System and a Dynastic State, 1967–1980

From 1967 North Korea followed an increasingly eccentric evolutionary development, that is, it began to deviate from other socialist states and became to what seemed to most outsiders as an increasingly strange society. That year saw the last major purge; after that the political leadership would remain stable. This purge was followed by a sort of "cultural revolution" which over the next few years created a monolithic political and social system and transformed the country into a dynastic state. The cult of Kim Il Sung was intensified and extended to his family, and his eldest son was designated as his successor. At this point the DPRK became ideologically as well as politically autonomous. It was also during these years, the late 1960s and 1970s, that the state achieved its fullest measure of control over all segments of society.

North Korea's Cultural Revolution

The Kapsan Purge

The first two decades of the DPRK were characterized by frequent purges; the last major one eliminated the Kapsan faction. These were veterans who had participated in the Kapsan Operations Committee and provided logistical support to the guerillas but were not themselves guerillas.

They were generally lumped together with the partisans and were glorified in the official accounts of the anti-Japanese resistance, along with Kim Il Sung and other fighters. Tensions arose between them and Kim Il Sung when they began to promote a rival or at least a secondary cult of Pak Kŭm-ch'ŏl, a founding member of the group and the fourth ranking member of the party. Early in 1967, Kim Il Sung called for a halt to these acts of "individual heroism" – meaning the development of any rival cults of personality. According to at least one defector, the Kapsan members were also critical of the regime's single-minded concentration on heavy industry, preferring to develop light industries and to improve living standards.[1] At a party meeting in May 1967 Kim had Pak and all other Kapsan members removed from official posts.[2] They then disappeared, presumably executed or imprisoned.

The Kapsan purge was followed by what can be called a "cultural revolution," not entirely dissimilar from the one Mao was carrying out in China. On May 25, 1967, immediately following the purge, Kim Il Sung ordered the inspection of all books. Officials then checked all printed material and anything that was not approved was confiscated and burned, including many literary classics and almost anything beyond a narrow range of official DPRK published materials.[3] Books were gathered – some had pages blacked out; most were destroyed. This was followed by works of art, sheet music, anything that had foreign influence; even Beethoven was banned. The cultural purge included some traditional Korean literature and artistic forms such as *p'ansori*, the beloved traditional music and storytelling performance.[4]

Already ubiquitous, the cult of Kim Il Sung was intensified. Instructions of the Great Leader were read at every meeting. Every article and publication, no matter what the topic, included his quotes in bold letters, and newspapers devoted a large amount of their space to coverage of him. One of the peculiar features of North Korea appeared at this time when party officials began wearing badges bearing his picture. Over the next few years the practice was expanded to include ordinary citizens until all North Koreans were expected to wear these badges when in public. All this bore a strong resemblance to China's Great Proletariat Cultural Revolution that Mao had inaugurated the year before – although the term "cultural revolution" was never actually used in the DPRK. But the

North Korean case differed – there were no Red Guards harassing teachers and going on rampages. North Korea's "cultural revolution" was more orderly and more gradual. There was another extremely important difference as well. Unlike in China, where the Cultural Revolution was moderated somewhat in the early 1970s and abandoned altogether with the death of Mao Zedong in 1976, Kim's "cultural revolution" only became more intense over time, remaining a permanent force that would shape the ideology, culture and politics of his society for decades.

Still another difference was that Kim Il Sung's cult extended to all his family. That had always been true to some extent. Unlike the Soviet Union or China where the great leaders' parents were almost never publicly mentioned, North Korean propaganda made reference to Kim's "revolutionary lineage." From 1967, however, homage to his family became a central part of the ideology. His mother, Kang Pan-sŏk, in particular became an object of veneration. A song in praise of her appeared that summer and, on September 4, an article calling her "the mother of us all" appeared in the party newspaper *Rodong sinmun*.[5] She came to be commonly called "the mother of Korea" (*Chosŏn ŭi ŏmŏni*). It is interesting to note that Kang was the mother not only of Kim Il Sung but of his younger brother Kim Yŏng-ju who was emerging as the designated successor. Her cult and that of all the Great Leader's relatives was useful for keeping the succession within the family. When Kim Jong Il emerged as the designated successor, the cult of his mother, Kim Jong Suk, became prominent.

Fundamental to Kim Il Sung's cultural revolution was the elevation of Kim Il Sung's thought into a comprehensive ideological system that provided the foundations for the state. In his Cultural Revolution Mao Zedong was transformed into a peerless thinker whose ideas were memorized and endlessly quoted. In a like manner, Kim Il Sung's thought emerged as the ideological basis of society. This was first presented as the "Monolithic Ideological System" (*yuil sasang ch'egye*). South Korean scholar Lim Jae-Cheon traces its origins to the same May 25, 1967 speech calling for censorship. He argues that while the speech, which discussed the transition to socialism and the dictatorship of the proletariat, contains no remarkable content, it does attempt to lay out a theoretical position that differed from Maoist or Soviet versions of Marxism-Leninism.[6]

It complemented and reinforced Kim's declaration of an independent position in the socialist camp the previous year. North Korea was becoming ideologically and politically autonomous.

Kim Yŏng-ju, Kim Il Sung's younger brother, was then given the role of drawing up the "Ten Principles for the Establishment of the Monolithic System." The principles presented Kim Il Sung as a great revolutionary thinker whose thought must be studied. They stressed the importance of ideological struggle, and most of all, of following the Great Leader's instructions.

The Ten Principles were:

1. We must give our all in the struggle to unify the entire society with the revolutionary ideology of Great Leader Kim Il Sung.
2. We must honor Great Leader comrade Kim Il Sung with all our loyalty.
3. We must make absolute the authority of Great Leader comrade Kim Il Sung.
4. We must make Great Leader comrade Kim Il Sung's revolutionary ideology our faith and make his instructions our creed.
5. We must adhere strictly to the principle of unconditional obedience in carrying out the Great Leader comrade Kim Il Sung's instructions.
6. We must strengthen the entire Party's ideology and willpower and revolutionary unity, centering on Great Leader comrade Kim Il Sung.
7. We must learn from Great Leader comrade Kim Il Sung and adopt the communist outlook, revolutionary work methods and people-oriented work style.
8. We must value the political life we were given by Great Leader comrade Kim Il Sung, and loyally repay his great political trust and thoughtfulness with heightened political awareness and skill.
9. We must establish strong organizational regulations so that the entire Party, nation and military move as one under the one and only leadership of Great Leader comrade Kim Il Sung.
10. We must pass down the great achievement of the revolution by Great Leader comrade Kim Il Sung from generation to generation, inheriting and completing it to the end.[7]

Their banal, repetitive content are beside the point. Kim Il Sung is not only the supreme and unquestioned leader; he demanded absolutely loyalty and obedience. Kim Il Sung told his party officials that, "You comrades should be able to read, not only the contents of words I speak, but also the thoughts in my head."[8] Furthermore, he was the ideological guide whose principles establish the basis of society. Over the years, 65 sub-clauses were added to the Ten Principles giving specific details on how the Monolithic Ideological System was to be implemented. They provided specific instructions on how to go about establishing the one-ideology system. For example, sub-clause 8.5 dealt with the need for regular meetings:

> The people shall participate actively in evaluation meetings every two days and fortnightly, wherein the Great Leader's instructions and Party policies should be used as the yardstick by which to set high political and ideological standards for the evaluation of their work and lives, carrying out ideological struggles through criticism, and forging revolutionary ideals and continuously improving themselves through ideological struggles.[9]

In April 1974 the party officially adopted the Ten Principles for the Establishment of the Monolithic System as guidelines for the conduct of its members. Reviews of them became a part of meetings and study sessions and they were used to measure the degree of loyalty to the regime. The Ten Principles were the yardstick for measuring conduct. All North Koreans had to memorize them. Not only that, they had to put them into practice; during regular evaluation meetings, people criticized themselves on the basis of whether or not they had been living up to the Ten Principles in their everyday lives. In fact, political arrests were made primarily on the basis of violating them.[10]

The Ten Principles were founded on *juche* (*chuch'e*). *Juche* is a vague term and scholars of North Korea differ on how to interpret it. Usually it is rendered simply as "self-reliance." At times *juche* was defined as a creative adaptation of Marxism-Leninism or socialism to the conditions of Korea, rather than slavishly following foreign models. Certainly, that was the original intent of the term when Kim Il Sung introduced it. *Juche* reflected the nationalist aspirations of Kim, which were shared by most Koreans and were the main impetus of the North Korea revolution – to create a nation-state that was strong and autonomous. North Korea never sought to be self-sufficient; the country was obviously too small and lacking in crucial resources for that. Self-reliance meant having an economy that was not dependent on another power as colonial Korea's was on Japan; not being dependent militarily on another power for its defense as South Korea was on the USA; and not being politically dependent on another power as North Korea was on the Soviet Union in its first years. This was not an unreasonable or unrealistic goal. Economic self-sufficiency was not unique to North Korea. In fact, the idea of import substitution was common to many developing countries after World War II from Brazil to India. It was bound up with the anti-imperialism that provided much of the impetus for nationalism outside Europe and North America.

Only after 1967, however, did *juche* thought occupy a central place in North Korea when it became the theoretical foundation for the Monolithic Ideological System and an instrument for the glorification of Kim Il Sung. At that time, official publications began to suggest that *juche* was a complete system of thought. There were several reasons for this change. Partly it was in emulation of Mao. Kim Il Sung having eliminated all possible rivals at home may have wanted to establish himself as a great thinker too within the broader international communist movement. The troubled relations with both the Soviet Union and China in the 1960s, which made the DPRK less certain of the reliability of its allies, only contributed to the tendency toward self-reliance. It was thus an attempt to achieve an independent position within the progressive, socialist movement – a sort of ideological autonomy that complemented and reinforced the country's political independence. Having its own anti-imperialist ideology also made the DPRK a credible candidate for the Non-Aligned Movement. In fact, Brian Myers has argued that *juche* was mainly intended for a foreign audience and was never really important as an internal system of thought.[11]

Promotion of *juche* continued throughout the 1970s. By then, theorists sometimes argued that it was a universal philosophy. It was interpreted in broad if vague ways, and volumes were written on it. Its study became the core curriculum in the schools and the subject of weekly study sessions at workplaces throughout the country. In 1979 an Academy of Juche Sciences was established in Pyongyang under the direction of party ideologist Hwang Jang Yop (Hwang Chang-yŏp) (1923–2011). It sought to ensure that the universal principle of *juche* was applied to every field: music, sports, science and so on. North Korea developed an ambiguity about its role in the world at large. At times its universality was highlighted. *Juche* study societies were organized around the world under the supervision of the Juche Research Center Tokyo which was created in 1978. "The Great Juche idea has become the thought of the time," the DPRK's international monthly *Korea Today* proclaimed in in 1979, "Many heads of state and people of all states … express their admiration, saying President Kim Il Sung shows mankind its way like the sun with his immortal Juche idea. The success of the experience of Korea serve all nations building a new society as a priceless model."[12]

In 1972 the DPRK created a new "juche" constitution to replace the one drawn up by Moscow. Article 1 declared the DPRK to be an independent socialist state. Article 4 stated "the Democratic People's Republic of Korea is guided in its activity by the Juche idea of the Korean Workers' Party [KWP], a creative application of Marxism-Leninism to the conditions of our country."[13] Other articles enshrined the Ch'ŏllima movement, the Ch'ŏngsan-ri method and the Taean system.[14] It concentrated state power with the president, a title Kim Il Sung now assumed. All leading posts were filled at the recommendation of the president, and the Central Court, the highest judiciary was also accountable directly to him. The president was the commander and chief of the armed forces and chair of the newly created National Defense Commission. Gradually *juche* and the cult of Kim Il Sung virtually replaced Marxism-Leninism altogether. By the end of the 1970s references to Marx, Lenin or any other thinker other than Kim Il Sung were rare. At the Sixth Congress of the KWP in 1980 Marxism-Leninism disappeared from the party by-laws.[15] North Korea continued to call itself socialist, used some of the language of communism but no longer called itself Marxist or Leninist, or even mentioned the terms.

The Cult of Kim Il Sung

Perhaps no development was more striking than the extreme elaboration of the cult of Kim Il Sung. His cult appeared as early as 1946 and was initially part of the Soviet promotion of him as leader. Kim had resisted de-Stalinization and maintained the adulation of the leader that was now out of fashion in the Soviet bloc. Yet the cult became something more than an anachronistic manifestation of Stalinism. From 1967 it grew in intensity without pause until North Korea emerged as what could be called a "cult-state." After that year Kim Il Sung was generally referred to the *suryŏng* (leader). This was a term originally used for Stalin and Lenin came to be applied also to Kim Il Sung. He had usually been referred to as *susang* (premier) or *changgun* (general). In the late 1960s it became standard to refer to him as the great (*widaehan*) or fatherly leader. Only Kim was given these exalted prefixes to his name.[16] In 1972 he added the prefix president (*chusŏk*), the same title as used for Mao Zedong (and usually translated as "chairman") but different from the term *taet'ong-nyŏng* used by South Koreans for president. Then there was the raising of his "thought" as the ideological foundation of the society.

In April 1972 Kim Il Sung reached 60, an important landmark in Korean tradition. Sixtieth birthdays, known in Korean as *hwan'gap*, are often elaborately celebrated. The fanfare that accompanied the Great Leader's 60th birthday, however, was unprecedented in Korean history. Amid enormous, well-choreographed demonstrations, a massive statue painted in gold was unveiled on Mansudae, a high hill overlooking the Taedong River in Pyongyang. This was a spot that, ironically, had once been the site of a shrine to the Japanese emperor. A vast marble museum opened at Myohyangsan, a famous mountain north of the capital, dedicated to recording the heroic deeds of the Great Leader. Its 92 exhibition rooms dealt with the milestones in recent Korean history: Kim's heroic and successful anti-Japanese resistance, his liberation of Korea, his direction of national defense during the Korean War, and his construction of the socialist state after the Korean War. Most interesting were the rooms filled with gifts sent from all over the world to honor the Great Leader, a tribute to his global stature and his many admirers abroad. Badges with the Great Leader's picture were mass produced for the April 1972 birth celebration. All North Koreans now wore these badges. There were three types of badges – those for students, for adults and for party members. They were worn everywhere except at home.[17]

By the time of his 70th birthday in 1982 the entire country had become dotted with shrines to Kim Il Sung. The places he visited, and he traveled frequently throughout the small country, became sacred sites marked with commemorative plates. His quotes were carved into prominent rock outcrops and mountainsides throughout the country. Songs in praise of him dominated the airwaves. On his 70th birthday, to celebrate this new milestone in his life, an Arch of Triumph, larger than the original arch in France that it was modeled on, was constructed. In addition, a Tower of *Juche* was built to honor his contribution to human thought. It was the tallest stone structure in the world, and is topped with a red torch. And the Kim Il Sung Stadium, a massive sports arena with a 100,000-capacity, was opened.

By the 1980s adoration of the Great Leader and his family came to pervade every aspect of North Korean society to an extent that it struck most foreign observers as incomprehensibly bizarre. His name was preceded by such honorifics as "Ever-victorious iron-willed brilliant commander," "the sun of the nation," "the red sun of the oppressed people of the world," "the greatest leader of our time." Kim Il Sung became the infallible leader, and his *juche* thought the infallible truth. The religious-like cult was a central feature of North Korean society. In every classroom, office and home his portrait was hung in a prominent place. At the base of these portraits was often a small cloth to clean the glass plate over his picture. Workers and students began their days bowing before his portrait and placed wreaths at his statues on holidays. It was nearly impossible to be out of sight of an image of him or a banner praising or quoting him. Huge inscriptions of his quotations on every subject appeared everywhere even in remote mountains. His birthday, April 15, was a major holiday. His hometown of Mangyŏngdae was a place of pilgrimage. His life and his various heroic activities were the subjects of much of the nation's output of movies, plays and operas. Kim Il Sung was portrayed as an international figure admired by the oppressed throughout the world. North Koreans were told of tributes to the Great Leader that constantly came in from abroad.

Initially modeled on the cult of Stalin and later influenced by that of Mao, Kim Il Sung's cult took its own unique elements. Most obvious were the family references. But perhaps what is most striking was the maternal imagery. Not only was there the veneration of Kim Il Sung's mother and his wife, Kim Chŏng-suk, but Kim Il Sung himself was often referred to in maternal, nurturing terms. He was less often referred to as the fatherly leader than as the "parental leader" (ŏbŏi suryŏng), a term that could include motherly as well as fatherly features. As Brian Myers and others have pointed out he was often depicted in caring rather than heroic poses: tucking in soldiers at night, hugging and embracing the troops, watching over them while they rested. Posters and paintings portrayed him surrounded by children in a bed of flowers. He loved, cared for and protected the people. Even his portraits and statues presented a somewhat rounded, almost maternal look, not the large, tough guerilla fighter that he actual was. North Korean propaganda showed him surrounded by crowds of adoring subjects basking in his benevolence, or as it was often stated, "bonded in his bosom."[18] This motherly imagery carried over to his son and successor Kim Jong Il.

Observers have often tried to analyze the traditional Confucian element in the cult. Considering how deeply Confucianism penetrated Korean culture this would be expected and yet in many ways the cult of Kim differed from traditional values. Certainly, the language of a ruler who loved and cared for his people, who ruled them with benevolence and protected them from the Yankee imperialists, echoed traditional Confucian language and imagery. In fact, the cult of Kim Il Sung was unprecedented in Korean history. Kings were less lofty figures than the Chinese emperors, they lacked the sacred aura of Japanese emperors or of Southeast Asian devarajas (god-kings). The cult had a more modern derivation – from that of Stalin and influenced by Mao's. It was also echoed and influenced by the emperor cult of prewar Japan. North Korean school children paid their daily obeisance to the Great Leader at the school's shrine to him much as colonial Korean school children attended shrines to the semi-divine Japanese emperor. The practice of bowing ceremoniously in the direction of the imperial palace in Tokyo, the ubiquitous Shinto shrines, and the tone of reverence expressed when referring to the emperor all had strikingly similar manifestations in North Korea. Even the glorification of the Kim family resembled that of the Japanese imperial family and its ancestors. Like the Japanese imperial cult, the cult of Kim Il Sung sought to inculcate an almost mystical sense of unity among the people and demanded their total loyalty to the leader. Whatever its traditional, colonial and communist influences, the cult of Kim Il Sung and his family had no real counterpart in any contemporary society.

Ultimately, *juche* combined with the cult of Kim Il Sung effectively isolated North Korea ideologically from its neighbors and helped to insulate it from the upheavals and collapses that swept the communist world in the late 1980s and early 1990s. It contributed to the ease by which Pyongyang was able to ignore the winds of reform in China and elsewhere in the remaining socialist countries.

Creating a Dynasty: The Rise of Kim Jong Il

After 1967 North Korea began to transform itself into a dynastic state. Indeed the emphasis on the Kim Il Sung family was so great the South Korean anthropologist Lee Moon-woong refers to North Korea as "a family state."[19] South Korean scholars Cho Ŭn-hŭi and Jae-cheon Lim, go as far as dividing North Korea into the pre-family cult before 1967 and the family cult after that.[20] This development which took the North Korean revolution in such an eccentric direction grew out of a serious challenge for Kim Il Sung: how to ensure a succession that would carry on his legacy. The attack on Stalin shortly have his death in 1953 by his "revisionist" successors made him aware of this problem early in his rule. The "deviant" path China took after the death of Mao in 1976 could only have reinforced his concerns. Early on he seems to have decided to keep the regime within his family. This is not entirely surprising, given the cultural deposition of Koreans to emphasize bloodlines and hereditary status. Even the social system constructed from the late 1940s to the late 1960s was to a large measure inherited. Furthermore, the cult of Kim Il Sung early on was extended to include his family.

At first Kim Il Sung seemed to be grooming his younger brother Kim Yŏng-ju as his successor. The younger Kim was appointed to a key position in the powerful Organization and Guidance Department (Chojikbu) of the KWP in 1959; and at the Second Party Conference in 1966 he was given another key position. At the Fifth Party Congress in 1970 Kim Yŏng-ju was ranked sixth in the party hierarchy. In 1972 the younger brother was sent to South Korea to represent the regime in the negotiations between the two countries that year. His rise caused some problems.[21] Besides the obvious fact that it was based on his blood ties to the Great Leader rather than any particular accomplishment, Kim Yŏng-ju played no important part in the guerilla movement, and in fact was not politically active before 1945. This was in contrast to the solid revolutionary and nationalist pedigrees of the rest of the Kim family. Both Kim Il Sung's father and his uncle were active in the nationalist movement, his other younger brother Kim Ch'ŏl-ju was killed fighting the Japanese, and his first wife was also an active member of the partisans. However, Kim Yŏng-ju in addition to his handicap of never having served in the guerilla movement, suffered from health problems, spending spells in hospitals.[22] Whether for these or for other reasons, he seems to have fallen out of favor in the 1970s and for a while disappeared entirely from the public, only to resurface much later but never to hold anything other than honorary positions. From the early 1970s Kim Il Sung instead promoted his eldest son Kim Jong Il as his successor. It is not clear when this decision was made. According to one defector this was discussed in a Central Committee meeting as early as December 1972.[23] Most likely the decision to make Kim's eldest son his successor was announced to party insiders in early 1974. In 1980 the decision was made known to the public.

Early Background of Kim Jong Il

Kim Jong Il, the eldest son of Kim Il Sung and Kim Chŏng-suk, was officially born on February 16, 1942, on Mount Paketu Mountain, Korea's highest peak, at the guerilla headquarters of Kim Il Sung's anti-Japanese forces. Not only his birth there but also the Paektusan guerilla base itself were a later fiction. Most likely he was born outside of Khabarovsk in eastern Siberia where his father was stationed at the time. Even his date of birth may also be fictitious since evidence suggests that he may have been born in February 1941. The later myth of his birth in a rudimentary mountain fortress with bullets flying overhead has the obvious purpose of dramatizing his arrival into the world and linking it to the heroic guerilla movement. It is not clear why his date of birth may have been moved up one year.

Perhaps by making it shortly before his father's 30th birthday the two events could be commemorated together every ten years.[24]

Kim Jong Il attended the elite First Pyongyang Middle School and the First Pyongyang High School. In elementary school he was elected chair of the Children's Union and in high school vice chair of the school's Youth League. In 1957 he accompanied his father to Moscow to attend a Soviet party congress. He seems to have always played the role of leader. As a student at Kim Il Sung University he is reported to have initiated a movement to read 10,000 pages a year focusing on the works of Kim Il Sung.[25] After graduation Kim Jong Il was placed in key positions in the party. His first position in 1964 was in the Organizational and Guidance Department of the Central Committee of the KWP. Since this department dealt with administrative affairs in the various branches of the party it meant that while still in his early twenties he was involved in important and sensitive work. In this and in his official capacities he would have worked with much older and high-ranking party officials including those at the ministerial and vice-ministerial levels.[26]

In the late 1960s Kim Jong Il became involved in the Propaganda and Agitation Department of the party. A man of artistic dispositions, he flourished in this post directing literature, theater and his great passion – film. Most of his work centered around elaborating on the cult of his father. This included restoring historical sites associated with his life such as Mangyŏngdae and Poch'ŏnbo and overseeing celebrations of his father's 60th birthday in 1972. Kim Jong Il directed the Paektusan Production group that produced films, the April 15th Literary Production group that wrote novels, the Mansudae Art Troupe that created theater productions and the Mansudae Art Studio that produced paintings. The main subject of these groups was the glorious life and deeds of Kim Il Sung or those who dedicated themselves to him. His was more than the chief propagandist, the younger Kim was an innovator and theoretician of the arts. Kim Jong Il is credited with inventing *pangch'ang*, a technique of offstage singing in operas which were most probably influenced by the revolutionary operas promoted by Mao's wife during the Cultural Revolution in China.[27] He developed his "speed war thesis" which stated that all writers and artists should in the shortest time possible produce works of high standards based on the unitary thought of Kim Il Sung.[28] And he wrote a treatise on film making which became the definitive work on the subject – that is in North Korea of course. In the early years this was done in the background. He was never mentioned in public. On his 31st birthday on February 16, 1973 the *Rodong sinmun* praised his new innovations in the arts but without referring to him by name.[29] Only insiders may have understood the reference.

While continuing to be czar of the arts, Kim Jong Il became the chief ideologist of the party. He emerged in this new role in 1974 with a speech given to propaganda workers on the "Kimilsungization of the Whole Society." Only a few years earlier his uncle Kim Yŏng-ju had promulgated the Ten Principles of a Monolithic Ideological System. Now, as the newly designated successor Kim Jong Il promoted their study. To carry out this ideological training he directed the further development and intensification of study sessions for party workers and for all citizens at offices, factories and farms. In the 1970s he established a complicated system of every-other-day, weekly, every-ten-day, monthly, quarterly, and yearly assessment sessions to instill ideological correctness among party members. Gradually, the young Kim built up an elaborate party guidance system that included loyal officials in every civilian organization. He introduced the "three-line and three-day" system in which officials from the party, the administration and the secret police directly sent him briefings every three days.[30] In this way he began building and overseeing a vast surveillance system.

In the 1970s Kim Jong Il also took on the task of improving economic development. He directed the Three Revolutions Team Movement (*Samdae hyŏngmyŏng sojo undong*) drawn up in 1973 or 1974 and implemented in early 1975.[31] Young people were dispatched in teams of 30 to 50 to factories and collective farms to assist and stimulate the workers and farmers. It was assumed their young idealism would invigorate production and cut through bureaucratic inertia. He then directed a second campaign labeled the Three Revolutions Red Flag Movement (TRFM). This was Kim Jong Il's own variation of the Ch'ŏllima movement. Just as his father had begun the latter with a visit to the Kangsŏn steel plant in December 1956, Kim Jong Il inaugurated the TRFM with a visit to the Kŏmdŏk coal mine in December 1975. There, like his father, he was able to lead the workers to heroic feats of production.[32] Kim Jong Il used the Organization and Guidance Department to consolidate power. This organization was the only one that had access to the activities of every branch of government. The younger Kim packed it with loyalists, many recruited from the Three Revolutions Team Movement.[33]

Kim Jong Il began to emerge in public during these campaigns, not by name but as the "Party Center," (*tang chungang*) a term that initially puzzled outside observers and only gradually began to be understood as referring to Kim Il Sung's eldest son. The great publicity given to the extraordinary accomplishments of these campaigns was clearly intended by Kim Il Sung to promote his son as well as to spur production. And from 1975 his portrait began to appear alongside his father's at military offices, although it appeared in party and government offices only after his official anointment as successor in 1980. A Party Center athletic field event was held on February 16, 1976, Kim Jong Il's 34th birthday.[34] Still his name was never mentioned in public nor did his picture appear anywhere in the media.

It is not clear why Kim Jong Il was promoted in such an indirect way. Kim may have been concerned about an unfavorable reaction from his two benefactors, the Soviet Union and China, and he might have been worried about undermining his efforts to achieve a leadership position in the Non-Aligned Movement. Kim may also have had personal doubts about his son's ability. Furthermore, there is some hint of internal opposition, although this is not known for certain. Oddly, between 1977 and 1979, reports of the Party Center nearly disappeared. One study of the party publication *Kŭlloja* found "the Party Center" mentioned 378 times in 1976 but only four times in 1978.[35] In 1977, when the reports of the Party Center began to diminish, Politburo member Kim Tong-gyu disappeared, apparently sent to a prison camp where he died seven years later.[36] Several high-ranking members were demoted. Perhaps, as some have speculated, there was opposition to Kim Il Sung's plan to name his son as his successor. It is possible that Kim Jong Il, with his rigorous party guidance system, may have been too hard on cadres, generating party unrest. Another possibility is that he may have been responsible for the August 18, 1976 axe murders. This may have been an effort to show his toughness and compensate for his lack of military experience. The incident, which resulted in Kim Il Sung's public letter of regret and the panicky evacuation of more than 200,000 people from Pyongyang, may have temporarily discredited him.[37]

Becoming the Dear Leader

At the Sixth Party Congress Kim Jong Il was appointed to each of the three most important organs of the party: the Politburo, the Military Affairs Committee and the Secretariat. In the Politburo he was placed on the Standing Committee where he was the fourth ranking member after his father and two guerilla comrades, Kim Il and O Chin-u. On the Military Affairs Committee he ranked third after his father and O Chin-u.[38] He was not clearly designated as his father's successor and curiously even then he was not referred to by name nor did he give public speeches. Only after 1980 was his name mentioned. From 1982 his photo began to appear regularly in publications along with poems, essays and stories praising him.[39] Yet even then when his photo became ubiquitous he did not speak in public. However, it was generally accepted that he was his father's designated heir. In June 1983 he accompanied his father on a ten-day trip to China where it is believed he was presented to the Chinese leaders as the future successor – a decision the Chinese leadership were less than enthusiastic about. Three years later, in May 1986, Kim Il Sung stated at the 40th anniversary of the Kim Il Sung Party School that the issue of succession had been satisfactory resolved.[40]

In the early 1980s Kim Jong Il became the definitive interpreter of this father's thought, a position signaled with the publication in 1982 of *On the Juche Idea*. It became required reading, a work that received the degree of admiration previously reserved for his father. This was added to his position as official arbiter of all cultural and artistic production. He was portrayed as a brilliant theoretician writing masterworks on cinema, and developing the "seed theory" of art and literature. This vague and somewhat incoherent theory seemed to imply in an abstract way that he as his father's "seed" was part of a natural process of progressive evolution.[41] On the eve of his 40th birthday in 1982 he was awarded Hero of the DPRK. In 1983 he then moved up to rank second in the official leadership hierarchy after his father; and in 1988 he was receiving a level of honorifics in public pronouncements similar to his father. By this time he was called *ch'inaehanŭn chidoja*, usually translated as "Dear Leader" in the Western press. His birthday, February 16, became a holiday. The "Song of General Kim Il Sung" was played at almost all public events and functioned as a kind of second national anthem. It now became the custom to follow this song with a performance of the "Song of General Kim Jong Il."[42]

Meanwhile, Kim Il Sung made sure that his son had the unquestioned loyalty of the military. This too was done through a long, careful process. As early as the 1970s a cult of Kim Jong Il began within the military before it appeared in the civilian or public sectors. His public emergence at the Sixth Party Congress was accompanied by a letter campaign in which soldiers pledged their loyalty to him. Kim Jong Il took his own measures to secure control of the military. In late 1974 he expanded the role of the Organization and Guidance Department to review military officers.[43] In 1983 he established a notification section, *t'ongbokwa*, to provide him with reports on the public and private lives of generals.[44] Kim Jong Il continued a gradual rise in profile and responsibility in military affairs. On December 1991 he was made commander-in-chief of the Korean People's Army and in 1993 chair of the National Defense Commission. According to the constitution the president served these positions so it was dutifully amended to make this legal.

Personal Life

Short and physically unimpressive, Kim Jong Il was very different from his father in build and personality. He was interested in movies, art and literature and in becoming an authoritative figure on those fields. His private life was as complicated—involving several wives. His father appears to have arranged a marriage to Kim Young Sook (Kim Yŏng-suk), the daughter of a high-ranking military officer and they had a daughter, Kim Sul-song (Kim Sŏl-song, 1974–). But early on he took up with Sŏng Hye-rim (1937 and 2002), a movie star five years his senior and a daughter of a former editor of the official party newspaper. She became his mistress in the late 1960s eventually divorced her husband, the son of a prominent North Korean writer. They had a son, Kim Jong Nam (Kim Chŏng-nam,

1971–2017). Their relationship is said to have been kept secret from Kim Jong Il's father, at least for some time. Later they separated and Sŏng is reported to have died at a Moscow clinic in 2002. The private lives of North Korean leaders are kept secretive, even their spouses rarely appear in public but Sŏng's sister, Sŏng Hye-rang, defected to Switzerland in 1996 and wrote a memoir that is an important source of information about the Kim family. Sŏng Hye-rim may have joined her and then decided to return. This sort of sharing of family history was not tolerated. Sŏng Hye-rang's son, Ri Il-nam, defected to South Korea in 1982. He was shot dead in Seoul by North Korean agents in 1997.[45] Kim next took up with a Japanese-born dancer, Ko Young Hee (Ko Yŏng-hŭi) (?1953–2004) and they had two sons, Kim Jong Chul (Kim Chŏng-ch'ŏl) (1981–) and Kim Jong Un (Kim Chŏng-ŭn) (1984–). Ko died of cancer in 2004. Kim Ok, who had been his personal secretary since the 1980s, became his last consort.

One complication in Kim Jong Il's rise was the existence of Kim Sŏng-ae, whom his father married several years after the death of his mother, Kim Chŏng-suk. Kim Sŏng-ae made her first public appearance in 1965, serving as vice chair of the Democratic Women's Union in late 1965 and chair in 1969. She began to be seen in photos with her husband and in the late 1960s began appearing in public, meeting foreign female delegates without the presence of her husband. Kim Il Sung had a daughter with her, Kyŏng-jin, and two sons, Kim P'yŏng-il and Kim Yŏng-il, who became known to the inner circle as members of the "side branch" (kyŏtkaji) of the family rather than the "main branch."[46] Kim Sŏng-ae was reportedly ambitious and ruthless to opponents, being, according to one account, responsible for the purge of Pak Chŏng-ae, one of the only high-ranking women in the regime who was not a relative of Kim Il Sung.[47] She also promoted family members to party and state positions.[48] But with Kim Jong Il's emergence as the clearly designated heir his stepmother largely disappeared from view and his half-siblings never became public figures. When Kim Il Sung died in 1994 Kim Sŏng-ae ranked only 104th out of the huge 273-member state funeral committee. Kim Jong Il's half-siblings, Kim Kyŏng-jin, Kim P'yŏng-il and Kim Yŏng-il, were not on it.[49]

With the rise of the son, the entire Kim family was further glorified across the media. This trend toward widening the cult of Kim Il Sung to include his family had already begun, but with the succession being passed on to a new generation propaganda increasingly emphasized the importance of the unique family in protecting and guiding the nation as well as embodying the revolution. Texts were rewritten to make the modern history of Korea the history of the Kim family. The official history, *Kŭndae Chosŏn yŏksa* (Modern History of Korea), claimed that in 1866 Kim Ŭng-u, his great-grandfather, bravely fought the US imperialists and led the local people in the attack on the *General Sherman*. This now became a major incident in Korean history, the beginning of the struggle against American and Western imperialism, with the Kim family at the forefront. According to the official histories his father, Kim Hyŏng-jik, in the 1910s and 1920s led a national liberation movement. Kim Jong Il's birth was now factiously located on the sacred Paektu Mountain. His mother, Kim Jong Suk, was elevated to the status of a national hero who had fought the Japanese alongside her husband, becoming known as the "invincible revolutionary."[50] Monuments to her and other members of the Kim family appeared throughout the country.

When Kim Jong Il succeeded his father as leader in 1994 he had an extremely long apprenticeship. By the time he had been designated to the inner circle as his father's successor he had already been actively involved in party affairs for a decade. He then continued to acquire key posts over the next 20 years. For 30 years he had been involved in most of the centers of power – party administration, propaganda, the security organizations and the military. Only in two fields was he not known to have been deeply involved: economic development and foreign affairs. For all his odd appearance and his personal eccentricities he had been extremely well prepared to assume power upon his father's death.

Kim Il Sung's Monolithic Society

By the 1970s North Korea was becoming a truly monolithic socio-political system with a distinct culture. It was a highly regimented, totalitarian society centered on the cult of Kim Il Sung and his family. Indoctrination reached a level of intensity perhaps found nowhere else. Virtually all art, literature, film and music was directed at glorifying Kim Il Sung, the revolution and the Great Leader's philosophy of *juche*. North Koreans learned very little of the prerevolutionary culture, or of art, music and literature from outside Korea. Every aspect of life was focused on or linked to the leader and his family.

It was a society that prevented the populace from having even a minimum of knowledge of the outside world. International news consisted mainly of reports of foreign praises of the Great Leader and meetings of *juche* study clubs in various countries. Foreign visitors to North Korea after 1980 were often amazed by the near total ignorance of what was happening beyond the country's borders by a generation that had grown up under the regime. Even access to printed materials from the Soviet Union and its allies was extremely restricted. This isolation can be explained by the need to seal off the country from the post-Stalinist and later post-Maoist changes in the communist world and especially from the developments in South Korea as that country began to economically prosper. The siege mentality of the Korean War contributed to this ideological hothouse. North Korea had become a cultist state, where the people were intensely bonded to the leadership and sealed off from the rest of the world.

A Hierarchical Society

One of the ironic features of North Korea is that it was founded on the egalitarian ideology of Communism, which advocated a classless society and yet developed one of the world's most sharply defined and unequal social systems. Indeed, it came to resemble the rigidly hierarchical, hereditary nature of premodern Korean society as a new class system emerged to replace the own society that had been dominated by the landholding *yangban* elite. The three classes (*kyech'ŭng*) – loyal, wavering and hostile – were subdivided in the mid and late 1960s into 51 *sŏngbun* (groups), each with their own ranking. There were 12 loyal groups belong to the loyal or core class. These comprised workers from working class families; former farmhands; former poor peasants; personnel of state organizations; KWP members; family members of deceased revolutionaries; family members of national liberation fighters; revolutionary intelligentsia (those who received education after liberation); family members of civilians killed in the Korean War; families of soldiers who were killed during the Korean War; families of servicemen; and families of war martyrs or heroes. Nine *sŏngbun* belonged to the wavering class and 30 to the hostile class. The latter included those who had served under the Japanese as officials; former landlords; businessmen; merchants; Christians; active Buddhists; shamans; those who had engaged in pro-Japanese or pro-American activities; and those who had family members who had fled to the South. These *sŏngbun* were all based on family background so that each became an inherited status. Discrimination against people of unfavorable backgrounds was common in other communist countries, and China under Mao in the 1950s had placed people in categories. But in no other modern society was such a well-defined, inherited system of social status created.[51] In 1980, 12 new *sŏngbun* were created to reclassify ethnic Koreans from Japan and those from South Korea, China and elsewhere.[52]

These were not officially publicized but everyone knew where they belonged. Young people discovered this when they went off to school and were denied permission to attend higher levels of education or join the party. These categories were hereditary and they mattered profoundly. Food rations, access to desired goods, housing, jobs, career advancement and admittance to higher education were determined by the classification, which was very difficult to change. For most people there was little chance of improving upon their inherited social status although people could be downgraded as a result of improper political behavior. Cases of upward social mobility were rarer. The privileged were able to live in Pyongyang. In fact, it was difficult for most North Koreans to visit the city other than on official excursions.

The real elite were the highest *sŏngbun* within the core class making up perhaps less than 1 percent of the population. This top tier of society lived in a separate and restricted section of the capital. The gap between the elite, or higher ranking KWP members, top bureaucrats and military officers, and the rest of the population became more pronounced over time. By the 1980s, if not earlier, those at the very top enjoyed a lifestyle unimaginable to ordinary people, driving expensive German cars, drinking French cognac, and having access to other imported luxuries. The hereditary nature of the ruling elite also became more pronounced over time. By the time of Kim Il Sung's death in 1994, most of the younger high-ranking officials were the sons, nephews or in-laws of the old guard. North Korean politics by then could be seen as rivalry among powerful elite clans.

Just as in traditional Korea, the education system reflected the hierarchical nature of society. At the top institute of higher education was Kim Il Sung University in Pyongyang followed by the technical-focused Kim Ch'aek University. Other schools were of lower rank. Admission was by family background and ideological purity as much as merit. In premodern Korea the civil examinations were used to select high officials but were only opened to members of the *yangban* elite. The DPRK school system functioned in a similar way. Prestige degrees were a means of reaffirming status rather than acquiring it. Youths from 12 to 18 could try to join the Socialist Youth Organization, an important gateway to better opportunities later in life. But membership in this too appeared to be linked to family status. Thus, the egalitarianism and social mobility of the early years were replaced by a rough replication of the rigid, ranked structure of society based largely on bloodlines that was characteristic of traditional Korea.

Family and Gender

Another way in which the DPRK resembled the traditional order was the absence of women from important positions. North Korea's revolution in the late 1940s brought about radical change in the legal status of women. Women enjoyed equality in education and, at least legally, in pay. Women could share equal inheritance, divorce was made easier, the taking of concubines was outlawed and all occupations were in theory open to women. In the late 1950s the state began to actively encourage women to take jobs outside of the home. By the 1970s women made up about half the workforce, and 70 percent of all those employed in light industry and 15 percent in heavy industry.[53] The government boasted of its achievements in advancing the career paths for women, claiming over 100,000 professional and managerial positions were occupied by women in 1971. "Women in our country enjoy a happy life under the sagacious leadership in the benevolent bosom of Comrade Kim Il Sung the genius leader of the revolution," it was proclaimed.[54] Women reportedly "Boundlessly adore the fatherly leader Comrade Kim Il Sung who had freed them from double and treble oppression and subjugation of the old society."[55]

The prime motivation to bring women into the workforce was a labor shortage. This was especially acute after 1953 and remained a problem since so many young men were in the military and because economic growth tended to rely more on increasing labor inputs rather than on improving productivity. While women were never forced to leave the home, those who did not work were penalized by receiving smaller rations. A law in 1946 provided 77 days' maternity leave and this was later extended to 150 days. The effort to free women for labor was accelerated with the 1976 Law on the Nursing and Upbringing of Children. This called for the creation of 60,000 kindergartens and pre-kindergartens that could accommodate 3.5 million children, virtually all in this age group.[56] The daycare centers also served the function of indoctrinating the young at an early age. They became a great source of pride; a visit to a model daycare center was part of the standard tour for foreign visitors.

But North Koreans were still conservative enough that women were expected to take care of the housework, to cook for their families and to raise children. Married women were often let out of work early to collect children and prepare dinner. According to the 1976 law women with children under the age of 13 were to be let out two hours early but paid for eight hours.[57] Most of the jobs filled by women were low-paid menial ones. Few women enjoyed high-status jobs; it was rare for them to hold jobs as managers. Many were school teachers but by one estimate only 15 percent were university professors. One-fifth of the delegates to the Supreme People's Assembly, the powerless legislature, were female, but there were few women in top positions. The former Soviet intelligence officer Pak Chŏng-ae stands out until she was purged in the 1960s. Hŏ Chŏng-suk, daughter of Hŏ Hŏn the prominent leftist intellectual, served as Minister of Justice for a while but she too was purged in the early 1960s. Women made up only 5 percent of the Central Committee members in 1961 and just 3 percent in 1980.[58] Later Kim Jong Il's sister, Kim Kyŏng-hŭi, wielded some power but mainly through her husband, Chang Sŏng-t'aek.

Most women wore simple traditional Korean clothes until April 1970 when Kim Il Sung gave instructions for women to dress more colorfully. Western clothes then became more popular but there was a limit reached in 1982 when women were warned not to wear clothes that were too revealing.[59] Marriages were commonly arranged using the Korean custom of a *chungmae* or matchmaker, much as was done in the South. By the 1980s love matches were becoming more common, again reflecting a pattern of change similar to its modernizing neighbors.[60] Visitors to North Korea noticed the change, with more young couples appearing together in public. But in many respects it was a puritanical society with premarital sexual relations strongly discouraged.

The state initially attacked familism – the Confucian value system that gave primacy to the family over all other forms of social organization. This gave way to the revival of traditional family values. Propaganda extolled the virtues of the family and the role of motherhood. The latter was especially praised as an important component for constructing a socialist society. This attitude was typified in a 1961 speech entitled "The Duty of Mothers in the Education of Children" in which Kim Il Sung stated: "At present, our mothers are charged with the important duty of rearing their children into fine builders of communism."[61] As in traditional Korea people were expected to get married and have children, and divorce while legal was not encouraged. In 1946 the Law of Equality between the Sexes made divorce by mutual consent extremely easy and for a decade divorce was fairly common. The rising divorce rate alarmed officials who in the mid-1950s began to require couples to go to a People's Court, pay a high fee and then adhere to a period of reconciliation. As a result divorce once again became uncommon.[62] Family bounds, between husband and wife and especially between parent and child came under official praise to an extent not found in other communist states. In 1966 the ethnological publication *Kogo Minsok* described filial piety as part of the country's cultural heritage worthy of preservation, calling on the country's "beautiful customs and virtues" (*mip'ungryangsok*). Interestingly, this was a stock phrase ironically used by conservative defenders of the social tradition in the South.[63] The 1972 Constitution stated: "It is strongly affirmed that families are the cells of society and shall be well taken care of by the State."[64] The nuclear family was idealized and supported.

Yet the cultural revolution after 1967 was also directed at the family. In 1968 the state called for the "revolution of the home" and in 1971 the propaganda organs heralded a plan to "revolutionize family life." The goal was to develop a spirit of collectivism that would replace selfishness. People were urged to raise children to become loyal socialists. They should learn, state propaganda taught, not to be more devoted to their family than to the nation, its revolution and its leadership. As the *Modern Korean Dictionary* (1981) explained under "domestic revolution":

> All families are to be educated to have unending devolution to the party and the Suryŏng [Leader] and all traces of old ideas remaining in their minds should be thoroughly uprooted. Families should always work and learn for the purpose of the revolution and in order to live life they should each dedicate their whole body to becoming a fighting revolutionary and communist for the party, Suryŏng, fatherland and people.[65]

To reinforce this link between the family and the revolution, from the 1970s the bride and groom at wedding ceremonies, wearing their Kim Il Sung badges of course, pledged "we, as an eternal husband and wife, commit totally to the Great Leader and swear that we will build a revolutionary home." In the 1980s they also pledged their devotion to the "Dear Leader."[66]

The birth rate was quite high in the 1940s, 1950s and 1960s, and then fell. This was partly due to government efforts. Early marriages were banned. In 1971 the marriage age was recommended at 28 for women and 30 for men.[67] The long years of military service, small apartments and the entry of women in the workforce all contributed to a decline in the birth rate. And it also reflected the normal demographic transition as the country became more industrialized, urbanized and better schooled. By 1990 the birth rate had fallen to the point that the ban on early marriages was relaxed.

The Arts and Letters

Art and literature served the state. This is, of course, true in every totalitarian state – but in few if any societies in the modern world was all artistic expression as restricted to so few themes and as completely harnessed to serve propaganda. In the early years North Korea followed the pattern of the Soviet bloc countries. From the very beginning of the regime art and literature were seen as the vehicles for propaganda. Many prominent cultural leaders voluntarily came to the North after 1945 and were willing to serve the new revolutionary government. Writers and artists came under the direction of the Federation of Literature and Art. From 1948 to 1962 this was headed by the novelist and short story writer Han Sŏr-ya (1900–1970?). However, the restrictions placed on artists and writers only intensified, and in the 1960s virtually every well-known one disappeared. Han, for example, who had been a successful writer associated with the proletarian literature movement in colonial times, was purged in 1962 as too bourgeois. Another prominent example was Ch'oe Sŭng-hŭi (1911–?), an internationally acclaimed dancer who introduced modern Japanese influences into Korean traditional dance during the colonial period and went to the North in 1946. She adapted Korean and modern dances to revolutionary themes, but she also fell out of favor in the 1960s and was not heard of again. Artistic expression became so constricted that it was difficult for any creative individual to flourish.

Literature was in the socialist realist mode to follow other communist countries. Stories had to be for the purposes of education and inspiring the masses. Writers who failed to adhere to the guidelines were reprimanded and forced to rewrite their stories. From the late 1960s restrictions were tightened to the point that most literature was reduced to panegyrics and crude, often violent tales glorifying the deeds of the Great Leader or the heroic struggles of peasants fighting the Japanese or other agents of oppression. Stories not centered on him were educational. Tatiana Gabroussenko, a North Korean specialist, reviewing rural literature in the 1990s found they were remarkably formulaic with the same unvarying stereotypes. Literary works often began with a mandatory quotation from the Great Leader or his son the Dear Leader or a *Rodong sinmun* editorial such as in the story "Wild Strawberry" that begins by citing a party newspaper editorial:

> In the agricultural area we must steadily implement the Party's revolutionary agricultural strategies which have confirmed their efficiency in practice, such as in the "seed revolution," the revolutionary strategy of double

cropping, the revolutionary strategy of potato growing, and the strategy of growing soybeans as well.

The story would then reinforce this lesson, resulting in perhaps the world's most didactic and boring literature. North Korean literature differed from Soviet and Chinese literature in its lack of conflict and tensions between major protagonists. There were no brothers or sisters divided by different loyalties that often populated the stories in those communist states. In DPRK literature class conflict among Koreans disappeared and all Koreans were depicted as good and united. Conflict was with outsiders. If Koreans were villainous or did bad things it was largely owing to the influence of foreigners.[68]

From the 1970s the stage was dominated by collectively composed revolutionary operas such as *P'i Bada* (*Sea of Blood*) first performed in 1971, the story of mass killings under the Japanese with lyrics said to have been composed by Kim Il Sung. Another work, *Kkotp'an Ŭnch'ŏnyŏ* (*The Flower Girl*), the story of oppressed villagers under the Japanese and a peasant woman turned revolutionary, first appeared in 1973 and remained a staple. These revolutionary operas were produced under the direction of Kim Jong Il when he served as head of the Culture and Arts Department in the Party Central Committee. The creation of model revolutionary operas was probably inspired by similar revolutionary model operas created in China in the late 1960s during the Cultural Revolution under the direction of Jiang Qing, Mao's wife. Although there are two differences: the North Korean operas were more Westernized in their music; and unlike the Chinese revolutionary operas that faded from the scene after Mao died in 1976, in Korea these were a staple of public entertainment for decades.[69] This is not surprising since North Korea's cultural revolution never ended.

Most musical output consisted of songs extolling the leadership such as "Song of General Kim Il Sung," "Long Life and Good Health to the Leader" and "We Sing of His Benevolent Love." One can hardly imagine an artistically more confined or sterile environment. Artists who tried to find any form of creative expression did so within extremely narrow parameters. A painter might express the beauty of nature through his or her depiction of falling snow as it fell upon Kim Il Sung in a winter scene from his wartime guerilla camp.[70] Only films were allowed a slight bit of creativity.

Living Standards

Although up until the early 1980s the DPRK citizens were probably better off in terms of basic health care, education and housing than many of those in developing countries, living conditions can best be described as spartan. Nor were there more than marginal improvements in the standard of living after 1970. Electricity was widely available but not necessarily indoor plumbing; most used communal toilets and baths. Goods available in the shops were very limited except for those who had access to foreign currency and could shop at a Rakwŏn (Paradise) store that sold higher quality or imported consumer goods for foreign exchange. Oddly enough, North Koreans unlike their counterparts in Stalinist Russia or Maoist China could own foreign exchange although very few did. Among the few who did have access to foreign exchange were those who had relatives in Japan who sent remittances. Locally made consumer goods were of low quality when available. Most country homes were extremely humble and urban dwellers lived in crowded apartment houses or even in wooden shacks.[71]

Still there were marked improvements in the daily lives of most DPRK citizens. Overall, housing, clothing, health and education improved, at least up to 1980. An area where life improved dramatically was education, one of North Korea's impressive achievements. By the 1960s almost all children were completing at least elementary school and the great majority of adults were literate. In the 1970s compulsory education was expanded to 11 years, although it is not certain when and if this target was actually met. Higher education expanded more until by the 1980s as many as one in five secondary school graduates went on to some form of higher education, mostly technical colleges. A much smaller number entered the comprehensive universities. Industrial enterprises maintained their own technical training schools. Admission to higher education was by recommendation which meant that family status was an important criterion. In 1980 an admission test was required for college entry; this did not end the restrictions on those with undesirable backgrounds but made college entry more competitive among the rest of the population, excepting, of course, the sons and daughters of the top elite.[72]

Life was probably hardest in rural areas that had the least developed infrastructure and best in Pyongyang. The capital had broad streets kept immaculately clean and an impressive subway system. Its skyline, squares and parks were dominated by monuments to the Great Leader; indeed, the city was a showcase to the regime and must have impressed those from the provinces. The best schools, hospitals and nicest housing for the elite were located there. However, away from the main streets and squares were muddy streets with crowded, modest housing where most ordinary citizens lived. Foreign visitors to the capital in the 1960s and 1970s remarked on the contrast between Pyongyang and the noise, dirt and chaos of Seoul; it was a clean, quiet city with some attractive buildings, efficient public transportation, and trees and parks. However, they also found it a strangely lifeless city. It was a city devoid of cars, busy markets or nightlife, striking many foreigners as grimly sterile. The streets were quiet except during the peak hours when people went back and forth to work. At night it was dark.

North Korea made great progress in improving basic health care. Although medical standards were fairly primitive by Western or Japanese standards they were adequate enough to raise the life span to about 70 by 1990.[73] DPRK health statistics have to be viewed with caution; still it seemed that North Koreans were, by the 1980s, healthier and living longer than their counterparts in most other developing countries. This progress in health care, however, began to be undercut in the 1990s, if not earlier, by food shortages leading to undernutrition and malnutrition.

A Regimented Society

In the 1990s famine, corruption and economic desperation weakened the state's ability to control society. But in the 1970s and early 1980s the DPRK had reached a level of regimentation that is truly remarkable. Kim Il Sung wanted his subjects to possess the will to resist an invasion with a ferocity that was absent in 1950. Therefore he saw to it that they were continually involved in military drills and exercises. A constant state of alert prevailed, as public rhetoric suggested that an invasion was imminent at any moment. Music, dramas, school lessons, every medium was used to promote a militarily ready society. The vocabulary of public announcements, no matter on what subject, were laced with fierce, militant rhetoric. International events were either interpreted as a sign that the USA and its allies were planning an invasion or used as warnings for the need for preparedness. In the wake of the Cuban Missile Crisis, Kim argued that the nation must be prepared to expel the "Yankee Imperialist" invaders and their South Korean allies as well as aid revolutionaries in the South. The increased US involvement in Vietnam, the breakdown of talks with the South in 1972–1973, and later the Gulf War of 1990–1991 also were occasions to increase combat readiness.

Military training and political indoctrination went together and began from childhood. Starting with preschool daycare centers much of schooling involved political indoctrination and military-like drills and exercises. Small children learned to march with toy guns and were taught dances such as "My Heavy Little Machine Gun." Even math lessons used problems such as how many American wolf-bastards remained after so many had been killed.[74] A lot of time was spent on carefully choreographed dances and marches that were like massive military drills. When boys reached the age of 16 they went into military service, except for a few that went on to college. Then, there was the extraordinarily long period of military service, which as we have seen reached a total of 12–13 years before it was shortened to "only" eight years.

Fewer aspects of life so well indicate the extreme indoctrination North Koreans were subjected to than the study sessions they were required to attend. Ordinary citizens spent much of their non-working time attending compulsory meetings. Everyone was assigned a work station at their factory, farm, office or shop. There they attended sessions where they read and discussed the newspapers before actually working. After work they stayed at their worksite to attend meetings or sessions where they reviewed the day's work and discussed future plans and how they would meet the goals assigned in the economic plans. North Korea initially followed the Soviet bloc practice of a couple of hours a week of indoctrination, but later study sessions became daily. Workers typically spent 30 minutes reading sections of the newspapers, articles, editorials and then 10–15 minutes discussing them in sessions led by low-level cadres. North Koreans had to study and memorize the teachings of the Great Leader and from the early 1980s the Dear Leader. In the 1960s North Korea adopted the Chinese practice of self-criticism sessions called *saenghwal ch'onghwa* (meetings on drawing upon the results of life). In the early 1970s they became weekly for city folks and every ten days for farmers. Although obviously modeled on Maoist practice they were later attributed to the innovative genius of Kim Jong Il.[75] And on top of this there were the constant mobilization campaigns to meet some special target in which people did "voluntary labor" on weekends and evenings.

So much time was taken with official activities that there appeared no room for any private life. Nor were there any non-official organizations of any kind. Religious life, other than the quasi-religious cult of Kim Il Sung and his family, was suppressed. By the 1950s there were no functioning churches. Buddhists and Ch'ŏndogyo temples were closed except for a few museum temples at historical spots. Any form of religious activity ceased to exist except at the most hidden level. There was an official Korean Christian Association but it was disbanded in 1960. In 1974 it reappeared apparently for propaganda purposes and to function as a means for Pyongyang to obtain contacts with Christian organizations in the South.[76] It served no actual religious role. Foreigners were sometimes taken to religious services at the several known churches but these seemed to take place only for their benefit. Overall the DPRK went further than most other communist states in suppressing all religious and, in fact, all state or party organization or activities of any kind.

Boys and girls from age 9 to 13 belonged to the Sonyŏndan (Children's Union). At 14 they could join the Kim Il Sung Socialist Youth. Membership to this organization was more selective, with those from bad family backgrounds excluded. The highly organized life of youth and the heavy indoctrination that characterized education were typical of communist countries. What distinguished North Korea was the intensity of the indoctrination over so long a period. Young people, especially secondary school and college students, often spent much of their time on "voluntary" service such as helping with the planting and harvest, or on public construction projects. Dating and romance were initially disapproved of but this began to change in the mid-1980s when themes of romantic love reappeared in literature, music and drama.

Access to any source of information other than that controlled by the state was so severely controlled that few North Koreans had much real awareness of the outside world other that the limited and distorted information they were given. Radios and, later, televisions were adjusted so they could only receive the official Central Korean Broadcasting Service. The chief newspaper, the *Rodong sinmun*, was devoid of any real news but was a vehicle for disseminating the official line on various aspects of life. Provincial newspapers were virtually identical in content to the main newspaper in the capital. By the 1960s North Korea had become a truly totalitarian society where almost every part of life was controlled by the state. Even university professors could be surprisingly ignorant of even basic developments in the world.[77]

The Surveillance System

By the late 1960s North Korea had constructed a system of surveillance and control that went beyond that of any contemporary society. This included incorporating traditional Korean and East Asian means of maintaining order as well as institutions and practices borrowed from other communist countries. In the late 1950s, during the great purge, the government created the *oho tamdangje*, the "five household-in-charge system." In 1971 it was renamed the *ogajo*, the "five-household team," but was not necessarily composed of five households as it could be much larger – up to 15 or 20.[78] Another institution that was formalized at that time was the *inminban* (people's *ban*). Typically they consisted of 30–50 families. In Korea the *ban* functioned as the smallest unit of local administration and in South Korea *ban* organizations called *banhŭi* conducted meetings to disseminate information and organized campaigns such as rat extermination campaigns. In North Korea the *ban* became an effective system for penetrating authority down to the neighborhood. It was a ubiquitous organization found on collective farms as well as in urban areas. Residents were given instructions on the latest state directives and participated in neighborhood cleaning and repairs supervised by an *inminbanjang*, usually a middle-aged woman. The collection of night soil and in rural areas manure was another responsibility of the *inminban*.

The *inminbanjang* checked all visits and kept track of all activities in the group. Andrei Lankov, when living in North Korea in the 1980s, was told by one *inminbanjang* that: "An inminban head should know how many chopsticks and how many spoons are in every household."[79] Residents of apartment buildings took turns as security guards.

Unannounced visits by security officials were routine. Every home was subjected to the *sukpak kŏmyŏl*, the midnight home check by police and the *inminbanjang*.[80] Security officials would check radios to ensure the mechanism that kept them fixed to state radio stations hadn't been tampered with, and that there were no unauthorized literature or goods. The KWP also formed a surveillance function, since the one-in-five adults who were members were under various kinds of supervision and control. All travel and movement was strictly controlled. People had to register to stay overnight at another home even if it was that of a relative. Travel of any kind away from one's city or town required a *t'onghaengjŭng* (travel permit).[81] Permission to travel was difficult to obtain for city dwellers. It was even more difficult for farmers. Fearing an exodus of farmers to cities and towns the state made it extremely difficult for rural people to travel anywhere. Since the collective farm had its own schools, store – or what might better be described as a distribution center – and medical clinic, there was little reason for a resident to leave, making them virtual prisoners on their collectives. Most restricted of all was any travel to Pyongyang.

All of these elaborate surveillance systems were supervised by the special security police. Originally they operated within the Ministry of the Interior which also included the regular police. In 1973 the State Political Security Department (*kukka chŏngch'i powibu*) became an independent branch of the government headed by Kim Pyŏng-ha, a distant relative of Kim Il Sung. In 1982 Kim Pyŏng-ha, along with many top security officials, was removed and perhaps imprisoned. The organization was then renamed the State Security Department (*kukka powibu*) and brought directly under Kim Jong Il's control. In 1993 it was again renamed, this time as the State Safety and Security Department (*anjŏn powibu*).[82] The security police, assisted by a network of informants including the *inminjangs*, watched over citizens in much the same fashion of all police states. A separate Military Security Command operated as a secret police system within the Korean People's Army.

An essential part of this system of control were the prison camps, including the political prison system often called the "Gulag" by outsiders, after the system of prison camps in Stalinist Russia. North Korea soon developed its own complex system, eventually consisting of four levels of prisons. For minor crimes involving a few weeks' or months' detention there were labor training centers (*nodong tallyŏndae*); for more serious offenses but still under two years there were labor education centers (*nodong kyoyangso*). For serious offenses of more than two years there were labor correction centers (*nodong kyohwaso*). Those charged with political offenses were sent to the *kwalliso*. The *kwalliso* can be translated as "place of custody" or "management or administrative center." Some were divided into the "revolutionization zones" (*hyŏngmyŏnghwa kuyŏk*) and the "total control zones" (*wanjŏn t'ongje kuyŏk*). The former were for prisoners with some chance of rehabilitation. They lived and worked under harsh conditions with a high death toll and spent their "free time" memorizing the works of Kim Il Sung. Those who survived and had showed "correct thought" could be released although they would have the stigma of being former political prisoners. The total control zones were death camps where conditions were the harshest and there was no attempt at rehabilitation and no hope of release. As in the Soviet Gulag, prisoners were often put to work in mines under extreme conditions; many mined coal. The number of political prisoners grew with the purges of the late 1950s but the number is not clear. Estimates are that by 1980 about 150,000 to 200,000 people were held in the camps, a number that may have remained the same over the next 30 years.[83]

Political prisons were gradually consolidated into a few enormous camps. In the 1980s there were about a dozen political prison camps but from 1989 that number was gradually reduced so that in the 2000s there were only six. The two largest were camp number 15 in Yodŏk and camp number 22 in Hoeryŏng; each held 40,000–50,000 inmates. Most of the camps were located in remote narrow mountain valleys where the steep mountain sides acted as a natural barrier. Rather than fitting a conventional image of a prison, they were more like a string of villages. Perhaps the most unusual feature of North Korean prisons was the *yŏn'goje* connection system by which whole families could be incarcerated together, from grandparents to children. Thus, prisoners often lived in huts with their families, children and even their parents. This meant that the DPRK exercised a collective responsibility system similar to that in premodern Korea but even harsher and more inclusive. Blood relations were most important. Sometimes a spouse of a political prisoner would be spared, forced to divorce his or her partner and to cease any contact. The large prison system was just part of the huge costs assumed by the state to maintain control over its citizens.

Paradise on Earth

One can charitably point to the improvements in living standards of what had been an even poorer population prior to the revolution. Yet, by the 1980s, North Korea was arguably the most oppressive society on earth.

North Koreans were taught that under Kim Il Sung's guidance they were marching "on the road to paradise." They had already achieved the essential material basics for happiness. "Throughout the nation's history," the official line went, "our ancestors thought a paradise to be a society where people enjoy three things: being able to eat white rice, live under a clay-roof, and educate their children. These three 'privileges' were the life-long aspiration for our ancestors. Now we have achieved all three under the wise leadership of the Great leader."[84] Children were taught to sing "we have nothing to envy in the world."

> We Have Nothing to Envy in the World
> Skies are blue and my heart is happy.
> Play the Accordion.
> Wonderful is my fatherland
> Where the people live harmoniously
> Our father is Marshal Kim Il Sung,
> Our abode is the bosom of the party,
> We are brothers and sisters, We have nothing to envy in the world.

And they sang the "The Song of Paradise."

> Let us all sing of our socialist nation
> Of the Paradise on earth free from oppression

The songs ends with:

> We are free from exploitation, even from any tax or levy
> Free from worries about food or clothing entirely,
> Oh, how blessed we are all in the grateful embrace
> That treasure man more than anything else.
> Oh, ours is a socialist nation best in the world.
> The great leader has built it."[85]

The North Korean press frequently reported on the admiration for their country expressed by foreign visitors. One supposedly typical remark was: "If there is a Paradise on Earth it is Juche Korea."[86] How much of this was accepted by non-elite citizens is difficult to assess but judging by accounts of refugees there was a deeply instilled respect, even love, for Kim Il Sung. And up to the early 1980s life in terms of education, health and basic necessities was improving for the major ity of people. They had little reason to doubt that the country was progressing toward becoming a modern, powerful, independent state and that the eventual liberation of their oppressed, impoverished southern compatriots was inevitable.

Notes

1   Lim, 2009, pp. 38–39.
2   Chŏng Ch'ang-yŏng, *Kyŏt esŏ pon Kim Chŏng-il* [close to Kim Jong Il]. Seoul: Kimyŏngsa, 2000, pp. 99–100.
3   Lim, 2009, p. 42.
4   Sŏng, Hye-rang, pp. 312–317.
5   Lim, 2009, p. 40.
6   Lim, 2009, p. 39.
7   "What Are the Ten Principles?" *Daily NK* August 9, 2013.
8   Hwang Chang-yŏp, p. 115.
9   "What Are the Ten Principles?" *Daily NK* August 9, 2013.
10 Lim, 2009, p. 66.
11 Brian R. Myers, *North Korea's Juche Myth*. Busan: Sthele Press, 2015.
12 "Great Juche Idea is Widespread among World People," *Korea Today* 277 (September 1979): 45–52.

13 Kim Sŏng-bo, *Pukhan ŭi yŏksa 2: Chuch'e Sassang kwa yuilch'eje* [North Korean History: Juche and the Monolithic Ideological System]. Seoul: Yŏksa Pip'yŏngsa, 2011, p. 75.

14 Christopher Hale, "Multifunctional Juche: A Study of the Changing Dynamic between Juche and the State Constitution in North Korea," *Korea Journal* 42, no. 3 (September 2002): 283–308.

15 Lim, 2009, p. 63.

16 Lankov, 2007, p. 31.

17 Lankov, 2007, p. 7.

18 See Brian R. Myers, *The Cleanest Race: How North Koreans See Themselves-And Why It Matters*. Brooklyn, NY: Melville House, 2010. for interesting illustrations.

19 Heonik Kwon and Byung-ho Chung, p. 18.

20 Cho Ŭn-hŭi, "Pukhan ŭi tapsa haenggun ŭl t'onghae pon hyŏnghae pon hyŏngmyŏng chŏnt'ong ŭirye mandŭlgi [North Korea's Making the Ritual of the Revolutionary Tradition Through Visits to Revolutionary Sites]," *Hyŏndae Pukhan yŏn'gu* [Modern North Korea Studies], 10, no. 2 (2007): 100–147; Jae-Cheon Lim, *Leader Symbols and Personality Cult in North Korea*. London: Routledge, 2015, p. 21.

21 Chŏng, p. 99.

22 Lim, 2009, p. 50.

23 Chŏng, p. 116.

24 Lim, 2009, pp. 11–12.

25 Kim Hakjoon, 2015, p. 67.

26 Lim, 2009, pp. 36–37.

27 David-West, Alzo, "Nationalist Allegory in North Korea: The Revolutionary Opera 'Sea of Blood,'" *North Korean Review* 2, no. 2 (2006): 75–87.

28 Kim Hakjoon, 2015, p. 74.

29 Lim, 2009, p. 54.

30 Kim Hakjoon, 2015, pp. 89–81; Lim, 2009, p. 68.

31 Takashi Sakai, "the Power Base of Kim Jong Il: Focusing on Its Formation Process," in Han S. Park, editor. *North Korea Ideology, Politics, Economics*. Englewood Cliffs, NJ: Prentice Hall, 1996, pp. 105–122.

32 "Komdok-A Great Leap Ten years," *Korea Today* 346 (July 1985): 29.

33 Daniel Tudor & James Pearson. *North Korea Confidential: Private Markets, Fashion Trends, Prison Camps, Dissenters and Defectors*. Tokyo: Tuttle, 2015, p. 93.

34 Lim, 2009, p. 70.

35 Morgan E. Clippinger, "Kim Jong IL in the North Korean Mass Media: A Study of Semi-Esoteric Communication," *Asian Survey* 21, no. 3 (March 1981): 289–309.

36 Kim Hakjoon, 2015, p. 86.

37 Chŏng, pp. 203–204; Lim, 2009, pp. 82–83.

38 Lim, 2009, pp. 83–84.

39 "Homage to Kim Jong Il," *Korea Today* 304 (January 1982): 36.

40 Lim, 2009, p. 84.

41 Suh, p. 285.

42 Lankov, 2007, p. 38.

43 Chŏng, p. 162.

44 Lim, 2009, p. 71.

45 Kim Hakjoon, "The Hereditary Succession from Kim Jong-il to Kim Jong-un: Its Background, Present Situation, and Future," in Sang-hun Choe, Gi-Wook Shin, and David Straub (eds), *Troubled Transition: North Korea's Politics, Economy, and External Relations*. Stanford, CA: Walter H. Shorenstein Asia-Pacific Research Center, 2013: 229–259.

46 Kim Hakjoon, 2015, pp. 67–68.

47 Sŏng,Hye-rang, *Tŭngnamu chip*, p. 323; Kim Hakjoon, 2015, p. 78.

48 Chŏng, pp. 111–112.

49 Lim, 2009, p. 106.

50 Kim Hakjoon, 2015, pp. 69–70; Lim, 2009, p. 89.

51 Robert Collins, *Marked for Life: Songbun, North Korea's Social Classification System*. Washington, DC: Committee for North Korean Human Rights. http://www.hrnk.org/uploads/pdfs/HRNK_Songbun_Web.pdf. Accessed April 24, 2015; Andrei Lankov, *North of the DMZ: essays on Daily Life in North Korea*. Jefferson, NC: McFarland & Company, 2007, pp. 68–69.

52 Collins, *Marked for Life*. http://www.hrnk.org/uploads/pdfs/HRNK_Songbun_Web.pdf. Accessed April 24, 2015, pp. 25–26.

53 Jin Woong Kang, "The Patriarchal State and Women's Status in Socialist North Korea," *Graduate Journal of Asia-Pacific Studies* 6, no. 2 (2008): 55–70.

54 *Korea Today* 175 (February 1971): 21.

55 *Korea Today* 175 (February 1971): 29.

56 Kang, 2008, p. 66.

57 Park Kyung Ae, "Women and Revolution in North Korea," *Pacific Affairs* 65, no.4 (Winter 1992–93): 527–545.

58 Kyung Ae Park, "Ideology and Women in North Korea," in Han S. Park, editor. *North Korea Ideology, Politics, Economics*. Englewood Cliffs, NJ: Prentice Hall, 1996, pp. 71–85.

59 Lankov, 2007, p. 116.
60 Lankov, 2007, p. 131.
61 Jin Woong.Kang, "The 'Domestic Revolution' Policy and Traditional Confucianism in North Korean State Formation: A Socio-cultural Perspective," *Harvard Asia Quarterly* 9, no. 4 (Fall 2005): 34–45.
62 Mun Woong Lee, *Rural North Korea under Communism: A Study of Sociological Change.* Houston, TX: Rice University Press, 1976, pp. 71–72.
63 MunWoong Lee, p. 81.
64 Kang, 2005, pp. 34–45.
65 Kang, "The Domestic Revolution."
66 Ilpyong Kim, p. 114.
67 Lankov, 2007, p. 133.
68 Tatiana Gabroussenko, "North Korean 'Rural Fiction' from the Late 1990s to the Mid-2000s: Permanence and Change," *Korean Studies* 33 (2009): 69–100.
69 Lankov, 2007, pp. 41–43.
70 Conversation with North Korean refugee, Seoul, May, 2013.
71 The large and growing body of literature by North Korean refugees is a good source of what everyday life was like. See the Bibliography for some suggestions.
72 Lankov, 2007, p. 215. Much of this and the following several paragraphs are taken from Lankov's *North of the DMZ* which is based in part on his experience living there as a foreign student.
73 Yim Sang-chŏl. *Pukhan nongŏp [North Korean Agriculture].* Seoul: Tosŏ Ch'ulp'an Sŏil, 2000, p. 28.
74 Lankov, 2007, p. 47.
75 Lankov, 2007, p. 35.
76 Lankov, 2007, pp. 207–208.
77 This is confirmed by the author's experience meeting North Korean academics in the 1990s.
78 MunWoong Lee, p. 54.
79 Lankov, 2013, p. 39.
80 Lankov, 2007, pp. 173–174; Hassig, Ralph and Kongdan Oh, *The Hidden People of North Korea: Everyday Life in the Hermit Kingdom.* Latham, MD: Rowman& Littlefield, 2009, p. 128.
81 Lankov, 2007, p. 181.
82 Lim, 2009, p. 73; Lankov, 2007, pp. 170–71.
83 There is a large literature on the North Korean "Gulag." One example is David Hawk, *The Hidden Gulag: The Lives and Voices of "Those Who are Sent to the Mountains,"* Second Edition. Washington, DC: Committee for Human Rights in North Korea, 2012.

84 Han S. Park, *North Korea: The Politics of Unconventional Wisdom*. Boulder, CO: Lynne Rienner, 2002, p. 43.

85 C.I. Eugene Kim, "Introduction: A Long Journey," in Kim, C.I. Eugene, and B.C. Koh, editors *Journey to North Korea: Personal Perceptions*. Berkeley, CA: University of California Press, 1983, pp. 1–23.

86 *Korea Today*, 292 (January 1981): 43.

5

From Stagnation to Crisis, 1980–1994

When the Korean Workers' Party (KWP) held its Sixth Party Congress from October 10 to October 14, 1980, North Korea was at a turning point. The achievements of the North Korean revolution were largely behind it. Economic growth was coming to a halt and any chance of unifying the country under its leadership had passed. It was falling behind its southern rival in terms of industrial output and standard of living. While South Korea was embarking on a path to economic prosperity, democratization and international respectability the DPRK was about to enter a period of economic decline and isolation. In a decade it would face a series of crises that would call its very survival into question. None of this was obvious at the time, however, least of all to the country's leadership.

The Sixth Party Congress: The View in 1980

Although the KWP congresses were supposed to meet every five years it had been a decade since the previous one, and the Sixth Party Congress would be the last for 36 years. Its main but unstated purpose was to confirm Kim Jong Il as Kim Il Sung's successor. Other than this development there was little change in the leadership. Eight of the eleven full members of the Politburo elected at the 1970 Congress were still full members. This was in contrast to the previous congress when three-quarters of the top positions were held by new people. The period of major purges was over and the composition of the political elite had become stable. Kim Il Sung was a robust 68-year-old surrounded by his old partisan comrades. Eight of the ten most senior ranking members were ex-guerillas.[1] In addition, there was Kim Jong Il who was co-opted into the ex-guerillas. Kim Jong Il at only 38 was by far the youngest member of the Politburo; the average age of the top leadership being in the early sixties. It was an aging leadership of narrow background, limited education and close ties to Kim Il Sung. It was not a group likely to carry out innovations, nor by experience and aptitude well prepared to deal with the challenges of the rapidly changing international environment of the 1980s.

Besides Kim Jong Il, other second-generation leaders were emerging from the families of the Manchurian guerillas. They included the 47-year-old O Kuk-yŏl also the son of a partisan and the second youngest member of the Politburo. Many of the younger members of the upper echelons of the KWP were graduates of the Mangyŏngdae School for Children of the Revolution where top officials sent their sons and daughters.[2] North Korea was emerging as a state ruled by a tiny hereditary elite largely consisting of Kim Il Sung and his family, his partisan comrades and those related to them by blood or marriage. The party, the state bureaucracy and the military were dominated by this small number of families and branch families. Each would develop their own patronage networks. Eventually elite families would be careful to place members in all the major centers of power and these powerful families formed alliances based on marriage.

The highlight of the congress was Kim Il Sung's lengthy address to the delegates which acted as a way of summing up the achievement and goals of the revolution. Kim spoke of "a brilliant victory in the building of socialism."[3] He was not without justification in examining the country's economic achievements with pride. Into the 1970s North Korea maintained an impressive level of economic development. Two and a half decades after the Korean War North Korea had become an industrialized nation. No more than a third of the population was rural; in Asia only Japan was as urbanized. Later, many North Koreans would look back on this time as one of promise and prosperity, at least compared to later periods. Refugees who later fled the country often see these as the good years. Hwang Chang-yŏp, the party ideologist who defected to South

Korea in 1987, recalls the years before 1980 as a time of comfort and high morale among party workers.[4] The system overall was working. People were receiving their food rations as well as other basic necessities; factories were turning out their products; education was still expanding; and immunization programs were improving health.

North Korea's revolution did not look like a failure to outsiders either. Pyongyang permitted a small number of journalists from non-communist countries to visit in the 1970s, taking them on carefully managed tours and sometimes granting them an interview with Kim Il Sung. They were often impressed with what they saw. Allan Bouc from the French newspaper *Le Monde* on a visit in 1971 commented favorably on the level of industrialization, noting that all the vehicles he saw from bicycles to trucks were locally manufactured. He described the countryside as characterized by "beautiful, well- irrigated rice paddies, worked on by tractor." The cities and towns were neat with central squares that had pretty flower beds. He saw "no idlers, street peddlers or useless occupations."[5] Another foreign journalist on a 20-day tour that year commented, "Three things impress the visitor: The well-cared-for children, the adoration of Premier Kim Il Sung, and massive construction."[6] Harrison Salisbury from the *New York Times*, the first prominent American journalist to enter North Korea since the Korean War, reported on his 1972 visit that the country had made a "tremendous technical and industrial achievement." Visiting the Hamhŭng–Hŭngnam area on the east coast, he saw "endless vistas of industrial smokestacks."[7] Another visitor that year, John H. Lee, observed "a well-organized, highly industrialized socialist economy, largely self-sufficient with a disciplined and productive labor force." He noted, "although consumer goods are sparse and factory equipment is sometimes outmoded, the overall industrial plant compare favorably to anything in Asia outside Japan." Unlike most developing countries, he commented, modernization seemed evenly developed without the usual disparity between the cities and the countryside.[8] Several years later, another Western journalist contrasted the orderly industrial society of North Korea with South Korea, noting the lack of slums, prostitution and children selling gum that could be seen in Seoul.[9]

After the early 1970s, access to the country was more difficult but the DPRK permitted several Western journalists to cover an international table tennis tournament in 1979. One, American journalist Bradley Martin, on his visit to North Korea noted, "the overriding impression was of Northern success, up to a point – not failure." Even though he was "deeply troubled" by the intense ideological indoctrination that he found carried out throughout society he was impressed by the level of industrialization. He observed that the "people appeared adequately housed and clothed," and that "there was austerity apparently rather evenly shared, but I saw no sign of destitution. All this seemed to set North Korea apart from other developing nations."[10] Another academic visitor to North Korea at the time noted that it was producing everything from metal lathes to large refrigerator ships, excavators, bulldozers, electric transformers and electric locomotives: "all signs that notable gains have indeed been made on the economic construction front."[11]

In contrast to these favorable reports in the 1970s, by the early 1990s most foreign observers saw North Korea as an anachronistic, impoverished society – a failed revolution on the verge of becoming a failed state.

Economic Stagnation

In the 1980s North Korea's economic expansion sputtered to a halt. It is difficult to calculate just when North Korea's economy slowed down and at what rate since there are so few reliable statistics for scholars to work with. Most outside analysts believe the economic slowdown began in the early 1970s and further slowed after 1980, with the economy ceasing to grow at all by the end of that decade. One estimate by South Korean economists calculates GDP growth rate at 4.4 percent for 1954–1989 and per capita growth at 1.9% which made it about the same as the Soviet economy for 1928–1985. Most estimates are much higher: at least 7 to 8 percent from the 1950s to 1970, lower in the 1970s and then much lower after 1980. South Korea's Ministry of Unification estimates that it slowed to GDP growth rates of 3.6 percent from 1980 to 1985 and only 1.4 percent from 1985 to 1990.[12]

Even before 1980 the North Korean economy was experiencing serious problems. The Seven-Year Plan for 1961–1967 was extended by three years, making it in effect a ten-year plan. As we have seen, it was a victim of the equal emphasis policy that diverted resources from development, and it suffered from the temporary reduction in Soviet aid in the 1960s as well as from the overly ambitious goals. Nonetheless, the rate of real growth – certainly lower than that reported – was still high. Pyongyang then launched a new Six-Year Plan for 1971–1976. To spur production the state launched endless speed battles and other campaigns. In 1971 these were aimed at exceeding targets before Kim Il Sung's 60th birthday on April 15, 1972. It then conducted new campaigns in 1973 and 1974, including the Three Revolutions Team Movement. In 1974 public exhortations and campaigns were aimed at the "glorious task" of fulfilling the Six-Year Plan ahead of schedule, specifically by the 30th anniversary of the founding of the party in October 1975. This was an effort to duplicate the achievement of the first five-year plan in the late 1950s when by mobilizing the population the country was able to meet economic targets one and a half years early. On the eve of the October 10 anniversary, Kim Il Sung proclaimed that this had been achieved. The Six-Year Plan had been completed 16 months ahead of schedule with industrial production having grown in the past five years at an annual rate of 18 percent, well over the 14 percent target.[13] Yet the attempt to repeat the achievements of the 1957–1961 five-year plan seemed unconvincing. At the end of 1975 the Three Revolutions Red Flag Movement was launched to spur production. And in early 1976 North Koreans were being urged to fulfill targets of the plan, despite the previous claim that they had already been filled. Then, 1977 was declared a "year of readjustment" (*wanch'ung ŭi hae*) whose major task was to ease "temporary strains" on the economy.[14] A second Seven-Year Plan was launched for 1978–1984, announced as "deepening and strengthening [the country's] socialist foundation by the juche-ization, modernization, scientific transformation (*kwahak-hwa*) of the people's economy."[15] Despite public exhortations to workers to double their efforts and complete the plan with "the speed of the 1980s" there were two years of adjustment in 1985 and 1986. This effectively made it a nine-year plan; and even then the announcement of its completion was buried in routine reports, interpreted by some foreign observers as a tacit admission of failure.[16]

Military production, referred to as the "second economy," was the main growth area, with the production of artillery, tanks, military vehicles and small arms expanding. In the 1980s military production made some strides toward producing more sophisticated weaponry. Overall, although the "second economy" may have outperformed the regular industrial sector its output was not sufficient to free North Korea from reliance on military aid from its socialist allies, but it did enable the DPRK to supply much of the arms for its huge military apparatus.

Economic Problems

North Korea's economy faced a number of problems. Not least was that much of the country's resources went toward supporting its vast military forces. In addition to this much of its industry was labor-intensive. Kim Il Sung relied on mass mobilization, such as *ch'ŏllima* campaigns in which workers competed for medals and fought speed battles to increase output, rather than improvements in productivity. Mass mobilization campaigns were carried out by other communist countries but none did so on the scale of the DPRK. People worked long hours, beyond the official eight-hour day, five-day official work week. North Korea made full use of all its potential labor, including employing women in light industry, sending soldiers to help with industrial production or construction projects, suspending classes to utilize student labor, and making use of the large prison population in industrial work. But the limits of mass mobilization had been reached.

Economic development was running into bottlenecks. The first was owing to out-of-date technology. North Korea relied on pre-1945 Japanese plans and Soviet technology from the 1940s and 1950s. Most of the country's power plants and steel mills were from the colonial period. North Korea's leadership appeared to have understood the need to modernize its industrial plants. Kim Il Sung was most likely also concerned about the new industries that South Korea was rapidly constructing under Park Chung Hee. In 1972 Kim began a buying spree of Western plants and machinery. But the equipment was too sophisticated, the country lacked parts and money to buy them, and the electricity supply was often unreliable, rendering much of these purchases of limited use. Furthermore, this modern equipment suffered the general problem that most North Korean industrial plant had of being poorly managed and maintained.[17]

Energy was another bottleneck. North Korea had considerable hydroelectric power inherited from the colonial period. For a number of reasons, including the fact that they often relied on rivers that they shared with China and Russia and thus there were political problems, the emphasis instead was on coal. However, North Korean coal mining techniques were primitive and productivity was poor. The fact that coal miners were often prisoners provided less of an incentive to improve the simple yet dangerous and inefficient methods of production. Petroleum was imported from China and the Soviet Union but as North Korea had limited foreign reserves to pay for this, it relied on below-market "friendship" prices. This helped, but the heavy industries were energy-intensive and petroleum was also needed for the country's intensive use of fertilizer.

Chronic food shortages plagued the economy. At no time after 1945 was North Korea able to accomplish more than barely meeting the population's minimum nutritional requirements. As was the case in many communist countries priority had always been given to industry but, nonetheless, the regime made heavy investments in agriculture. At first the DPRK relied on the economies of scale that resulted from consolidating farms into large cooperatives and some mechanization. This was clearly insufficient. In the 1960s Kim launched his "four modernizations" in agriculture, which consisted of mechanization, electrification, irrigation and chemicalization (chemical fertilizer and pesticides). Still even with this heavy and costly investment, agriculture production lagged behind basic needs.

Kim Il Sung appeared to have had no desire to change. His address to the delegates at the 1980 party congress praised the traditional methods of economic development and organization: the Ch'ŏllima movement, the Ch'ŏngsanri method and the Taean work systems. Each he hailed for its great successes. He also singled out the Three Revolutions Team Movement for strengthening the ideological foundations for production. In fact, Kim attacked self-serving economic officials, which may have been a veiled criticism of those who were more pragmatically inclined in economic affairs.[18]

It must have been particularly alarming to the regime that this economic slowdown occurred while the South Korean economy was booming. In the 1980s the ROK broke into new export markets such as steel, automobiles and electronics. Propelled by successful exports its growth rates reached an average of 12 percent a year in 1986 through 1988 when they were the highest in the world. In the DPRK, by contrast, exports appeared to have declined in the early 1980s. For an industrialized state it exported few manufactured goods. Most of its manufactured goods were too low in quality to be marketable. Even the Soviet bloc nations found them so shoddy that they did not want to import them. As a result, North Korea's exports to its socialist allies were mainly raw materials – minerals such as copper, lead and zinc. North Korea was rich in mineral resources. The DPRK contains over 80 percent of the peninsula's mineral wealth, including iron, coal, gold, copper, silver, molybdenum, manganese, magnesite, nickel and tungsten. But poor mining practices and the country's isolation from international markets hampered their exploitation.[19] Because of modest exports earnings, North Korea suffered from a shortage of foreign exchange. This caused problems for Pyongyang when it entered global financial markets in the early 1970s to purchase new industrial plants and was unable to service its debt. This problem was compounded by some bad luck. Its tepid venture into the capitalist world to buy industrial equipment coincided with the oil shock of 1973, which depressed the price of its mineral exports. The DPRK rescheduled its debts with Western Europe in 1980 but quickly fell behind the repayment schedule and had to reschedule its debts with Japan in 1982. Again in 1984 it rescheduled its foreign debt only to cease making payments almost immediately afterward.[20]

Remittances from Koreans living in Japan provided some hard currency. Since its formation in the 1950s the Chosoren (Korean: *Choch'ongnyŏn*), a pro-Pyongyang organization among the Koreans in Japan, had provided an important source of revenue. There were approximately 600,000–700,000 Koreans residents in Japan, many of them brought over during World War II to work in factories and mines. As a result of an agreement worked out between Tokyo and Pyongyang 80,000 Korean residents in Japan including some Japanese spouses migrated to North Korea mainly between 1959 and 1967. After 1967 the agreement ended and migration slowed to a trickle.[21] Family members back in Japan sent money to support their relatives in North Korea. There are widely differing estimates of the size of these remittances. Whatever the amount, they were an important source of foreign exchange but far short of what the country needed.

In the 1970s the DPRK began to engage in counterfeiting and drug smuggling through their foreign embassies under the cover of diplomatic immunity to acquire badly needed foreign currency. In the mid-1980s the state inaugurated a number of new efforts to earn foreign exchange. It instructed all organizations from factories to handicraft shops to find ways to produce exportable products. Rural folks were ordered to pick medicinal herbal plants, and children to raise rabbits to sell their skins. The KWP, various branches of the military and the government maintained separate trading companies to promote trade.[22] Officials pressured the Japanese-Korean returnees to write to their relatives in Japan to send more money. In the late 1970s the regime created a special bureau known as "Room 39" (sometimes called "Office 39"), to help earn foreign exchange. This became notorious for carrying out illegal activities such as drug manufacture and smuggling. Even before the creation of this office, North Korean diplomats were expelled from several countries around the world for heroin smuggling. All these efforts produced only modest results while damaging the country's international reputation.

North Korea's difficulties were only compounded by the misallocation of manpower and other resources in ill-conceived gigantic projects. In 1981 the state launched the Four Projects for Nature Remaking. The most ambitious one was the West Sea Lock Gate. This effort to deal with the severe shortage of arable land in many ways typified the regime's approach to economic problems – achieving solutions through huge, showy and labor-intensive undertakings. The West Sea Lock Gate was an 8-kilometer sea wall with three lock gates and three dams at the estuary of the Taedong River. It was intended to make possible the reclamation of a considerable amount of land, including 490,000 fertile acres at the mouth of the country's most important river. Completed within five years it was one of the largest projects of its kind in the world, and became an object of great pride – one of the standard sights foreign visitors were taken to see. It created only a fraction of the new land expected which turned out to be too salty to farm, rendering the whole project fairly useless. Furthermore, it interfered with the drainage of the river causing industrial, farm and urban waste to back-up. A similar fate fell to the other projects. One of these was a massive undertaking to build power plants along tributaries of the Taedong River. Streams were diverted to the river so that it could generate enough electricity. This required a 130-foot (40-meter) tunnel underneath a mountain. But the whole project proved costly and impractical and was never completed.[23]

Enormous amounts of resources were squandered on prestige-based projects of little economic value but which enhanced the image of the leadership. In 1983, for example, a costly Loyalty Festival was announced that commenced on Kim Jong Il's birthday on February 16 and culminated with his father's birthday on April 15. In the late 1980s vast construction works were carried out in preparation for the 13th World Festival of Youth and Students held in Pyongyang in 1989. These included a virtually unused Pyongyang–Kaesŏng Express Highway. Perhaps nothing better symbolized these wasteful prestige projects as well as the regime's love of the gigantic than the awsthetically tasteless Ryugyŏng Hotel. The project was reportedly conceived of in 1986 as a response to the completion of the Westin Stamford Hotel in Singapore, a 226-meter (741-foot), 71-story, phallus-shaped structure built by the South Korean Ssangyong construction company that year. Not to be outdone the Ryugyŏng Hotel was to be a 330-meter (1085-foot) monster with 105 stories and over 3,000 rooms with multiple revolving restaurants. It would be the tallest hotel ever built and one of the world's tallest buildings. Construction started in 1987 with completion set for the opening of the 13th World Festival of Youth in the summer of 1989. One estimate put the construction cost at 2 percent of the nation's entire GDP. The building's strange, elongated pyramid-shaped structure ran into serious structural flaws, including elevators that would not work, and its opening was long-delayed. It reached its full height in 1992 when further work was halted. Instead of becoming the symbol of success, it became an embarrassing emblem of the country's economic failures: an unavoidable and, to many, strikingly ugly presence looming over the city's skyline.[24]

Kim Il Sung's response to the economic problems was to mobilize more labor. He sent students to labor projects or to work on farms, and he utilized soldiers to work on construction and help with harvesting. Fridays became Friday Labor Day in which government workers were to work on farms and construction sites.[25] Old methods of increasing labor inputs were renewed. But these efforts only made life harder without stemming the country's economic slowdown.

False Steps Toward Reform

Faced with a slowing economy, many observers expected that the DPRK would follow the reforms being carried out in China under Deng Xiaoping. At this time Beijing introduced the "Responsibility System," which in effect meant dismantling the collective farms and returning to family farming. It opened Special Economic Zones where foreign investors were welcomed and private businesses permitted. Examples of North Korea emulating developments in the People's Republic of China were numerous: it had borrowed from the Great Leap Forward, adopted self-criticism sessions, and inaugurated the Red Guard-like Three Revolutions Teams. When Beijing and the USA began rapprochement in 1971, Pyongyang followed suit with its own moves toward cooperation with Seoul. The regime gave some public praise for the Four Modernizations policy of economic reform launched by Deng. The KWP periodical *Kŭlloja*, for example, reported favorably on the increases in agricultural and industrial production in China.[26] Interest in reform was suggested by a flurry of high-level visits. Premier Zhao Ziyang visited Pyongyang in December 1981 and the following April both Hu Yaobang and Deng Xiaoping made unpublicized visits. Kim Il Sung visited China later in 1982, his first visit in many years. Kim Jong Il made his first official visit in June 1983. He traveled to Shanghai and was introduced to signature sites of their economic reforms. The following year a number of North Korean officials including the foreign minister and then Premier Kang Sŏng-san also made tours of the Special Economic Zones.[27] Shortly after these visits, in September 1984, the Supreme People's Assembly enacted a Joint Venture Law.

Little came of Pyongyang's tepid move toward opening up the country to foreign investment. North Korea did not have the infrastructure or experience of dealing with foreign investors and made only half-hearted attempts to encourage then. Between 1984 and 1989 the DPRK signed one hundred contracts for investments. These, however, were far from the type of large-scale international investments that characterized the Special Economic Zones in China. Seventy percent were with Korean residents in Japan, mainly from the pro-DPRK organization there. There were twenty from other socialist countries and only ten from the West. Only half the contracts were ever implemented and they were mostly very small scale.[28] Even this small trickle of investments petered out after 1987 and pro-communist Koreans living in Japan found doing business in the North Korea difficult. As the Chosoren stated, "the provincialism and inefficiency in the Democratic People's Republic of Korea is a real problem."[29] One reason for the failure to develop a major foreign investment zone may have been geographic. When China opened up Special Economic Zones it mostly located them on the southern coast far from the capital and from most Chinese population centers, making them easier to quarantine and control foreign influences. This was more difficult for North Korea to do. Kim Jong Il later recalled telling the Chinese Communist Party general secretary Hu Yaobang that North Korea because of its small size could not so easily open areas to foreign investment.[30]

At the same time as the Joint Venture Law, the DPRK carried out another act that suggested, at first, a move away from the centralized, heavy-industry orientation of the economy. On August 3, 1984 Kim Jong Il inaugurated the August Third People's Consumer Goods Production Movement, an effort to increase basic light industries – clothes, soap, furniture and household goods – through production at the local level. The purpose was not only to increase light industry but also to decentralize industry so that each region produced the basic consumer goods needed. It also shifted much of the responsibility for light industry to the local officials. To be self-reliant, factories were encouraged to use local materials and to recycle scrap. "Side-job work teams" and "household work teams" utilized part-time rural workers and housewives.[31] Yet this was really the old policy of making the local areas more self-sufficient to enable the state to concentrate resources on heavy-military production. It was not even a modest step toward any real market-based reform. Another measure taken in 1984 was the established of the independent accounting system (*Tongnip ch'aesanje*), which gave factory managers more independence in decision making on labor, equipment, materials and funds but proved to be a minor and ineffective modification in the economic system.

Rather than embracing China's path in carrying out economic reform, North Korea took advantage of an improvement in ties with the Soviet Union to avoid them. Relations between Moscow and Pyongyang had never been close. The North needed the military and economic aid the Soviets provided but since Khrushchev's reforms, Kim Il Sung had not felt comfortable with them. The Soviets, for their part, found North Korea an unpredictable ally and considered it as being closer to China. Yet, as China seemed to tilt toward the West, Moscow took a new interest in the strategic value of cultivating closer cooperation with North Korea. In the spring of 1984 Kim Il Sung paid a six-week visit to the Soviet Union. Soon after, Moscow stepped up economic aid, much of it in the form of trade on favorable terms.

This new injection of Soviet aid was extremely important in propping up the flagging economy. There were more than 5,000 Soviet technicians in North Korea, helping among other things with plans to double steel capacity at Kimch'aek. North Korea began to rely more and more on Soviet trade to prop up its economy as well as aid. Trade with the Soviet Union increased in the 1980s, almost doubling between 1980 and 1988.[32] In 1980 the Soviet Union accounted for 24 percent of the DPRK's foreign trade, a figure that rose to 37 percent in 1987.[33] Soviet economic support made it easier for Kim to ignore the basic structural problems of the economy and continue with his accustomed methods of development. This was reflected in the third Seven-Year Plan for 1987–1993 which closely followed the model of previous ones.

Yet even in these peak years of Soviet aid, in the late 1980s, the economy grew by very little. In fact, North Korea from the beginning had trouble with the third Seven-Year Plan. The influx of Soviet aid helped disguise the real nature of a failing economy. The industrial plants were becoming obsolescent, food shortages were becoming more severe and efforts to increase foreign trade failed. Meanwhile, consumer shortages were dealt with by encouraging the people to get by with less. Meanwhile, much of North Korea became a Potemkin village to impress outsiders and hide the country's backwardness. In one example, after foreign visitors complained of the lack of public phones and taxis in the 1980s, some public phones were installed in areas of the capital where foreigners were likely to visit, although they were found nowhere else and not used by the public.[34]

Facing the Rise of South Korea

In 1980 the DPRK leadership still believed that they would eventually reunify Korea. But South Korea's economic and political rise in the coming decade would challenge this notion. Already by 1980 South Korea had caught up and surpassed North Korea in economic output and certainly in living standards. Its 9 percent annual growth rate in the 1970s was probably much higher than the real rate in the DPRK; its education system was expanding at a greater pace; its exports earnings were many times higher; and even its military was modernizing faster. In the 1980s the gap in economic strength between the two countries would widen enormously as the ROK broke out of its international isolation and established a stable democratic political order.

Yet at the start of the decade Pyongyang could still find signs that history was on its side. Kim Il Sung never accepted the outcome of the Korean War as anything other than a temporary setback, and he never gave up the goal of reunification; nor did he waiver in his belief that his regime was the true bearer of Korean nationalism. The South, whatever its economic achievements, was occupied by foreign troops and was economically in debt to its former colonial master, Japan; furthermore, it was ruled by a military whose officer corps had served the Japanese and who were now subordinate to the American military. Student radicals, labor and social activists, and intellectuals in the South often challenged the ROK's political and social order. They often echoed the DPRK's own propaganda in questioning the legitimacy and nationalist credentials of their government. Since Kim Il Sung regarded himself as the true, legitimate leader of all the Korean people it was not hard for him to interpret the dissent in the South as signs of popular support for this claim. Meanwhile, state propaganda continued to depict South Korea as a hell on earth. Reports of famines appeared regularly, along with those of oppressed farmers and workers living under extremely harsh conditions who could only dream of the standard of living the people of the DPRK enjoyed. People suffered from hunger, farmers were swindled out of their land, and workers labored in appalling conditions and suffered horrific punishments if they complained. All this while under the brutal rule of the American imperialists and their South Korean puppets.[35]

Not all of this propaganda was completely false. South Korea's remarkable industrial transformation had come at a heavy social cost. In the late 1970s there was considerable social and political unrest from political, student and labor groups and from a burgeoning middle class uncomfortable with the restraints of Park Chung Hee's increasingly authoritarian rule. In 1979 tensions led to labor strikes, demonstrations and confrontations by a younger generation of political opposition leaders. In the midst of an internal debate on how to handle the situation Park's intelligence director, Kim Chae-gyu, shot and killed him. This led to a period of political openness called the "Seoul Spring" that ended with a crackdown under General Chun Doo Hwan who led a military group that seized power. The arrest of a leading opposition member, Kim Dae Jung, in May 1980 resulted in an armed uprising in the city of Kwangju in his home province. Hundreds were killed when Chun sent paratroopers to put down the uprising. Amidst the turmoil South Korea's GDP dropped by 6 percent in 1980, aggravated by poor harvests and a steep jump in oil prices.

All these events suggested the South Korean system might be unraveling. As with the fall of the Rhee regime in 1960, the death of Park and the political turbulence that followed opened the possibility that the situation in the South could develop in a way that allowed for greater influence of the North in its internal affairs. Perhaps it would even lead to the emergence of a South Korean government that would call for the removal of US troops. The political turmoil in South Korea from 1979 to 1980 offered some promise for the rise of revolutionary forces. Mass rallies throughout the DPRK took place in 1979 in support of striking workers in South.[36] Assuming the role as the main champion of national unification, Kim Il Sung reintroduced his call at the Sixth Party Congress for a Confederal Republic of Koryŏ which he had first proposed two decades earlier. Fishing in troubled waters, the DPRK proposed the resumption of talks and even used the official name Republic of Korea for the first time. Seoul responded by referring to the North as the Democratic People's Republic of Korea. A series of low-level talks were held from February to August 1980 to prepare the way for a meeting of prime ministers. However, the consolidation of power by the new military rulers and the crackdown on dissent removed the opportunities for the North to exploit the political divisions in the ROK and dashed immediate hopes that the system might unravel. The consolidation of power by the Chun Doo Hwan regime and the resumption of the economic boom in 1981 further dimmed those prospects. The DPRK broke off all talks in September 1980 and resumed its loudspeaker tirades along the DMZ which it had suspended in 1972.[37]

Seeking to hasten the inevitable collapse of the ROK's political and economic system and promote the latent revolutionary forces in the ROK, North Korea tried to contribute to this instability by keeping tensions along the DMZ high and creating incidences. In 1982 it carried out an assassination plot against the visiting President Chun Doo Hwan in Gabon. The most dramatic attempt to create a crisis in the South was on October 9, 1983 when it attempted to kill Chun during his visit to the Burmese capital, Rangoon. A platform where ROK and Burmese leaders were to speak was blown up, killing 17 senior ROK officials including four cabinet ministers as well as members of the Burmese government, although failing to harm Chun. This was a carefully planned operation that was probably approved at the highest levels and perhaps directed by Kim Jong Il to prove his credentials as a warrior.

China, apparently alarmed at this incident, encouraged Kim Il Sung to open up a dialogue with the USA and the South. The USA also indicated that it would talk directly with Pyongyang if the talks included the ROK. North Korea agreed to the three-way talks between the DPRK, the ROK and the USA. Little, however, came of this since North Korea insisted that the talks lead to a bilateral agreement with the Americans, excluding the ROK, a demand that was acceptable to neither Seoul nor Washington. In September 1984 the DPRK Red Cross offered assistance to the South after severe floods struck that country. Seoul accepted the offer of food, textiles, cement and medicine to the victims, taking it as an opportunity to resume talks. A discussion about a joint Olympic team, of family reunions and other issues continued into 1985. North Korea rejected an offer to open the country for trade and the South rejected a proposal for a non-aggression pact. Talks came to an end when Pyongyang objected to the Team Spirit military exercises.[38] Held every spring the joint exercise between US and ROK forces was a sore point with Pyongyang. They were useful for domestic propaganda since they highlighted the presence of American troops in the South and could support the picture that the imperialists were always plotting an invasion. They also provided an excuse whenever North Korea was negotiating with its southern counterparts for ending or delaying talks. Negotiations resumed, leading to an exchange of art performances and family union visits in the summer and fall of 1985. But this minor thaw in relations soon ended when the DPRK demanded a non-aggression pact between the two countries and the ending of joint military exercises between the ROK and US forces.

The Losing Struggle for Legitimacy

Historical trends were working against North Korea in its competition with the South for legitimacy. North Korea began suffering setbacks in a kind of international diplomatic war with the ROK. Since 1965 it had sought, with some success, to gain the support of the Non-Aligned Movement, which regularly passed pro-DPRK resolutions at summits and meetings of foreign ministers. But South Korea was launching its own diplomatic offensive to climb out of the USA's shadow. By the early 1980s the ROK was presenting itself as a model of successful development to other members of the Third World. And, it was also becoming an important trading partner for many developing nations. Meanwhile, North Korea's unsophisticated diplomacy, its sponsorship of terrorist activity, its default on its international loans, the extremism of its leadership cult, and its promotion of a hereditary succession, all cost it some respect and legitimacy among the international community. In 1981 at a Conference of Foreign Ministers in New Delhi the representatives of the Non-Aligned Movement failed to place the Korean unification issue on its agenda despite DPRK efforts. The next year, in June 1982, at a foreign ministers' meeting in Havana, the Movement did not support a DPRK-sponsored resolution which called for the withdrawal of US troops from Korea and the dissolution of the UN command.[39] The Rangoon bombing and the bombing of Korea Air Flight 858 further undermined sympathy for North Korea in international circles. The latter occurred when North Korean agents, on November 29, 1987, placed a bomb on a plane returning to Seoul from Baghdad. All 104 passengers, mostly South Koreans working in the Middle East, and the 11 crew members were killed. The two agents were traced to Bahrain: one committed suicide but the other, a female agent, confessed and her testimony suggested that the incident was again planned from the top level.

No incident more dramatically marked the changing realities of the rivalries on the peninsula than the 1988 Seoul Olympic Games. South Korea, which won the bid to host the games in 1981, saw the Olympic Games as an opportunity to demonstrate its achievements much in the way Japan had used the 1964 Tokyo games to highlight its recovery from World War II and its emergence as a dynamic, economic power. North Korea's reaction to the awarding of the games to Seoul was to protest that the ROK was unfit to host them, citing tensions on the peninsula and internal problems in that country. Its propaganda organs warned of a widespread AIDS epidemic and general instability. Its official news magazine reported: "'What's the use of going to somewhere where AIDS is so widespread, at the risk of our lives' people are saying."[40]

In 1985, adjusting to reality somewhat, the DPRK changed its position to a demand to co-host the Olympics. The International Olympic Committee considered the DPRK's proposal for a "Pyongyang–Seoul, Korea, Olympiad," and in 1986 provided a more modest proposal: an offer to hold the table tennis, archery, soccer and cycling events in the North. Pyongyang rejected this. It then tried to frighten away participants with a bombing on October 14, 1986 at Seoul's Kimpo airport and the destruction of Flight 858 in 1987. Meanwhile, it began a campaign to boycott the games. However, almost every country, including China, the

Soviet Union and its Eastern European allies, indicated their willingness to attend the games in Seoul. In fact, the games provided an opportunity for the ROK to work toward establishing relations with the People's Republic of China and the Soviet Union. As early as 1984 Beijing began to establish sporting relations with South Korea when it invited the ROK national tennis team to an international tournament it was hosting. From the mid-1980s Chinese and Soviet athletes were arriving into the ROK for athletic practice meets. There was a brief time in 1987, during a wave of anti-government demonstrations, when the games were in jeopardy but with a peaceful resolution to the political crisis in South Korea the way was prepared. One hundred sixty nations participated in the games in Seoul in September 1988 – a record number. Only Albania, Cuba, Ethiopia, Madagascar and the Seychelles answered North Korea's call for a boycott. The games, the first in 12 years in which all major countries participated, were a great success, enabling South Korea to show off its economic achievements. That same month the DPRK was celebrating its 40th anniversary. For a regime that loved to celebrate anniversaries the symbolism could not have been lost. Isolated and ignored by the world, North Korea hosted the 13th Festival of Youth and Students 1989 as a way of compensation. Some 22,000 young people from 177 countries attended. But the games were a costly burden that the state could hardly afford and whatever domestic purpose they may have served, they drew little international attention.

Meanwhile, Seoul made some efforts to improve relations with its northern rival. The new president of the ROK, Roh Tae Woo, who took office in July 1988 issued a Six-Point Declaration which defined the DPRK as part of a "single national community" not as an adversary.[41] In subsequent addresses he called upon both Koreas to work on a Korean Commonwealth. This was not a new idea and resembled the DPRK's own proposal of a Democratic Confederal Republic of Koryŏ. Pyongyang, while not embracing the idea, proposed interparliamentary talks between the two sides in 1988 but the conditions it set for those talks made them unacceptable to Seoul. North Korea did not ignore these overtures completely and in December 1988 high-level talks occurred between the South Korean prime minister and the northern premier; there were more talks in 1989 that led nowhere.[42]

North Korea and the Collapse of Soviet Communism

Even more challenging for North Korea than the rise of South Korea was the collapse of the Soviet Union, a calamity that threatened the very survival of the regime. That the two developments occurred simultaneously dramatically altered the DPRK's geopolitical position in just a few years. Even before the unraveling of the Soviet empire, Gorbachev's reforms in the late 1980s brought about a series of shocks to Pyongyang. Gorbachev, concerned with reforming his country's economy and reducing military commitments, sought to improve relations with its former adversaries. As a result of this change in policies, the Soviet Union established economic ties with South Korea. In 1988 Moscow established direct economic contacts with Seoul through the Soviet Chamber of Commerce and Industry. In September 1988 Hungary and South Korea exchanged ambassadors and began negotiations toward full diplomatic recognition. The Soviet Union and the ROK exchanged trade missions in 1989 and in September 1990 President Roh and the Soviet leader Mikhail Gorbachev met and agreed to establish full diplomatic relations. In April 1991 Gorbachev went on an official visit to South Korea. The Soviet Union's trade with the ROK increased after 1988, while its trade with the DPRK sharply declined.

North Korea's strategic importance, of such concern to Moscow a few years earlier, now appeared less important than establishing economic ties with South Korea. Meanwhile, 1989 saw the collapse of most of the communist regimes in Eastern Europe, the extraordinary pace of change in the Soviet Union and talk about the "collapse of Communism." In 1989 the Soviet Union ended major weapons shipments to and joint military exercises with the DPRK. In September 1990 Foreign Minister Shevardnadze officially informed the DPRK that Moscow was suspending further large-scale investments.[43] The Soviets began insisting on payment for oil and imports in hard currency. This was an enormous economic blow since the Soviet Union accounted for half of the DPRK's foreign trade, much of its oil and most of its new technology inputs. North Korea's faltering economy had been briefly buoyed by the increase in Soviet aid; but that aid was drastically reduced until it came to an end altogether. Then, in December 1991, the Soviet Union itself was dissolved. The impact of this can hardly be exaggerated. For all its trumpeting of "self-reliance" North Korea remained dependent upon Soviet economic and military support. When relations between Moscow and Pyongyang soured after 1962, the DPRK economy was hard hit. Kim Il Sung quickly improved relations after 1965, and while never really comfortable with the Soviets after that he was careful not to rupture relations and actively sought to keep the aid flowing. Now it stopped.

North Korean relations with China were culturally, historically and ideologically closer. But Beijing too was moving toward better relations with South Korea, proceeding at a slower more deliberate pace. In fact, the decision by the Chinese government to send in troops to crush protesters in Tiananmen Square in June 1989 had the effect of assuring the North Koreans that the communist regime in China was not about to collapse nor were they about to experiment with democracy. Furthermore, Beijing still found North Korea a useful communist ally. As China continued to seek improved trade and other ties with South Korea its officials assured the North Koreans of their continued support. Trade between the two countries continued. However, North Korea's geopolitical position remained greatly weakened. The pragmatic Chinese saw the advantage of increasing trade with and seeking investment from booming South Korea and continued to improve relations. Meanwhile, the Chinese were either unable or unwilling to make up for the loss of Soviet trade and aid.

Improved relations with Japan offered some hope for North Korea to strengthen its deteriorating strategic and economic position. A peace treaty with Tokyo could pave the way for reparation payments as well as trade and economic assistance. But establishing diplomatic relations with Japan was not easy. A Japanese parliamentary mission visited the DPRK in 1990. Bogged down over issues of reparations, Japan's worry over North Korea's nuclear program and its failure to meet demands for the release of captive Japanese fishing crew members, little progress was made in improving relations between the two countries.[44] Thus, the opportunity of partially offsetting its strategic and economic setbacks by improving relations with Japan was lost to Pyongyang.

Holding Fast to the True Path

Facing the decline in Soviet aid and pressure from China to open itself up to Western trade and investment, in 1991 North Korea created the Free Trade and Economic Zone in the Rajin-Sŏnbong (Rasŏn) area. The UN Development Program provided some seed money. During 1992–1993 the DPRK enacted laws and regulations governing the free trade zone and held seminars to promote the zone among foreign investors. Again, as in 1984, the country appeared to be cautiously embracing some measure of reform following Beijing's example. But little came of this. The free trade zone was located in the remote northeast corner of the country. The far-off location of this site perhaps reflected the regime's ambivalence about the project. It lacked port facilities that could handle container vessels; and while near both the Chinese and the Russian borders it was connected to them only by dirt roads. It also had erratic electricity supplies.[45] Not surprisingly, few firms were attracted. Chinese entrepreneurs built a casino but the Chinese government soon cracked down on cross-border gamblers. At any rate, this, like the 1984 initiative, was not followed up by other market-friendly measures.

Despite deteriorating economic conditions, the North Korean leadership did not opt for any significant reform. Instead the regime held fast to traditional methods of economic and social management. During the early 1990s it carried out more mass mobilization campaigns. It continued to rely on all the old ideological movements such as the Three Revolutions Team Movement, the Chŏllima, and the Taean industrial system to spur economic production. Severe food shortages were met by cutting rations and reaffirming the principles of agricultural production spelled out by Kim Il Sung in his 1964 *Rural Theses*. The regime's commitment to its traditional ways of doing things was suggested by its propaganda. The media began referring to *urisik sahoejuŭi* (our style of socialism). The North Korean leadership could not make it clearer that it had no intention of changing from its economic or ideological policies. The message was clear: avoid reform or revisionism and adhere to ideological purity. On April 18, 1992 Kim Il Sung, in an interview with the *Washington*

Times, emphatically stated that North Korea was not going to emulate Chinese reforms:

> On detailed method of socialist construction, each country should develop a method reflecting their own situation because [the] environment for socialist construction varies in accordance with each country's size and level of development. We acknowledge that Chinese policy of economic construction reflects Chinese situation and register strong support."[46]

Two days later representatives from communist parties in 30 countries invited to celebrate Kim's 80th birthday met. They signed a document, "Let Us Defend and Advance the Cause of Socialism." Known as the "Pyongyang Declaration" it called for the "ultimate victory of socialism." Yet, whatever the internal propaganda purpose it may have served, the very obscurity of the signatories bespoke of Pyongyang's isolation. Tiny and powerless communist parties of Jordan, Cyprus and Malta attended, while the Chinese ignored it. It is interesting to note that Pyongyang, while reaffirming its commitment to its way of doing socialism, was careful not to antagonize its sole remaining ally after 1991. Kim Il Sung in 1993, for example, told a visiting delegation from Beijing that China's economic reforms were a "tremendous success."[47]

Meanwhile, Kim Il Sung began to accelerate the slow process of con-solidating Kim Jong Il's position as the unchallenged, inevitable successor and guarantor of the continuity of the regime. On December 24, 1991, at the 19th Party Plenum of the Sixth Congress of the KWP he was named the Supreme Commander of the Korean People's Armed Forces. Two months later, on his 50th birthday, February 16, 1992, was celebrated as a national holiday. On April 20, 1992, Kim Jong Il was promoted to Marshall (Wŏnsu), one week after his father became a Generalissimo (Taewŏnsu).[48] Kim Il Sung appeared to be turning over power, or at least much of the day-to-day governance, to his son. In 1992 Kim Il Sung, after publishing the first volume of his autobiography *Reminiscences with the Century*, stated that he now had the time to write since "a large part of my work is done by [KWP] Secretary for Organizational Affairs Kim Jong Il, I have been able to find some time."[49] When Kim Il Sung's birth-day was celebrated in 1993 the speeches in his honor centered around his "remarkable foresight" in making arrangements for his succession. The main focus of the propaganda was on his brilliant son. In late 1993 various organizations held rallies pledging loyalty to Kim Jong Il and emphasizing the need for a "single-minded unity" around him.[50] The process appeared to go smoothly with few major shake-ups in the leadership. What few changes that did take place, such as the reappearance of Kim Il Sung's younger brother Kim Yŏng-ju after 17 years of absence from the public to the number-seven position in the party hierarchy, suggested continuity rather than any new departures for the regime.

The Ultra-Nationalist Turn

North Korea's revolution was always driven by a fierce nationalism. Yet this was tempered somewhat by its Marxist-Leninist ideology. With the effective replacement of Marxism-Leninism with *juche* as the ideological basis of society, its nationalist character became less constrained. Then, in the late 1980s, there was a shift to a more strident racial-ethnic nationalism. This was accompanied by a revival of many traditional elements in Korean culture, including traditional holidays and ceremonies; and characterized by an increasing link between the regime and Korea's historical past; an emphasis on racial purity; and a heightening of xenophobia. This ultra-nationalist turn was the result of the isolation of North Korea, the need to insulate itself from threatening external events, and a way to explain and ideologically deal with its economic problems.

North Korea had a mixed relationship with its cultural heritage. Many traditional works of literature had been discarded. Musical performances such as the revolutionary operas showed strong Russian but almost no traditional influences. Yet there was no Maoist destruction of historical sites or a complete rejection of traditional culture. Korean curved roofs topped some buildings, and women wore traditional *hanbok* dresses on special occasions and learned to play traditional instruments such as the *kayagŭm*, a Korean zither, along with Western ones. In the 1950s a People's Classics Research Institute translated the many-volume *Richo Sillok* (Veritable Records of the Yi Dynasty) into *han'gŭl* so that they could be more readily accessible.[51] But the regime also attacked its Confucian and "feudal" past, and in 1967 the state went on a rampage destroying many old texts. A significant change took place in 1989 when the government reinstituted the traditional holidays of *Ch'usŏk*, the Korean fall thanksgiving festival, and the lunar New Year celebration. These had always been the two most important holidays of the year and had remained so in the South. It also reintroduced the celebration of *hansik* 105 days after the winter solstice, and *Tano* (*Dano*) the fifth day of the fifth lunar year, two traditional festivals that were no longer observed south of the DMZ.[52] On August 1991 Kim Il Sung, in a speech published in the party newspaper *Rodong sinmun*, praised "genuine nationalism" which he stated differed from "bourgeois nationalism." He went on to declare: "Our nation that has the same blood relation and the same language, and [that] has developed the great national culture is a highly patriotic, independent nation."[53]

The DPRK began to identify itself more with its historical past. "Our people have a long history of five thousand years and are an intelligent people who possess a glorious culture," went a frequently repeated quote by Kim Il Sung.[54] North Korean histories had continually pushed back the start dates for earlier Korean states. The second edition of the *Chosŏn t'onga* (General History of Korea) in 1962 pushed back the date for the first Korean state, Old Chosŏn, to the fifth century BCE, several centuries earlier than most historians outside the DPRK accepted. The third edition pushed it back even further to the eighth century BCE.[55] In the early 1990s, following instructions from the Great Leader, archaeologists searched for and discovered the ancient Taedonggang civilization that predated even the earliest known urban society in China. Shortly afterward, they made a more amazing discovery: the tomb of Tan'gun, the mythical founder of the first Korean state. According to tradition he was born in 2333 BCE. South Korea, which had its own tendency toward racial-nationalism, honored Tan'gun as a symbol of the nation's uniqueness and homogeneity; his birth on October 3 was a national holiday. However, most textbooks and professional historians treated him as a myth. In the DPRK Tan'gun had also officially been regarded as a feudal myth. This changed when North Korea announced, on the eve of National Foundation Day 1993, that its archaeologists had excavated the bones of Tan'gun and his wife as well as a gilded bronze crown and some ornaments. These remains were stated to be 5,011 years old. Few South Korean archaeologists or other scholars outside of North Korea took these claims seriously, generally assuming the findings were most likely fabricated. That no bronze work had previously been found on the peninsula dating early than the first millennium BCE only added to the skepticism. It seemed that not only were the North Koreans creating a fictitious national founder but were pushing back the earliest bronze society by at least two thousand years.[56]

North Korea's propagandists may also have been attempting to link the Kim dynasty to the ancient progenitor of the Korean people, even if indirectly. Official mythology had it that Kim Jong Il was born in Paektu-san on the China–North Korea border, a sacred spot and considered the birthplace of Tan'gun. The regime was implying that it was the successor to the founder of the Korean nation and upholder of the national spirit. By the late 1990s Tan'gun's name was frequently asserted as a symbol of the Korean nation. October 3 became "the nation's day," with memorial services to "King Tan'gun." Official statements from Pyongyang often termed Korea as the "Tan'gun nation." For example, when North Korea launched the Taepo-dong 1 missile on August 31, 1998, it announced the launch as "a great pride of the Tan'gun nation."[57] In public statements Kim Jong Il urged the Korean people to follow the "spirit of Tan'gun." And Kim Il Sung was called "a great sage of Tan'gun's nation born of heaven, and [the] sun of a reunified country."[58]

North Korean official histories presented an increasingly xenophobic racial-nationalist interpretation of the past. Korea's history became the story of the constant struggle of a racially pure, virtuous people against outside invaders. This narrative in a more toned-down version could also be found in South Korean textbooks and in popular culture in the South. But North Korea's version of history was more extreme and more racist. The acknowledgment of foreign borrowing or assistance was rarely given. For instance, texts dropped all references to the Soviet Union's role in lib-erating the country from the Japanese. Full credit was given to the heroic Korean people under the great leader, Kim Il Sung. Those in Korea's past who had sought foreign support were criticized for failing to rely on the Korean people instead. Kim Il Sung had previously used this accusa-tion of being subservient to foreign powers to attack his opponents. He was influenced by the rejection by the colonial-era nationalist writers of *sadaejuŭi*, the Korean tradition of serving the great which had made Korea a loyal tributary state of China until the nineteenth century. This now was given a more racist tinge. As B.R. Myers points out this can be seen in the imagery of propaganda posters that routinely depicted foreigners, even when they were friendly visitors from Third World countries, as darker, uglier and sometimes almost grotesque in appearance, compared to the gentle, fair and pleasing look of Koreans.[59] Furthermore, propaganda increasingly used the language of racial purity. Interestingly, the term "*inmin*" (people), normally used in socialist rhetoric and embedded in the name Democratic People's Republic of Korea, generally was replaced by the more nationalistic and ethnically/racially tinged *minjok*.[60]

The purity and antiquity of the Korean race were reconfirmed by another extraordinary archaeological discovery in the early 1990s: Pithecanthropus. Dating to 1 million years ago, these remains, also found in the Taedong basin, suggested that Tan'gun and the Korean nation had descended from a distinct line of humans. It was now maintained that the basin of the river Taedong was "the cradle of mankind," since the remains of Pithecanthropus were found to date back to 1 million years ago. "Scientific evidence," one publication declared, "supports the claim that there is a distinctive Korean race and that the foundation of the first state of the Korean nation by Tan'gun was a historic event, which laid the groundwork for the formation of the Korean nation."[61] North Korea it appeared exceeded even the extremes of National Socialism in its effort to establish a biological basis for its national identity. However, it is interesting to note that North Koreans were not claiming racial superiority in any physical and mental way, but subtly suggesting a purity of virtue, and more importantly, a vague specialness that set them apart from other peoples. This purity and specialness needed protection from contamination from foreigners. North Korean propaganda increasingly focused on the vulnerability of the Korean race, its need for unity in the face of foreign aggressors and the indispensable role of its brilliant leadership as its protectors. In propaganda paintings Korean women facing foreign aggressors on the battlefield were depicted in white traditional *hanbok*, symbolizing their ethnic purity.[62]

Accompanying this heightening racial-nationalism was an increasingly xenophobic tone in the propaganda. This too was not new to either Korea since for all its opening to the world's markets and greater cosmopolitanism, a xenophobic streak also ran through South Korean nationalism. However, in the DPRK it was intensified in literature, children's stories and in propaganda to a degree that set it apart from the South. It was embedded in the historical narrative that blamed all past troubles on foreign invaders. As Tatiana Gabroussenko has explained, literature almost never portrayed Koreans as doing anything bad unless they were corrupted by contact with outsiders.[63] This xenophobia was linked with the history of foreign aggression against Korea, a history still going on since the DPRK was currently under siege from imperialist forces – primarily the USA which occupied South Korea.

A Regime in Crisis

In the early 1990s North Korea faced a series of interconnected crises so severe that they threatened the survival of the regime: the geopolitical challenge caused by the fall of the Soviet Union and the rise of South Korea; the economic crisis from the loss of Soviet aid; a growing food shortage; and a nuclear confrontation with the USA.

The end of the Soviet Union was a calamity for North Korea. Strategically, Pyongyang had been able to balance its relations with Moscow and Beijing, sometimes leaning to one or the other. This 30-year strategy of playing off its two neighbors no longer seemed possible. In 1992 the new Russian state, under President Yeltsin, made it known that the Soviet–North Korean Treaty of Friendship and Mutual Cooperation of 1961, especially Article 1, which committed Moscow to the defense of the DPRK in the case of armed conflict, was no longer in effect.[64] The treaty was formally nullified in 1996.

By far the most severe setback for North Korea that came with this turn of events was to its economy. Trade with Soviet Russia made up about 50 percent of its foreign trade in 1985–90 but only 6.6 percent in 1994. Oil exports, which amounted to 440,000 tons in 1990, fell to less than 40,000 in 1991.[65] The loss of subsidized oil was especially traumatic. Pyongyang did not have the foreign exchange to pay for imported oil, and it was no longer receiving cheap, below-market-value oil from Russia. China provided some, but not enough. In a meeting with Deng Xiaoping in 1992, the Chinese leader made it clear that Beijing was too busy with its own reconstruction to offer more help.[66] Blackouts, always common, became so frequent that they had a crippling effect. Tractors and trucks stood idle, homes went through winter with little or no heat and shortages of fertilizers hindered agriculture. Severe energy shortages, along with aging equipment, led to a decline in industrial output. It also came at a bad time when most sectors of the economy were already in trouble. Agriculture was threatened by flooding from deforestation; resources had been squandered on unproductive, ill-conceived projects; and there was the burden of a vast defense system. Food shortages worsened, and hunger and malnutrition were a serious problem. In a January 1994, in his New Year's address, Kim Il Sung admitted to his people that there were economic problems. Previously such an admission would be unthinkable. What he did not admit, but which must have been obvious to all North Koreans, was that the economy was undergoing a severe contraction. From 1990 to 1994 it may have shrunk by as much as 20 percent, possibly more. North Korea's economic problems in the early 1990s were reaching a crisis point.

The Nuclear Crisis

North Korea developed a formidable weapons industry. Although it was never self-sufficient in military hardware it did produce an impressive array of tanks, artillery, small arms and military vehicles. Besides conventional weapons, the DPRK also worked on developing biological, chemical and nuclear weapons, and a missile delivery system. These were probably always an important part of their military development plans but the DPRK became more reliant on them as the country's economic and geopolitical position became less favorable. These weapons of mass destruction were of great concern to South Korea, the international community and especially to the USA.

North Korea had started work on chemical and biological weapons perhaps as early as the 1950s. From the 1970s the Second Economic

Committee operated chemical weapons factories that produced mustard gas, sarin and other chemical agents.[67] North Korea, through a Germ Research Institute, developed biological weapons including, it was believed, anthrax, botulism, cholera, hemorrhagic fever, the plague (Yersinia pesitis), yellow fever and smallpox.[68] Work on biological and chemical weapons was a concern for the USA and South Korea. While the DPRK joined the Biological and Toxin Weapons Convention in 1987 and signed the Geneva Protocol in 1989 banning the use of biochemical weapons, it remained one of only five countries that did not sign the Chemical Weapons Convention.[69]

Of greatest concern to both its adversaries and its allies was its program to develop nuclear warheads and a missile delivery system. In 1959 the Soviets agreed to a North Korean request to develop nuclear energy and constructed a small "furniture factory" near the town of Yongbyon (Yŏngbyŏn). North Korea had always been interested in nuclear energy and had sent hundreds of technicians to study at the Nuclear Research Center at Dubna near Moscow. But the Soviets were reluctant to provide too much help. When the Chinese detonated an atomic bomb in 1964 Pyongyang turned to them for assistance but was rejected.[70] Nonetheless, technicians increased the capacity of the nuclear research reactor at Yongbyon and constructed a new one. In 1977 Pyongyang allowed the International Atomic Energy Agency (IAEA) to inspect its first reactor; but in the 1980s it began a secret project to build a facility for reprocessing fuel into weapons-grade material. It also began testing chemical high explosives for detonating a bomb. Under Soviet pressure, Pyongyang signed the Nuclear Non-Proliferation Treaty in 1985 but not the safeguards agreements.[71] The USA was becoming increasingly worried that the DPRK was developing nuclear weapons when, in 1990, satellite photos revealed a new structure that appeared to be capable of separating plutonium from nuclear fuel rods. American, South Korean and Japanese officials were now increasing nervous about North Korea's potential to become a nuclear power and to have a missile delivery system. Supported by the international community they pressured the DPRK to sign safeguards with the IAEA in January 1992.

There was nothing irrational about North Korea's desire to become a nuclear power. In fact, as early as the mid-1970s South Korean president

Park Chung Hee began secretive programs to acquire advance weaponry, including nuclear weapons. He twice worked out deals with France, in 1975 and 1978, to build a processing facility only to have it blocked by Washington. Despite this, the South Korean government carried out a clandestine project to develop its own nuclear weapons, but this too was terminated when the Americans found out about it. Washington, which did not want to see either an arms race on the peninsula or a militarily independent South, forced the cancellation of this program.[72] With the transition to democratic government in the late 1980s the South Korean government and public opinion became committed to a nuclear-free program, although it developed a major nuclear energy program. North Korea played to South Korean concerns over nuclear weapons by working out a Joint Declaration in December 1991 not to test, manufacture, produce, receive, possess, store, deploy or use nuclear weapons.[73] This followed an easing of tensions.

But in spite of the Joint Declaration it was soon apparent that North Korea was continuing to work on nuclear weapons development, and optimism about the nuclear issue was soon undermined by events. IAEA inspectors were not satisfied with the declaration of materials Pyongyang submitted in May 1992. They and the USA suspected that there was much more to the nuclear program than it was revealing, including two additional sites where nuclear waste was being stored. The biggest concern was over fuel that experts believed had been removed from the 5-megawatt (MW) reactor when it was shut down for 70–100 days in 1989. This could be enough material to make one to three nuclear bombs. North Korea turned down an IAEA request for access to these sites. As tensions rose over this dispute, in February 1993 North Korea announced its intention to withdraw from the Nuclear Non-Proliferation Treaty in June of that year.[74] The UN Security Council then passed a resolution calling for the DPRK to reconsider its withdrawal. Concerns about the nuclear program were coupled with worries about North Korean missile development. Missiles were important to the DPRK not only to maintain a creditable military threat and to act as a deterrent but also to provide a source of foreign exchange for a country with few marketable products. Pyongyang's interest in developing missiles dates from as early as 1971 when the DPRK signed a wide-ranging agreement with the People's Republic of China on cooperation in weapons acquisition, production and development, including missiles.[75] However, when its allies, showed no enthusiasm for assisting the North Koreans, they managed to buy Soviet Scud missiles from Egypt. From these they were eventually able to reverse engineer and produce their own, longer-range rockets.

The Clinton administration announced that if North Korea reprocessed plutonium it would be crossing a "red line" that could result in military action. And indeed, the administration was so concerned that it seriously considered a military strike on the main reprocessing facility. A military contingency plan was presented to Clinton in December 1993 known as USFK-OpPlan 502716. The prospect of such a military operation had frightening consequences. Seoul was within the range of over 8,000 long-range artillery pieces and an estimated 2,400 rocket launchers. A massive retaliation by Pyongyang could devastate the city of 10 million.[76] It would involve tens of thousands of American and hundreds of thousands of South Korean casualties. Of course, neither side wanted war but North Korea's brinkmanship was escalating tensions to dangerous levels. The arrival of Jimmy Carter in June 1994 led to a defusing of the crisis, as the two sides began working out an agreement that was satisfactory to both nations. Kim Il Sung also agreed to an unprecedented summit conference with South Korean president Kim Young Sam. Then, on July 8, 1994, Kim Il Sung died suddenly of a heart attack. His robust appearance during the negotiations and in a rare interview with Western journalists made his death all the more unexpected.

Nonetheless, negotiations went forward and what was known as the Agreed Framework was worked out. This was a legally non-binding agreement between the USA and the DPRK but not a treaty since the USA had no official relations with North Korea and would not negotiate formal treaties with that country until the Korean War officially ended. North Korea agreed to remain a party to the Nuclear Non-Proliferation Treaty and to its terms for international inspection. This meant it agreed to place its 5 MW nuclear reactor and two larger reactors it was constructing under IAEA inspection. North Korea also agreed it would take steps to implement the Joint Declaration on Denuclearization of the Korean Peninsula which it had made with the ROK at the end of 1991. All of its spent nuclear fuel stocks would be stored and eventually disposed of and not reprocessed. Thus, its capacity to produce weapons-grade plutonium would be eliminated, and its existing plutonium would be removed from harm's way. Since North Korea's nuclear reactors were ostensibly for the purpose of generating electric power, in return for shutting them down two 1,000 MW light water reactors were to be built as gifts by the USA and other outside parties. These would supply electricity but be incapable of producing weapons-grade material.[77]

The Death of Kim Il Sung

No sooner had the 1994 nuclear crisis passed than the DPRK faced another crisis; on July 9, 1994, as they were gathered around the radio during their lunch hour, North Koreans heard the following announcement: "Our Great Leader Kim Il Sung has left our side."[78] His death, which came only two weeks after Carter's visit, came as a shock. Kim Il Sung, although 82, seemed in vigorous health. In fact, among the elite in the North rumors circulated that his death was caused by Kim Jong Il impatient to assume full power, but few historians take this seriously.[79] The elder Kim, as he had so carefully planned, was succeeded by his eldest son.

Kim Il Sung's death brought the end of a remarkable half-century of rule. Few people succeeded in shaping a society to the extent that he did. His impact on North Korean society can hardly be exaggerated. His rule had been exceptionally long – the longest of any modern dictator (surpassed only by Fidel Castro a few months before he stepped down in 2006). Kim ruled a decade longer than Lenin and Stalin combined, and nearly twice as long as Mao Zedong. He was both the founder of the state and its only ruler. When he died he was for the vast majority of North Koreans the only ruler they had ever known. For all the promise and achievements of his regime, he left behind a country that was poor, hungry and isolated. The final years of his rule saw the country move from stagnation to economic decline, from one setback to another. For decades it had portrayed itself as the vanguard of progress for the entire Korean nation, North and South. By 1994, however, the North Korean regime no longer had much to offer Koreans outside its borders.

Observers abroad were now waiting for the country's collapse, and its absorption by the South was seen as likely if not inevitable. Kim Il Sung's goal was to create a unified, prosperous, strong, independent and progressive nation. For his successors, the main goal was survival.

Notes

1 Lim, 2009, p. 84.
2 Lim, 2009, pp. 83–84.
3 Buzo, p. 109.
4 Hwang Chang-yŏp, pp. 115–116.
5 Allan Bouc, "A Visit to North Korea," *New York Times*, June 14, 1971.
6 Benedict S. David, "Visitor to North Korea Describes Vast Building Drive," *New York Times*, August 10, 1971.
7 Harrison Salisbury, *To Peking and Beyond: A Report on the New Asia*. New York: Quadrangle Books, 1973, p. 200.
8 John H. Lee, "By Any Standards Industry is Powerful," *New York Times*, June 4, 1972.
9 Harrison, Selig S. *Korean Endgame: A Strategy for Reunification and U.S. Disengagement*. Princeton, NJ: Princeton University Press, 2002, p. 27.
10 Martin, p. 156.
11 B.C. Koh, "North Korea: Old Goals and New Realities," *Asian Survey* 14, no. 1 (January 1974): 36–42.
12 Kim, Byung-Yeon, Suk Jin and Keun Lee, "Assessing the Economic Performance of North Korea, 1954–1989: Estimates and Growth Accounting Analysis," *Journal of Comparative Economics* 35, no. 3 (2007): 564–582.
13 Young C. Kim, "The Democratic People's Republic of Korea in 1975," *Asian Survey* 16, no. 1 (January 1976): 82–94.
14 Byung Chul Koh, "The Impact of the Chinese Model on North Korea," *Asian Survey* 18, no. 6 (1978): 626–643.
15 Kim Sŏng-bo. *Pukhan ŭi yŏksa* 2, p. 122.
16 Young Whan Kihl, "North Korea in 1983: Transforming 'The Hermit Kingdom'," *Asian Survey* 24, no. 1 (January 1984): 100–111.
17 Buzo, p. 89; Donald S. Zagoria and Young Kun Kim, "North Korea and the Major Powers," in William J. Barnds, editor, *The Two Koreas in East Asian Affairs*. New York: New York University Press, 1976, pp. 177–189.
18 Buzo, pp. 109–110.

19 Yim, Sang-chŏl, *Pukhan nongŏp [North Korean Agriculture]*. Seoul: Tosŏ Ch'ulp'an Sŏil, 2000, pp. 24–35.
20 Buzo, p. 122, p. 140.
21 Tessa Morris-Suzuki. *Exodus to North Korea: Shadow from Japan's Cold War.* Latham, MD: Rowman & Littlefield, 2007, pp. 190–192, pp. 235–236.
22 Pyong-il Kim, pp. 106–107.
23 Hy-Sang Lee, pp. 138–139.
24 Lankov, 2007, pp. 84–87.
25 Pyong-il Kim, pp. 50–51.
26 Hy-Sang Lee, p. 157.
27 Kihl, Young Whan, "North Korea in 1984: 'The Hermit Kingdom'," Turns Outward! *Asian Survey* 25, no. 1 (January 1985): 65–79.
28 Lim, Jae-Cheon, "Institutional Change in North Korean Economic Development Since 1984: The Competition Between Hegemonic and Non-hegemonic Rules and Norms," *Pacific Affairs* 82, no. 1 (Spring 2009): 9–27.
29 Hy-Sang Lee, p. 158.
30 Hy-Sang Lee, p. 157.
31 Il-pyong Kim, p. 10.
32 Brazhanova, Nadia, *Koro e sŏn Pukhan kyŏngje [North Korean Economy at a Crossroads]*, trans Yang Chun-yong. Seoul: Han'guk kyŏngje sinmunsa, 1992, p. 96.
33 Brazhanova, p. 97.
34 Sŏng Hye-rang, pp. 471–473.
35 "Miserable Aspects of South Korea," *Korea Today* 348 (October 1985): 42–45.
36 Young C. Kim, "North Korea 1979: National Unification and Economic Development," *Asian Survey* 20, no. 1 (January 1980): 53–62.
37 Buzo, pp. 123–124.
38 Buzo, p. 150.
39 Koh, 1984, p. 224.
40 "South Korea-Danger Spot for the Olympiad," *Korea Today* 357 (June 1986): 49.
41 Buzo, p. 178.
42 Kim Hae-wŏn, *Pukhan ŭi Nambukkhan chŏngch'I hyŏpsang yŏn'gu [Research on North Korea's Political Negotiations with South Korea]*. Seoul: Sŏnin Publications, 2012, p. 129.
43 Buzo, p. 188.
44 Byung-chul Koh, "Ideology and Pragmatism in North Korean Foreign Policy," in Dae-Sook Suh (ed.), *Korean Studies: New Pacific Currents*. Honolulu: University of Hawaii Center for Korean Studies, 1994, pp. 207–226.

45 Hassig and Oh, 2009.
46 Kim, Yongho, p. 86.
47 John Merrill, "North Korea in 1993: In the Eye of the Storm," *Asian Survey* 34, no. 1 (January 1994): 10–18.
48 Armstrong, 2013, p. 12.
49 Buzo, p. 209.
50 Merrill, 1994, p. 18.
51 Kim Sŏng-bo. *Pukhan ŭi yŏksa* 1, p. 258.
52 Lankov, 2007, p. 120.
53 Kang, Jin Woon, "Historical Changes in North Korean Nationalism," *North Korean Review* 3, no. 1 (2007): 86–104.
54 Jorganson, John, "Tan'gun and the Legitimization of a Threatened Dynasty: North Korea's Rediscovery of Tan'gun," *Korea Observer* 27 (1996): 273–306.
55 Yong-ho Ch'oe, "Reinterpreting Traditional History in North Korea," *Journal of Asian Studies* 45, no. 3 (May 1981): 503–517.
56 *Korea Newsreview*, October 16, 1993, pp. 30–31.
57 *Agence France-Presse*, September 11, 1998.
58 *Korean Central News Agency*, March 1, 2000, BBC Worldwide Monitoring.
59 Myers, *The Cleanest Race*, p. 131.
60 Armstrong, *Tyranny of the Weak*, p. 279.
61 "Pyongyang-Capital of the Korean Nation," *Korea Today* no.2 (1995): 43–45, 45.
62 Sung Minkyu, "The biopolitic of North Korea: Political Crisis, the Body and visual Power," *Seoul Journal of Korean Studies* 28, no. 2 (December 2015): 231–257.
63 Tatiana Gabroussenko, "North Korean 'Rural Fiction' from the Late 1990s to the Mid-2000s: Permanence and Change," *Korean Studies* 33 (2009): 69–100.
64 Buzo, p. 224.
65 Buzo, p. 214–215.
66 Chen Jian, "Limits of the 'Lips and Teeth' Alliance: An Historical Review of Chinese-North Korean Relations," Asia Program Special Report no.115 Washington D.C. Woodrow Wilson International Center for Scholars, September 2003.
67 Bermudez, Joseph S. Jr. *The Armed Forces of North Korea*. London: I.B. Tauris, 2001, pp. 222–231.
68 Bermudez, pp. 231–233.
69 Victor Cha, *The Impossible State, North Korea, Past and Future*. New York: Ecco, 2012, p. 233.

70 Walter Clemens, "North Korea's Quest for Nuclear Weapons: New Historical Evidence," *Journal of East Asian Studies* 10, no. 1 (2010): 1–27.
71 Cha, pp. 249–250.
72 Bermudez, pp. 240–241.
73 Kim Hae-wŏn, pp. 130–135.
74 Hy-sang Lee, pp. 182–183.
75 Bermudez, p. 239.
76 Hy-sang Lee, pp. 183–184.
77 The Arms Control Organization, "The Agreed Framework at a Glance," https://www.armscontrol.org/factsheets/agreedframework Accessed January 14, 2017.
78 Kwon, p. 21.
79 Fujimoto Kenji, *Kim Chŏng-il ŭi yorisa* [Cook of Kim Jong Il], trans. Sin Hyŏn-do. Seoul: Wŏlgan Chosŏnsa, 2003, p. 233.

6

Famine and Survival, 1994–2005

Shortly after Kim Il Sung's death North Korea experienced the worst famine ever to occur in an industrial nation.[1] The famine transformed society to a greater extent than had been seen since the completion of the socialization of the economy in the 1950s, marking a new era in its history. The regimented system of economic distribution and political control so carefully constructed gave way to a more chaotic semi market-orientated economy, and a more corrupt political system. This transformation differed from previous ones in that it came from below, not above. It was a grassroots response by millions of desperate, hungry people to cope with the breakdown of the state economy, and by opportunistic military and civilian officials. North Korea recovered from the famine by the end of the decade, but it became a changed society. Meanwhile, the regime under Kim Jong Il survived by requesting foreign aid, adjusting its ideology, modifying its constitutional structure, giving greater emphasis to military strength and by tacitly accepting and fitfully adapting to the new economic realities at home.

North Korea under Kim Jong Il

When Kim Il Sung died in 1994 the survival of the DPRK was in doubt. The economy was in a near freefall; the international situation was bad on all fronts; relations with Russia were frosty at best; China, its only ally, was pressuring it to carry out reforms to stave off collapse; a possible military confrontation with the USA had just been averted; and the South, under its democratically elected government, was cautiously waiting for change. Food shortages were critical and North Korea was on the eve of the worst famine ever suffered by a modern industrialized state. Yet the regime survived, and by 2005 was secure enough to retreat from some of the modest compromises it had made owing to economic and social realities, and to reimpose elements of the old order.

The Successor

Kim Jong Il's succession to power, which had been many years in the planning, went smoothly. The former Dear Leader, become the Great Leader but with a different Korean term (*Widaehan Ryŏngdoja*) to distinguish him from his father (*Widaehan Suryŏngnim*), also translated into English as Great Leader. Although a purge of military officers in the KPA's Sixth Corps, who may have been plotting a coup, took place in June 1995 there were, in general, no major shake-ups in the top leadership.[2] Whatever internal opposition there might have been to this unusual father-to-son transfer of power had long been resolved years earlier. Kim Jong Il had been groomed as his father's successor for more than two decades during which time he had wielded enormous and growing power. Contrary to the predictions of many foreign observers, Kim Jong Il appeared to be firmly in power. Lacking the revolutionary credentials or physical stature of his father, he seemed an unlikely candidate for supreme leader. His heavy drinking, his fondness for women and luxurious living, his artistic temperament, his elevated shoes and bouffant hairstyle compensating for his short height, and his sometimes bizarre behavior made him the subject of ridicule and contempt abroad. One example of his strange behavior was linked with his great love of cinema. He reportedly possessed a vast movie collection. In 1978 he had agents kidnap a famous South Korean movie actress, Choi Eun Hee (Ch'oe Ŭn-hŭi) (1926–), in Hong Kong and then lured her ex-husband, the well-known director Shin Sang-ok (Sin Sang-ok) (1926–2006), to North Korea.[3] The couple were reintroduced at a party, and Kim Jong Il asked them to make movies for him, complaining about the quality of North Korean films. After making several North

Korean films, while attending a film festival in Vienna they managed to seek political asylum in the US embassy there and return to South Korea. Yet, while there were many other reports of his eccentric behavior and his lavish and decadent parties, he had a shrewd intelligence and had learned well how to firmly grasp and maintain his hold on power.

Kim Jong Il's legitimacy depended on maintaining the cult of this father. While extravagant praise was heaped on Kim Jong Il, the veneration of his father, Kim Il Sung, who remained the founder, builder and towering figure of the Democratic People's Republic of Korea, continued unabated. Indeed, Kim Jong Il ruled by what was called *Yuhun t'ongch'i* (governance based on the teaching left behind by Kin Il Sung) which meant that the cult of Kim Il Sung had to be intensified.[4] Following traditional Korean Confucian practice, Kim Jong Il adhered to a three-year period of mourning punctuated with a hundred-day observance and annual observances. On the hundredth day of his father's death he assured the nation that Kim Il Sung was still with them. Kim Il Sung was placed in the national pantheon with Tan'gun. The latter was the founder of the nation, the former of the socialist nation.[5] On the first anniversary of Kim Il Sung's death his body went on display at Kŭmsusan Assembly Hall which had been his main place of work and residence, now renamed Kŭmsusan Memorial Palace. Russian specialists were hired to preserve his body which was now open for view in the manner of Lenin's. At the end of the three-year mourning period on July 8, 1997 elaborate ceremonies were held marked by the completion of the Tower of Immortality with the inscription "Great Leader Kim Il Sung is eternally with us." Monuments with this inscription appeared throughout the country. A new *juche* calendar was adopted in 1997, with year one being that of Kim Il Sung's birth, 1912. The current year, 1997, became the year 86. That same year Kim Jong Il assumed the position of the General Secretary of the Korean Workers' Party (KWP). He never became the head of state. Instead, in 1998 the constitution was revised making Kim Il Sung the "eternal president." In 1996 the media began to trumpet "the Red Banner Thought." It announced that this "profound philosophy," the creation of Kim Jong Il, was based on *juche* and was somehow a further advancement of it. However, the Red Banner Thought soon faded away; Kim Jong Il remained the interpreter of his father's thought rather than an innovative thinker.

Famine and the Arduous March

Soon after succeeding his father Kim Jong Il faced a new crisis. From 1995 through 1998 North Korea underwent a horrific famine. In many ways this was a historically unique event. It was history's first major famine suffered by an industrial state not at war. The immediate cause of the North Korean famine was the widespread flooding in August 1995 that destroyed much of the nation's rice crop. The summer monsoon rains that come each year were especially heavy. Starting on June 26 it rained for ten days, dumping as much as 58 centimeters (23 inches) on parts of the country. Satellite photos suggest that a quarter of the nation's rice paddies were under water.[6]

The dimensions of the catastrophe are not fully known, but between 1995 and 1999 thousands perished from causes directly or indirectly related to food shortages. Determining deaths in famines tends to be difficult. It can be calculated based on the number who die of direct starvation, or on higher rates of deaths from illness due to lowered resistance of under- or malnourished populations. And there is the fact that in times of famine people relocate and famines are often accompanied by chaos and confusion. In North Korea the secretiveness of the regime and the lack of publicly available statistics both prior and after the famine make the calculations especially difficult.[7] Therefore it is not surprising that estimates of the death toll vary widely. Western reports commonly gave figures of some 2 million, sometimes higher. The Buddhist charity Good Friends estimated 3 million deaths directly or indirectly resulted from the famine; and World Vision, a Christian charity, gave an alarming report in 1997 of a wildly improbable 7 million deaths. Foreign experts tried to measure the death toll by asking refugees in China how many family members died and extrapolating from there. From these surveys a figure of 2.5 million was produced. But most of the interviewees were from North Hamgyŏng province, which was perhaps the most severely affected region.[8] Some more recent estimates are much lower. At the low end, North Korean officials in 1999 and 2001 gave a figure of 220,000 for famine-related deaths.[9] Marcus Noland and Stephen Haggard in their study have placed the probable figure as between 600,000 and 1 million due to food shortages.[10] Even if the more conservative estimates of

600,000 to 1 million or more deaths out of 20 million are accepted this is a truly appalling number, amounting to 3–5 percent of the total population. And this does not count the number who suffered from long-term under-nutrition, probably millions.[11]

Failed Agriculture Policies

Whatever the immediate causes, North Korea's famine was, above all, the product of years of failed agricultural policies. Agriculture was the weakest sector of North Korea's economy. Despite considerable effort the country never was able to feed itself and suffered from chronic food shortages. This was partly down to geography. The country possessed limited farmland and a short growing season. Geographic limitations were made worse by years of economic mismanagement and the problems inherent in North Korea's socialist system of agriculture. Agricultural planning was too centralized, there was a lack of incentive for individual farmers, too much reliance was placed on capital inputs, and some policies were poorly conceived to the extreme. Agriculture production quotas were drawn up by the Central Planning Commission and approved by the State Council and the KWP. Their directives filtered down to the provinces and from there to the counties and finally to the cooperatives. Farms had their managers but decision making was supposedly made collectively, with farm members (*nongjangwŏn*) holding meetings to discuss the implementation of duties. *Hyŏpdong nongjgang kŏmsa wiwonhoe* (inspection committees) of 5–15 members were appointed for one-year terms among the farm workers to see that all rules and regulations were adhered to.[12] In reality, however, farmers had little control over their work. Rigid regulations made it difficult for farms to adjust policies to local conditions. Officials issued detailed instructions to each collective farm on what and when to plant. Farmers could only make a few basic decisions such as what crop mixtures to plant. Furthermore, the Central Planning Commission set targets unrealistically high, especially for key crops such as rice, wheat and corn. Not only did they almost always result in falling far short of the target, but they diverted efforts from the production of other crops that might have been more suitable for local conditions.

North Korean agriculture was almost completely socialized, with only tiny family plots (*t'ŏtpat*) permitted. Farmers could sell some surplus, but not grain, in designated farmers' markets (*nongmin sijang*) which opened on the 1st, 11th and 21st days of the month.[13] In the Soviet Union and Vietnam private plots accounted for a substantial proportion of the food produced, but the ones in North Korea were too small to provide a significant supplement to the state farm.[14] These plots were so small that they really only provided very modest additions such as chili peppers or squash for farm families. Farmers mainly had to rely on their allotment of grain and other staples for survival. Since the typical grain left over to farmers after harvest was similar to that of workers this meant that in reality they were little better off than salaried workers. This was a deliberate policy stemming from Kim Il Sung's concern that the peasants become in practice workers without any cultural or ideological gaps. The government contributed to further food shortages by its practice of collecting more crops from farmers when supplies were scarce, assuming farmers could make up the difference with their existing tiny private plots. This encouraged farmers to preharvest and hoard crops if they anticipated a poor harvest thus aggravating the food shortages. Preharvesting could mean premature harvesting, thereby only lowering yields.[15] As an added disincentive the state resorted to extra food seizures during times of food scarcity.

A number of efforts were carried out to make the work on farms more efficient. Starting in 1965, for example, the state experimented with creating small sub-teams (*punjo*) that would be able to work semi-independently and sell their surpluses to the state, but this was undermined by the low prices that were set.[16] The sub-teams were provided with land, farming animals and other resources. The idea was to give them incentives by purchasing their surpluses. But these purchases were often at prices too low to be effective incentives.[17] Since the state was not willing to provide real economic incentives it relied on the same mix of propaganda, indoctrination, popular campaigns and mass mobilization to spur agricultural production as it did for other sectors of the economy. Farmers attended regular ideological meetings. Propaganda teams usually consisting of young party workers, often college students from the city, arrived, setting up red flags and playing music, shouting slogans and exhorting peasants to work harder. Competition between collectives was encouraged. None of these efforts were very effective.

Agriculture was approached as part of the nation's industrialization. The basic policies were spelled out in Kim Il Sung's 1964 *Theses on the Socialist Rural Question in Our Country*. This document, which became a canonical text, attacked the problem of agriculture in four ways: electrification, irrigation, mechanization and "chemicalization." Mechanization of agriculture focused on the use of tractors. In early 1950, just before the start of the Korean War, the first five Agriculture Machine-Hire Stations were established with 70 tractors. After the war, tractor production was a high priority and by 1960 there were 89 tractor stations with 5,214 locally manufactured and imported tractors.[18] Plans called for the production of 10,000 a year by the 1970s, a target that was never reached. Nonetheless, visitors to the country were impressed by how many they saw in use. Huge amounts of chemical fertilizers were applied to obtain high yields, and elaborate irrigation methods were employed. All this resulted in what one study calls "one of the world's most input-intensive agricultural systems."[19]

But all four aspects of Kim's plan for agricultural development proved difficult to achieve. Electrification, irrigation, mechanization and chemicalization fell far short of the goals set for them. Irrigation projects were carried out but never to the extent planned. Tractor production remained modest; there were never enough tractors to carry out farming on the mechanized scale Kim envisioned. This was partly due to the priority given to military production, which meant tractor production competed with the demand for army vehicles and weaponry. Electrification efforts suffered because of the country's chronic and worsening energy shortages. Fertilizer production, although fairly high, never reached the enormous quantities needed to produce sufficient yields from small plots of land. Mechanization, fertilizer production and irrigation required large energy inputs that came increasingly from petroleum imported from China and especially the Soviet Union at bargain "friendship" prices. When Moscow demanded payment at the market price for its oil after 1989 North Korean agriculture suffered. Unable to afford the necessary fuel pumps for irrigation, systems ceased to operate and tractors stood idle. Fertilizer production, which was dependent on petroleum for its manufacture, fell by two-thirds from 1995 to 1997 to a level of only one-fifth of what was needed.[20] China may also have been a significant factor in turning chronic food shortages into critical ones. In 1993 it was supplying North Korea with 77 percent of its now-reduced level of fuel imports and 68 percent of its food imports, but in that same year China began to demand cash payments. The following year, in 1994, it reduced its corn exports to the DPRK, perhaps as a sign of displeasure over the country's nuclear program.[21]

In an effort to gain greater yields per hectare officials ordered seeds to be planted closely together. This, however, made the crops vulnerable to pests and exhausted the soil. The greatest problem was deforestation. From 1947 the regime had carried out reforestation projects. Regular tree-planting campaigns took place around Kim Il Sung's birthday, under the banner that each tree planted "carried the love of the Great Leader."[22] However, these efforts were undermined by the need to clear land for farming. The wooded hillsides of this mountainous country turned into farmland, even in areas too steep to be suitable for planting crops. One aid official, in 1997, observed entire hillsides torn away by erosion due to these shortsighted policies.[23] Even earlier the effort to bring the most marginal land into production was striking. American journalist Don Oberdorfer, in 1989, noticed when traveling outside Pyongyang that farmers were "cultivating practically every available square inch of arable soil."[24] Even the most marginal lands were used. Farmers were instructed to create "unification fields" (*t'ongil p'ojŏn*) on the least productive land and turn these into fertile fields but this often involved futile efforts to plant where crops simply could not grow, wasting labor and resources.[25] In a measure to deal with the scarcity of meat, the state encouraged live-stock raising, especially poultry and pigs, but this required feed. The state launched a campaign to encourage raising goats; "Let's expand Goat Rearing and Create More Grassland in Accordance with the Party!" the campaign proclaimed.[26] However, the country had limited grazing land and goats further contributed to erosion. Deforestation and erosion con-tributed to the disastrous floods that were the immediate cause of the severe famine of the 1990s.

As a result of all this from the earliest years of the regime targets for production fell far short. By one calculation the first Seven-Year Plan's goal of 6–7 million tons of grain was reduced to 5–7 million but was actually less than 5 million. Grain production probably peaked between 7 million and 8 million tons in the early 1980s. This was more than double what it was in the 1960s but only a little above the population growth rate.[27] Then it began to fall. Grain production fell sharply after 1989. According to South Korean estimates it fell from 5,482,000 metric tons in 1989 to 4,125,000 tons in 1994. Then it dropped to 3,451,000 in 1995.[28]

A Famine in Slow Motion

North Korea made being self-sufficient in rice a measure of the success of its revolution and began to boast of its ability to produce enough of this basic staple. The diet of North Koreans (and of all Koreans) traditionally centers on white polished rice. Indeed *pap*, a common word for meal in Korea, literally means cooked rice. Rice is served with dishes of fresh or pickled vegetables (*kimchi*), soup and, when available, fish and small pieces of meat. Barley and other grains have traditionally been substituted for or mixed with *pap* when not enough rice was available. The ideal diet was expressed by Kim Il Sung when, using an old Korean expression, he told his people that under socialism they would be "eating rice and meat soup."[29] The importance of providing rice for the North Korean diet was expressed in his widely publicized slogan "rice is socialism."[30] When in the 1970s an industrializing South Korea was importing food, propaganda broadcasts from Pyongyang chided the South for buying rice from abroad when the DPRK had plenty to spare. Again, in 1984, when floods in the South damaged the rice crop Pyongyang offered the ROK Red Cross rice as aid, which as a gesture of goodwill it accepted. However, this was sheer propaganda. There was probably never enough rice to supply its own demand. Kim Il Sung promoted corn as a substitute for rice, but corn was less nutritional and was regarded by North Koreans as an inferior grain. It was often mixed with whatever rice was available to make it more palatable. In the 1990s Kim Jong Il promoted potatoes to supplement the grain shortfall, but potatoes did not grow well in the acidic soils of the country, were more difficult to store,

proved vulnerable to insect pests and diseases, and failed to gain acceptance as a substitute for rice.[31]

Food in North Korea was distributed through the public distribution system (PDS). Farmers received their rations after their crops were
harvested. The non-farming population, which accounted for about 70
percent of total, received coupons (*yanggwŏn*) every 15 days that could be
redeemed at a state store. These were primarily for grain, although sometimes coupons for cooking oil, vegetables and, on rare occasions, princi-
pally major holidays such as Kim Il Sung's and later Kim Jong Il's birthday,
meat was also distributed. The amount of grain allowed depended on
occupation and status. Soldiers, miners and workers in heavy industry
were allotted 900 grams, party members 700, non-party office workers
somewhat less. Women over 55 and men over 61 received 400 grams,
children 200 to 300 grams. Status also determined what percentage of
this was rice. Only officials and military officers received mostly rice.
Ordinary North Koreans received mostly mixed grains with the percentage of rice in their rations declining over time. By the late 1980s and
early 1990s, the most people were receiving only 10 to 30 percent of
their grain rations in rice, the rest was usually corn.[32] The rations for most
people, at best, barely covered basic nutritional needs and, when possible, were supplemented by purchases in the very limited and restricted
markets for meat and vegetables.

The problem for most North Koreans became not the quality of food
but obtaining enough. Starting in the 1970s, rations were periodically
cut. They were restored in the early or mid-1980s only to be cut again by
10 percent in 1987.[33] Further cuts in rice rations were labeled as "patriotic rice" donations to the military.[34] Evidence suggests that by this time
malnutrition was becoming widespread, and that many children were
underweight and short for their ages. Visitors noticed the absence of live-
stock other than beasts of burden, although they did not see obvious signs
of malnutrition. Then the situation worsened. By the early 1990s the
country may have only produced enough to cover 60 percent of its food
needs. In 1991 the people were presented with the slogan, "Let's eat two
meals a day."[35] But getting even two full meals was becoming a problem.
Rations were cut again in 1993. In a survey of North Korean refugees
conducted in the 2000s, nearly 50 percent stated that by 1995 they were

receiving either less than half or no food at all though the PDS.[36] Since these refugees were disproportionately from the poorest and most remote parts of the country this may not have been true everywhere.

Yet it is clear that the situation was becoming grave prior to the floods. In 1994 a Chinese official reported that the food shortage was the worst in the DPRK's history, and rumors that the situation had become severe circulated in the West. North Korea denied these reports; a spokesman for the Agricultural Commission called them "a wicked deception to degrade the socialist image of the DPRK."[37] However, hunger was becoming all-pervasive before the start of the famine. One North Korean agricultural researcher who escaped to South Korea gave the following report to Human Rights Watch in 1995:

> Except for the elite class, no matter what your occupation was, your access to food was more or less the same. In other words, pretty much everyone was always short of food. Researchers, professors, and other educated people were not an exception. Even if you got paid more than farmers, if your salary bought you only a few days' worth of food each month, it didn't mean much. Starting in the mid-1980s, they began delaying distribution of rations. By the late 1980s, delays became normal.[38]

With the floods the entire PDS system broke down, causing ordinary people to often refer to the famine as the "age of non-distribution [of food]" (*pibaegŭp sidae*).[39]

Perhaps nothing so dramatized the failure of DPRK to adequately feed its people than the physical contrast between North Koreans and their cousins to the south. The contrast in nutritional levels between North and South Korea was quite dramatic by the 1980s. Stark evidence of this can be found in the growing height cap. Originally North Korean males and females were on average 0.8 cm taller than southerners but after the 1950s they became far shorter – a clear testament to the failure of North Korea to feed its people.[40] This came to the attention of Kim Il Sung who started a "Movement to Become Taller," ordering all primary and secondary students to undergo exercises to stretch them.[41] This pathetic campaign illustrated the unrealistic attitude of the DPRK to the problems of a failing economy that could not feed its people. And the height difference only became greater.

The Relief Effort

Even before the 1995 floods the government made some gestures toward seeking food assistance. A UN World Food Program assessment team was invited to the country in 1991 but was presented with no evidence of food shortages. This odd episode may reflect policy differences among the leadership over whether or not to accept aid. At the very least it reflected the extreme reluctance to openly ask for assistance. In 1994 North Korea approached Japan for food aid, yet did so without any display of urgency. Then, in 1995, it publicly reported the floods and openly sought help from foreign governments and international relief organizations. A number of foreign relief agencies came in, such as the UN-related World Food Program, the Food and Agricultural Organization (FAO), the UN International Children's Emergency Fund (UNICEF) and the World Health Organization. Some European countries also offered aid. By 2000, these international agencies were providing 40 percent of North Korea's food needs. The USA became a major aid donor with aid increasing in the late 1990s and then declining in 2000. By then South Korea had replaced the USA as a major donor. Japan provided some aid, the European Union (EU) very modest amounts.[42] From 1997 to 2004 foreign food donations fed one-third of the population.

However, unlike other states who have called upon the international community for massive assistance, the regime imposed extensive restrictions on the relief efforts. As a result international aid workers confronted a historically unprecedented situation. There was widespread starvation, but unlike the usual chaotic conditions that accompany famine, they found a tightly controlled police state determined to limit interactions between relief workers and the people they were helping. Concerned in part with keeping their citizens ignorant of the outside world, North Korean officials insisted on managing the distribution of food. Aid workers complained about a lack of access to victims and were frustrated over their inability to determine just where the food was going. Food was often transported in KPA trucks. This was because they were the only vehicles available with fuel, but it caused worries that relief supplies were going to the military rather than to the people – that they were being used to feed the army and party at the expense of others in more dire need, especially children. The extent to which this was true, however, could not be verified. There were also some disturbing reports that rice being supplied by Japan and South Korea was being resold abroad to earn foreign exchange.

Whole regions of the country were closed to international relief workers, including the northeast province of North Hamgyŏng, believed to be the most severely stricken by famine. The ability of international aid groups to understand the situation and assess needs was hindered by the North Korean government's efforts to limit the number of Korean speakers they could employ. Only slowly, and after considerable negotiations, was access to much of the country possible for the aid community. By the close of 1997 World Food Program officials had gained access to only 110 of the country's 200 counties. By 2000, after the worst of the famine was over, they had access to 167 counties but even in these the regime placed heavy restrictions on movement and activity.[43] Many of the activities that famine relief workers normally carried out, such as random nutritional surveys to determine need, were prohibited by the government. Relief workers often found themselves cooped up in the capital with lengthy waiting times for permission to venture out into the countryside. Frustrated by this lack of access, many agencies, including Médecins Sans Frontières, Oxfam and CARE International, pulled out of North Korea in 1998. Japan also withdrew its assistance.[44] Other groups, by accepting these limitations and carefully steering away from politics, remained in the country.

The most acute hunger was found in the industrial cities of the northeast. Reports by refugees talk of people abandoning work and school to search for food. Factory and office workers headed for the hillsides and collected whatever they could. Many crossed over the border illegally to China to sell anything they had for food to bring back to their families. Dogs and livestock of various kinds disappeared. People consumed what were called substitute or alternative foods, such as "green porridge" made from ground-up leaves and other vegetable matter mixed with a little grain.[45] Alternative foods were also made from tree bark, leaves, grasses and twigs ground and mixed with whatever else was available. The result was not only of little nutritional value but resulted in diarrhea, dysentery and internal bleeding. Abandoned children, known as *kotchebi* ("swallows"), whose parents had died, or were off in search of food, or too incapacitated to help them, wandered city streets and occupied abandoned factories and rail stations.[46] Especially hard hit was the industrial city of Chongjin which became a virtual ghost town as people left in search of food or were too weak to leave their homes.[47] Aid workers visiting one community saw only young people. They were told that older people gave food to their grandchildren and were themselves too weak to move about.[48] Only in Pyongyang, the relatively privileged capital, was food generally available, but starvation took place even there.[49]

Children were especially hard hit. The 1998 joint EU–UN International Children's Emergency Fund–World Food Program survey estimated that 62 percent of children were stunted (low height for their age) and 61 percent were underweight.[50] Children exhibited signs of long-term undernourishment, including lassitude, susceptibility to minor illness and infection, increased mortality and impaired cognitive functions. Foreign aid workers commented that children often appeared several years younger than their real ages. After 1998 conditions improved and starvation was rarer, but chronic undernourishment remained a problem, especially for children. The limited foreign access to some of the most severely affected areas makes the impact of the famine a matter of guesswork. In 2004 the UN's Fifth Report on World Nutrition found a sharp reduction in the number of underweight and stunted children although the figure was still high.[51]

Despite the magnitude of this disaster the North Korean government did not seem very concerned about reforms. In public statements it viewed the problem as the result of natural disasters and problems of external trade not policy failures. Efforts by the World Food Program to deal with the basic causes through a roundtable talk with DPRK officials in 1998 were simply used by the North Koreans as a platform for requesting more aid.[52] A disturbing possibility was that the leadership may not have been as concerned about many of the victims of the famine. This was not only due to the insularity and callousness of the elite but also because many of those hardest hit were from the hostile class. This possibility was supported by the fact that the northeastern region, which was most severely affected, was an area where members of the "hostile" class were often relocated. The country's priority was to feed those the regime depended on: the military and the state and party functionaries – the members of the "core" class. It is not certain to what extent this was the case, because many priority groups including soldiers also suffered.

The Unusual Nature of the North Korean Famine

North Korea's famine, although precipitated by natural disaster, was primarily political in its origins. This is true of almost all twentieth- and twenty-first-century famines, in the sense that they were caused by war, upheavals or misguided state policies. Mass famines resulting from failed policies happened in other communist regimes. Both of North Korea's two principal patrons –the Soviet Union and China – underwent massive famines due to state policies. Between 6 million and 8 million Ukrainian peasants perished in 1932–1933 during the Soviet collectivization of agriculture. The Great Leap Forward in China in 1958–1962 resulted in the greatest famine of modern times – 20 million may have died from starvation in rural China; some calculations are even as high as 30 million or more. Proportionately, the scale of North Korea's famine, if we assume 3–5 percent died directly from food deprivation, may be no greater than either of those. And it was proportionately less than the at least 1 million out of a population of 6 million who died from hunger in Cambodia under the Pol Pot regime (1975–1979).[53]

Yet North Korea's famine, which it called "the Arduous March," differed from these cases since it was not the result of upheavals caused by the implementation of radical new economic policies. Unlike other "political" famines it was the culmination of a long decline in agriculture and in nutritional levels. Perhaps the most unusual aspect of North Korea's famine was that it occurred in a modern industrial, largely urbanized state and struck the urban population especially hard. Major modern famines have taken place in predominantly rural societies and have impacted the countryside more than cities. The North Korean famine was also unusual in that it took place in a state that was determined to maintain full control over the population. In fairness to the regime it did at least, in contrast to China's Great Leap Forward famine in the late 1950s, admit to a food crisis and open the country to aid. This in itself was a tremendous threat to the regime's legitimacy, but to the surprise of many observers it was one it seemed to weather without losing its grip on power.

Recovery was slow, with grain production levels in 1999 only reaching the very low 1994 level.[54] It was not until 2004 that the North Korean government began to close the offices of many foreign aid agencies. However, there were no fundamental changes in its agricultural policies. Food shortages continued. Thus, North Korea had become an anomaly among modern states. An urban, literate, industrialized state with the technical know-how to develop nuclear weapons and missiles but one that suffered from chronic hunger, malnutrition and threats of famine. Perhaps nothing is as shocking as the regime's seemingly callous attitude to its own people's hunger. Rather than purchase food on the international market it conserved its scarce foreign exchange for higher priority resources such as military-related supplies and luxury goods for the elite. It is reported that even at the height of the famine millions of dollars were spent on imported Swiss watches and Mercedes-Benzes. Millions were spent on entertaining the elite. In one notorious incident Kim Jong Il is reported to have spent $15 million bringing American pro-wrestlers to the country in 1995 to put on an exhibition for him.[55] Extravagant expenditures on propaganda efforts such as massive parades and performances to mark the birthdays of Kim Il Sung and Kim Jong Il took place during the famine, totaling enough to feed a large proportion of the population.

Breakdown of the Old System

One impact of the famine was that the regime's all-embracing grip over society began to loosen. With the breakdown of the PDS people had to fend for themselves, searching for food, opening up small businesses such as making bean cakes or selling items on the black market. Workers did not show up to their workplaces and managers cannibalized their own factories to sell scrap on the black market. Smuggling goods from China became an important part of the economy. Underpaid and sometimes hungry, police and border guards, and local officials who themselves were often struggling, became complicit in this effort. Rules could be circumvented through bribery. The relatively efficient totalitarian system of state control that characterized the country before the famine was weakened somewhat yet not completely undermined.

Military-First and Detente

The famine and general near economic collapse posed major challenges to the very legitimacy of the regime. Kim Jong Il responded to this in part by placing more emphasis on the military. This was first articulated in 1998 when Kim Jong Il began to espouse the "Military First" (*sŏn'gun*) policy, which made it clear that military needs would have priority. While this policy was not a break with North Korea's military-centered society, the structural change in government was new. By establishing his power base in the military and keeping his generals happy, Kim Jong Il was probably securing his own position. He appointed many military men to key positions in the state. Significantly, the 1972 constitution was amended in September 1998 to make the National Defense Commission, the highest organ of the state. Kim Jong Il was its chair.

The new military emphasis was formalized in the new constitution of 1998 – technically an amended version of the 1972 one. It was an unusual document. First, no communist state had ever made the military the highest governing organ. But then the DPRK could hardly be called a communist state by this time. Second, it essentially eliminated the position of head of state. The preamble stated that Kim Il Sung is "the founder of the Democratic People's Republic of Korea and socialist Korea." He is "the sun of the nation," "the eternal President of the Republic" and the DPRK Socialist Constitution was the Kim Il Sung Constitution.[56] By making Kim Il Sung the eternal president, it not only reinforced the continuity of the state, but it also alleviated Kim Jong Il from the ceremonial duties of being president. The latter is an interesting development. More reclusive than his father, Kim Jong Il was clearly uncomfortable with this ceremonial role, but it also reflected the fact that the regime no longer found a steady stream of Third World heads of state as important to the aggrandizement of the leader and to the legitimacy of the state and its revolution.

In the late 1990s the military and military virtues were extolled to an unprecedented extent. Propaganda promoted the notion that the nation, the people and the military were bound together as one. This militarism was, of course, linked with the cult of the Kim family. An example was the "barrel-of-the-gun philosophy" (ch'ongde ch'ŏlhak). In 1926, the story went, upon the death of his father, Kim Il Sung was given two pistols wrapped in red cloth that had belonged to him. During the Korean War, a ten-year-old Kim Jong visited his father on the battlefield where he was given one pistol in red cloth, a day that was also his grandfather's birthday. So, the "gun-barrel family" continued, always ready to defend the nation.[57] Internal politics accounted for some of the rise in the power of the military. Long and firmly in charge of most party organs Kim Jong Il was careful to cultivate support within the military. His formal ascension as party head in 1997 was accompanied by some purges and another investigation into citizens' backgrounds similar to those in the late 1950s and 1960s but on a smaller scale. Led by a team of officials from the security bureaus known as the simhwajo (deep investigation team) over the next three years 25,000 people were accused of being spies for South Korea or the USA, and then imprisoned, exiled to remote areas or executed.[58] In April, that same year, he promoted 123 of his top generals.[59]

These moves did not necessarily mean a significant shift in power among the elite since many prominent families had members in the military, the party and the bureaucracy. Thus, the military was not a separate caste but rather top officers belonged to the same elite families as key officials in the party and bureaucracy. And all generals were party members. North Korean politics was increasingly based on rival families not institutions. Just as the sŏngbun system of inherited status resembled the society of premodern dynastic Korea's society, so the domination by powerful "aristocratic" families who jostled for "court" positions and favor with the "royal" Kim family resembled its politics. Rather the military-first policy was a greater emphasis on defense as a source of legitimizing the regime, an emphasis that was a response to the country's economic failures. In the past, to use a phrase popular in modern China and Japan, as well as in Korea, the regime's goal was to create a "rich country, strong military." When growth rates, even if officially inflated, were impressive the march toward a rich and prosperous state where everyone lived and ate well seemed to be inevitable. Achieving prosperity had been a source of legitimacy. Now the regime had to rely more on its success in creating a militarily strong state.

The regime also insulated itself from the horrors of famine and the pain of economic setbacks by blaming these on foreigners who kept the country in a state of siege. The famine itself was by implication linked to the activities of foreign imperialists and their attempts to destroy the society. It was up to the military and the brilliant and dedicated leadership to keep the country independent and the Korean people from being violated by *waeguksaram* (foreigners). In fact, North Korea's famine only reinforced the country's peculiar ideological evolution away from Marxism-Leninism to a racial-nationalism, an evolution that helped to protect it from the challenges presented by the famine and from the changing international situation. Pyongyang's call for international help and the presence of international relief workers, as restricted as their movements were, were a challenge to the regime. This was met by warning the population of the dangers posed by outside powers taking advantage of the situation and by the presence of foreigners in the country. Kim Jong Il, for example, announced that the people of North Korea must "sharpen their vigilance against infiltration by all manner of anti-socialist ideas and bourgeois modes of life, reject them categorically and staunchly defend the socialist ideology and our socialist system from the abuses, slander and subversive moves of the enemies of socialism."[60]

The centrality of nationalism as the basis both for the state and for national unity was made clear in a speech in which Kim Jong Il declared that "the Korean nation is a homogeneous nation that has inherited the same blood and lived in the same territory speaking the same language for thousands of years." The people of both North and South share the "same blood and soul of the Korean nation," and are "linked inseparably with the same national interests and a common historical psychology and sentiment." Therefore, "the reunion of our nation that has been divided by foreign forces is an inevitable trend of our nation's history and the law of national development."[61] That the nation was the basic unit of society, not class, was so far removed from the basic principles of Marxism that the North Korean regime could only be called an ultra-nationalist one. More than ever, the nation was defined along ethnic-racial terms. Kim Il Sung and Kim Jong Il were viewed as the great protectors of the Korean race – a race that throughout history had been subject to invasion and violation by outsiders, such as the Japanese in colonial times and the USA in more recent years.[62] Another central aspect of this ideological stance was that the unity of the Korean race meant that the division of the country was unnatural and its reunification a necessity and inevitable once the South Koreans were free from their enslavement by the Americans.

From Crisis to Summitry

North Korea's relationship with the outside world was complicated. It needed foreign aid. Yet it needed to keep tensions fairly high to reinforce the idea that the nation was under imminent threat of invasion, protected only by its strong military and vigilant leadership. Pyongyang also sought to maintain China as an ally, having lost the support of Russia while resisting Chinese pressure for reforms. Relations with China were complex and contradictory. Beijing at times signaled its displeasure with the DPRK's lack of economic reforms, with its nuclear program and its provocative actions toward the South. Still, it chose to maintain influence in the country by supplying foreign aid and some military support. The People's Republic of China continued to supply economic aid – food, coal and oil – but Chinese aid was far smaller than that which Moscow had previously provided. Interestingly, from 1991 to 1999 there were few high-level exchanges between the two countries. This changed in 1999 when a 50-member delegation went to China. It consisted almost entirely of military men and unlike visits in the past, this group did not travel to any special economic zones. Beijing, although clearly frustrated with the DPRK, reaffirmed its commitment to the 1961 Treaty of Friendship.[63]

The greatest source of tension between North Korea and its neighbors continued to be over the problem of nuclear weapons. During Kim Il Sung's final days, war had narrowly been averted as the Clinton administration considered taking military action against North Korea. Implementation of the Agreed Framework proved difficult. In the USA, shortly after it was signed, control of the US Congress passed to the Republican

Party which was not supportive of the Framework, with some Republican leaders calling it appeasement. Consequently, the US government had difficulty funding the fuel oil shipments, which often were supplied late. Even more difficult was finding international funding for the light weight reactors, causing more delays.[64] Ground breaking for their construction took place in 1997 but construction on the first reactor did not start until 2002 and then was halted in 2003 when the USA accused the North of operating a secret uranium enrichment program. After only a modest start the project was abandoned in 2006. North Korea may have sought to lift US economic sanctions that had been in place since the Korean War. If this was the case, they were disappointed since congressional opposition in the USA made lifting economic sanctions difficult for the Clinton administration. In addition, a high level of distrust remained on both sides. The USA and the IAEA remained concerned about the plutonium that had been removed from the Yongbyon reactor, thought to be enough for two bombs. Pyongyang was not able to account for it.

Another issue was the DPRK's missile program. In May 1993 North Korea tested a Rodong-1 (or Nodong-1) missile. The Rodong-1 missile developed in the mid-1980s was a single-stage rocket fashioned from the Soviet SS-1 (popularly called "Scud") missile. With a range of about 1,000–1,300 km it was capable of reaching any target in the South and carrying a payload of up to 750 kg. Its purpose was unclear. Since it was not very accurate it would not be useful as a tactical weapon against a military target but could carry a biological, chemical or small nuclear weapon to bring terror and destruction on civilian populations. The fact that the missile was tested by firing it into the Sea of Japan (or "East Sea" as Koreans call it) in the direction of their main island of Honshu alarmed the Japanese.

North Korea test-fired seven of these missiles on July 4, 1999. The Rodong-1 was a lucrative export item – Libya, Syria, Iran and Pakistan bought them and they became the basis of Pakistan's Ghauri and Iran's Shahab-3 missiles. The DPRK was also developing a medium-range rocket, the Taepo-dong I. In August 1998 it test-fired a Taepo-dong 1 ballistic missile that flew over Japan and crashed into the Pacific Ocean 1,500 km away. US intelligence believed it was a failed attempt to launch a satellite, but the military implication was clear. Short-range missiles threatened South Korea, and this medium-range missile was capable of targeting Japan's major cities.[65] The provocative trajectory of the missile led to government and public outrage in Japan, where North Korea was perceived as its most serious security threat. Japan responded by suspending its 20 percent contribution to the cost of the Agreed Framework nuclear reactor program.

The USA's policy toward North Korea comprised two paths. The first was to negotiate a set of verifiable agreements with North Korea that it was not establishing nuclear weapons and that it would reduce or cease the production and testing of missiles. These negotiations would be carried out in consultation with Seoul and Tokyo. In return for these agreements it would offer economic aid and diplomatic recognition and possibly a peace treaty. If efforts at negotiation failed, the second path was to impose economic sanctions and diplomatic isolation which would cripple the regime and lead to its collapse. In pursuit of the first path the USA offered food aid, economic relations and full diplomatic recognition if the DPRK would agree to discontinue its development of weapons of mass destruction. Negotiations with Washington were attractive to the North Korean leadership since besides resulting in aid and the end of US-imposed economic sanctions, it could lead to its long-sought withdrawal of US troops from the South. Yet, at the same time, it could not bargain away the threat of weapons of mass destruction that gave it leverage in negotiations and symbolized its strength to its people. And peace undermined internal legitimization as a protector against the imperialists.

Meanwhile, in 1998, the new South Korean president, Kim Dae Jung, inaugurated what he called the "Sunshine Policy" toward North Korea. Kim Dae Jung had been South Korea's leading dissident politician, hated by the military rulers who governed the country before 1987. His election to the presidency in December 1997 in a close contest and his peaceful and uncontested inauguration the following year were a sign of how successful the country's democratic transition was. The new president sought to break with the decades of confrontation with the North, attempting peaceful engagement that aimed to expand trade, economic and cultural links between the two countries and to gradually coax the DPRK toward reform, thus reducing tensions and easing the transition to the day when the two Koreas could unite. This too presented a dilemma for

Pyongyang. Improved relations with the South could lead to the withdrawal of US troops but also threatened to destabilize the regime. What if people found out just how prosperous South Korea was? Or that there was no longer an enemy at the border?

North Korea met these dilemmas by pursuing two contradictory policies: engaging in negotiations with Seoul and Washington and making moves in the direction of cooperation; while also continuing bouts of confrontations, breaking off negotiations, carrying out provocations and proceeding, often covertly, with its nuclear and missile programs. North Korea continued to create tensions with the South. Its propaganda organs poured out anti-Seoul and anti-US rhetoric espousing a militant stance toward the imperialists and their South Korean puppets. In 1998 a North Korean mini-submarine that was retrieving an infiltration team got tangled in the net of a South Korean trawler; the body of an infiltrator washed up later. The most serious incident was a naval clash on June 7, 1999. The Northern Limit Line that formed the sea boundary between the two states was established in 1953 unilaterally by the USA and the ROK. For two decades it remained accepted or at least unchallenged by the DPRK, but from 1973 it became a cause of tension.[66] The North seized stray fishing craft from the South, and its own vessels sometimes deliberately sailed beyond the line. ROK naval ships would then send them back in a kind of game of chicken. Pyongyang, finding this a convenient area to stir up trouble, began claiming a new sea boundary that ran further south. On June 7, 1999 North Korean naval ships escorted a fleet of northern fishing vessels that crossed the Northern Limit Line in an especially provocative move. This led to a naval clash eight days later. One North Korean warship was destroyed and several seriously damaged in the brief but deadly naval battle off the island of Yeonpyeong (Yŏnp'yŏng).[67] To work together in responding to Pyongyang's belligerence the USA, South Korea and Japan created the Trilateral Coordination and Oversight Group in the spring of 1999.

These actions toward South Korea, its infiltration teams and its fiery rhetoric sometimes puzzled outsiders since it was obvious that Pyongyang needed South Korean aid. Incidents it created seemed self-defeating. But North Korea continued to portray itself as the true, legitimate and free representative of the Korean people who seek unification under its leadership. The people of the North were told that their southern relatives were waiting for liberation from the imperialists and their collaborators who were repressing them. Such propaganda and the need to maintain a constant state of semi-war were both needed to legitimize the regime and explain its economic hardships. At the same time it could use renewed negotiations as the price for continued aid.

South Korean president Kim Dae Jung was determined to improve relations with North Korea. In March 2000 he gave his "Berlin Declaration," in which he offered North Korea security guarantees, economic assistance and help in supporting the DPRK internationally. He then secretly arranged an aid package to encourage a summit conference. On April 10, the surprise announcement came that the leaders would meet for the first summit conference between the two Koreas. In June, Kim Dae Jung traveled to Pyongyang with an entourage of South Korean reporters and concluded a five-point agreement on peace: reunion visits for separated families; and for the expediting of economic, social and cultural exchanges. Removing an old stumbling block to negotiations, the two sides accepted that creating one system of government for all of Korea was a task for a future generation, agreeing only to work for a federation. It was, on the surface, an acceptance that the division of Korea into two very different states was a long-term reality. An exchange of family unions occurred in August and September, and the North and South Korean Olympic teams marched together at the games in Sidney in the fall of 2000. Meanwhile, Kim Dae Jung's visit was followed by visits from Russian president Vladimir Putin in July, American Secretary of State Madeleine Albright in October, and by officials from China and the EU. There was talk in the USA of a possible visit to Pyongyang by President Clinton. It appeared the North Korea was breaking out of its long isolation.

The unprecedented visit of Kim Dae Jung to the DPRK caused great excitement in South Korea. But the high expectations that followed the summit were not met. When a ground-breaking ceremony took place in September 2000 for the construction of a rail link between the two countries, no DPRK officials showed up. Nor was there a follow-up visit by Kim Jong Il to South Korea as promised. Instead the DPRK placed more missiles near the border, apparently in an attempt to extract more economic aid from South Korea.[68] Relations became more strained in late 2001. Planned family reunions did not take place and there was no significant progress in dialogue between the two Koreas. Meanwhile, the thaw in relations with the USA was short-lived. The new George W. Bush administration in 2001 took a hard line toward North Korea. Efforts to improve relations between the DPRK and Japan also ran into trouble. The Japanese prime minister, Junichiro Koizumi, made a historic visit to Pyongyang in September 2002, where the two sides signed the DPRK–Japan Pyongyang Declaration, in which North Korea accepted that Japan "keenly reflected" upon its past and "apologized from the heart" for the damage and pain inflicted by colonial rule.[69] However, in an ill-calculated gesture of goodwill, Kim Jong Il admitted that the DPRK had kidnapped 13 Japanese citizens; eight had died and the remaining five could return to Japan. This admission that North Korean agents had come to Japan and abducted its citizens confirmed long-held suspicions by the Japanese public who reacted with anger at the revelations. Then the DPRK only further outraged them by its reluctance to repatriate the remains or allow children of abductees to visit Japan. As a result, Tokyo found it publicly difficult to provide any significant aid concessions.

Deteriorating relations with the USA turned to a new crisis. In November 2001, however, American analysts completed a report asserting that North Korea had begun construction of an enriched uranium plant. In October 2002, US envoy James Kelly, on a visit to the DPRK, presented the North Korean authorities with evidence that American intelligence had found of a highly enriched uranium program. When the North Koreans appeared to have admitted (accounts of this are confusing) that they had been secretly working on what was a second path to developing nuclear materials, the USA reacted strongly and suspended the Agreed Framework. Pyongyang then decided to up the tensions. It announced that it would lift its freeze on nuclear facilities in Yongbyon and told IAEA inspectors to leave by the end of the year. Even more provocatively, on January 10, 2003, Pyongyang declared it was withdrawing from the Non-Proliferation Treaty on the Non-Proliferation of Nuclear Weapons, the second time since 1993. Perhaps nervous after the US invasion of Iraq in March 2003 that removed the regime there, North Korea attempted to use the crisis as an opportunity to establish bilateral talks with the USA. Pyongyang then offered to eliminate its nuclear program in exchange for economic assistance, security guarantees and diplomatic normalization. Although the USA refused to meet in bilateral talks, seeing this as a reward for bad behavior, it did engage in a series of six-nation talks starting in August 2003. These also involved China, South Korea, Russia and Japan. All of North Korea's neighbors sought to cool the crisis. Over the next several years there were several rounds of six-party talks, but little progress was made. North Korea sought diplomatic recognition from the USA and an agreement not to use military force against it, while the Americans insisted on nuclear dismantlement first before any agreements were made. Meanwhile, the US Congress passed the North Korean Human Rights Act of 2004, committing the USA to aid and protect North Korean refugees.

It seems that North Korea may have miscalculated the reactions to some of its moves. In particular, it probably genuinely sought economic aid and support from Japan as it started carrying out its own economic reforms in 2002 only to fail to anticipate the public outrage in Japan over its admission to kidnappings. And it may have antagonized the USA more than it had intended with its admission of a uranium enrichment program. It did not abandon attempts to gain aid from its neighbors and continued to work with Seoul during the Kim Dae Jung administration and that of his successor, Roh Moo-hyun, who came to into office in 2003.

Tinkering with the System, Adjusting to New Realities

The 1990s was a near catastrophic decade economically. The Bank of Korea, estimates that the GDP from 1990 to 1998 fell by 40 percent.[70] In the wake of the economic crisis, major changes took place in North Korean society. Famine conditions in the mid and late 1990s resulted in a breakdown of the carefully controlled PDS by which food and goods of various sorts were allocated. People were forced to look for food where they could find it. Small private plots appeared and informal markets for agricultural products emerged. Even efforts to control the movement of people became more ineffective as individuals wandered to wherever they could find food or work. Thousands crossed into China illegally, where they took whatever work they could find and smuggled money and goods back into North Korea. Many of these refugees lived under appalling conditions in China, but they often managed to earn money to bring back with them when they returned home. This contributed to a flourishing black market in food and smuggled goods. Authorities tended to ignore these developments. Still, those who crossed into China were subjected to extortion, intimidation and arrest.

It seemed imperative that North Korea reform its failing economy. But the regime showed little sign of doing so during and immediately after famine. To the contrary it publicly reaffirmed its "style of socialism." In September 17, 1998 the two principle papers the *Rodong sinmun* and *Kŭlloja* in a joint editorial, "Let US Adhere to the Line of Building an Independent National Economy," called for the repudiation of reform and labeled the opening of the country the "honeyed poison of imperialists."[71] Another editorial warned the people that the "corrupt ideas" the imperialists were spreading were more dangerous than atomic bombs to the cause of building a socialist society.[72] Rather, the government's response to economic decline was to launch in 1999 what it called a "new" or "renewed" Ch'ŏllima movement. This began at the Sŏngjin Steel Company where a "Sŏngjin torch" was passed on.[73] Mass mobilizations to concentrate as much labor as possible on needed projects along with the usual speed battles were carried out as if little had changed – as if the PDS had not broken down, the factories had not ceased functioning and much of the population was not out foraging for food.

Yet there were always some signs that the door to reform was being left open. In 2001 Kim Jong Il went to China where he visited the bustling commercial city of Shanghai and its international commercial hub Pudong. There he remarked on the "unbelievable change" it had undergone since his last visit in 1983. He made visits to Shanghai Stock Exchange, clearly interested in the financial aspects of China's economic reforms. Soon after, a North Korean economic delegation toured Malaysia where they visited a Samsung Electronics Industrial Complex. Another economic delegation led by Vice Foreign Minister Kim Kyekwan visited several US cities to study banking and finance. In July Kim Jong Il went on a 24-day state visit to Russia. Considerable attention was drawn to the luxurious special train he took and the elaborate security precautions carried out much to the inconvenience of Muscovites. But more significant was the interest he showed in Russia's economic transformation. In October 2001 Kim Jong Il issued new instructions, calling for a thorough review of economic policies and the pursual of "*silli*" (practical benefits) while adhering to the principles of socialism. Prime Minister Hong Song-nam made reference to "dramatic measures" in a March 2002 speech.[74]

Then, on July 2002, the DPRK announced a series of radical economic reforms. These "7.1 measures," as they were called, consisted of several different sets of new policies. First, consumer prices were raised dramatically; citizens were billed for items such as housing, food and fuel that had previously been provided by the state at virtually no cost. The purpose was to bring the artificially low prices in line with real market values. Wages increased 20 times to compensate for these changes. Second were increases in the power and independence of managers of enterprises to purchase materials, market products and institute worker incentives such as bonuses to improve performance. Third, they permitted "general markets" (*chonghap sichang*) where all sorts of items including industrial products could be sold. This was only acknowledging reality, since the markets were widespread by this time. The reforms placed North Korea on a more money-based economy and introduced economic incentives and accountability for managers. The price reforms of 2002 were designed to end the distortion in the relative prices of goods, to eliminate the gap between state and market prices so that farmers would sell their products to the state instead of only in private markets, and to encourage the production of goods that could be sold abroad for hard currency. They may also have been intended to alleviate the drain on state finances caused by heavy subsidies on certain staples such as rice. The reforms had another benefit for the state – they enabled it to gain some control over the growing black market and to tax it. Thus, the measures served both to make the economy more flexible and to be able to gain greater state control over what was an increasingly market-driven economy. Although by North Korean standards these new policies were a bold measure, the regime was careful not to label them reforms – "Improved Economic Management Measures" became the favored term.

It appeared that the types of economic reforms that were introduced in China over the span of a decade were implemented in North Korea all at once. Because their introduction was so sudden they created many problems. The price reforms resulted in severe inflation. Wages could not keep up with items such as rice which increased 50 times over the next year. Hyperinflation became a problem until 2005 when prices began to stabilize. The clumsy nature of these reforms can be contrasted with some analogous measures carried out in China in 1979 which drove up the price of rice by a mere 25 percent.[75] Yet the North Korean state seemed in its awkward way to be adjusting to the reality of an economy that was increasingly characterized by markets and on-the-spot decision making by desperate or corrupt local actors. This move toward a more flexible, partially money-based market economy was accompanied by the emergence of a new generation, in their forties and fifties, into administrative positions. Most prominent was Pak Pong-ju (1939–), a former minister from the chemical industry, who replaced the older and less economically experienced Hong Song Nam (1929–2009) as premier. A mini consumer boom appeared, at least in Pyongyang, where the ownership of bicycles and electronics increased. A few privately owned automobiles were sold, although traffic in the capital was still extremely light. And the food situation improved somewhat, as the economy experienced modest growth.

The DPRK also generated two new sources of foreign currency, both suggesting an opening up of society toward a market economy. One was the inauguration of a tourist resort in the Kŭmgang (Diamond) Mountain area near the west coast. The resort, which was constructed and operated by Hyundai, proved popular with South Koreans and became a significant source of revenue for the DPRK. Tourists, however, had to cross the border in groups and stay within carefully fenced areas. The Diamond Mountains were long famed for their beauty, and the subject of numerous paintings and poems. But if South Koreans were able to finally visit them, they saw nothing else of the country, nor did they have any interaction with North Koreans. A second even more radical development was the creation of the Kaesŏng Industrial Complex just north of the DMZ. Established in 2004 several South Korean companies were to open plants, promising thousands of jobs for North Koreans. Troubles with the North Korean government and a lack of profitability raised doubts over the long-term prospects for the industrial zone. Still, this was all part of change that would be difficult to have conceived of a decade earlier. In 2005, 1,000 South Koreans crossed the border a day, and 3,000 were working in the North. By 2009, 40,000 North Koreans at Kaesŏng were working for about 100 South Korean companies. Direct flights from Seoul to Pyongyang were inaugurated by the DPRK's state airline, Air Koryo. Trade with the South increased, growing six-fold from 2000 to 2005.

The reforms did not generate as much revenue for the state as hoped. In response the state issued People's Life Bonds in March 2003. They carried no interest and could only be redeemed in installments. Lucky numbers on the bonds were periodically announced for cash prizes. So they functioned more as lottery tickets. People were urged to buy them as their patriotic duty.[76] These strange bonds, which fell short of expectations in generating revenue, illustrate how measures taken were often designed to sidestep real market reforms and resort to gimmicks to raise revenues. Other measures were clumsily executed. In 2002 the Supreme People's Assembly approved a Special Economic Zone at Sinuiju (Sinŭiju) next to the Manchurian border. Beijing, which was apparently not consulted, did not want a Special Economic Zone draining away investment from an area near its border. Premier Zhu Rongji suggested another site would be more appropriate. Then Chinese authorities arrested Yang Bin, the Chinese-Dutch businessman that the North Koreans had put in charge of the plan, on charges of corruption.

To sum up, North Korea's reforms, while significant, were often poorly conceived, inconsistently implemented and avoided fundamental changes to its economic system. They were at best attempts to adjust to the new economic realities of the country where factories were shuttered, food rations were not being distributed to workers and thousands of families were engaging in sideline activities to survive. Nonetheless, there was some real if modest economic growth in the early 2000s. By 2005 the DPRK was asking the World Food Program to switch from relief assistance to development aid. However, North Korea was still dependent on food aid as it still made up a substantial portion of its basic needs. And while improving, overall economic output and living standards were well below what that they had been 20 years earlier.

The Impact of the Famine: Breakdown of the Old System and the Marketization of North Korean Society

The famine was a turning point for North Korea. The near total command economy that provided for its citizens' every need and enmeshed them in a system of surveillance and control broke down. In its place was a harder to characterize society which combined the institutions and rhetoric of the old system with a more chaotic, improvised system of getting by through any means. The famine had caused the state's strict control over society to loosen somewhat. People forced to fend for themselves became less dependent on the state for their basic needs. In a 2004–2005 survey of North Korean refugees 700, accounting for 78 percent of the total, reported to have worked in the informal economy, including 74 percent of those with jobs in the official economy.[77] They reported that earnings from the informal economy accounted for three-quarters of their total income during 1998–2003. All communist countries had some form of informal economy but this was extraordinarily high. While these refugees may have been more engaged in the private economy than most of their fellow citizens, all evidence suggests that most people were dependent on this informal economy for survival. A few grew rich on it. These included people with access to trucks, officials able to accept bribes and with connections that helped them play the markets, and state enterprise managers who sold items through the "back door." Most government workers reported that market activities were conducted by their units.[78] Some officials were able to accumulate large fortunes, at least large by North Korean standards.

In their study of refugees Marcus Noland and Stephen Haggard found that the reforms led to significant social changes: increasing inequality, greater corruption and changed attitudes about the most effective pathways to higher social status and income.[79] The state lost some control over assigning social status and privilege. North Korea's strictly hierarchical society based on background and kinship was challenged, at least to some degree. While the highest status was still determined by proximity to Kim Jong Il, his family and close associates, and the power, wealth and privilege of the elite remained unchallenged, lower down the social scale the new markets brought changes. People at the margins of society, such as Japanese-Koreans with relatives in Japan, those with relatives in China, and the tiny local ethnic Chinese community, were all able to prosper relative to the general public. Women working in the market often made far more than their husbands at the factory or office. Especially entrepreneurial and lucky individuals sometimes did well financially despite having undesirable family backgrounds. This was even reflected in literature which was ambivalent about family background, emphasizing instead the racial-ethnic unity of the Korean people.[80] The *sŏngbun* that articulated everyone's status did not disappear but it was less all-determining of one's position than in the past.

Controls on movement within the country were less enforced. People often took to the road in search of food and work. Government and military trucks supplemented the decrepit and often non-functioning rail network as a means of travel, with passengers paying for rides. Border guards along the Chinese frontier would often look the other way in exchange for food or money as thousands slipped into Manchuria to look for work. Workers abandoned their factory sites since they were no longer receiving substantial or any wages at all, sometimes hitting the road and joining roaming groups in search of employment. Widespread corruption meant that many formerly strictly enforced regulations could be circumvented. Many other controls loosened. The *inminban* system of neighborhood surveillance became less effective. In 2002 even the self-criticism sessions were reduced in frequency.[81]

The country was no longer hermetically sealed from the outside world, although the population of the DPRK was still the most isolated of any modern country. Old VCRs started to enter the market from China. At US$50–60, a large sum for most people yet within the price range of many, they sold well. Along with these came a lively market in pirated South Korean videos. These must have been a revelation for most North Koreans. The slickly produced TV soaps from Seoul presented dramas about Koreans like themselves with family relations and personal problems they could identify with yet who were living in a modern, prosperous society with beautiful people. While watching them was risky, many took their chances and they were extremely popular. A few North Korean students began to dye their hair in South Korean fashion.

Still, for all the disruptions the famine caused, the North Korean system did not break down completely. The state still maintained a degree of totalitarian control greater than perhaps any other contemporary society. By 2005, against the predictions of many foreign observers, the state had survived intact without undergoing any radical transformations. Yet North Korea seemed to be changing in ways that might undermine the state's ability to determine the direction of internal developments. There was abundant evidence to suggest that it might be set to evolve into a more open society with a mixed economic system such as that found in China and Vietnam. This, however, was not to be the case.

Notes

1   By "industrial nation" it is meant a state with a high level of industrial development where the majority of the population is urban dwelling.

2   Kim Hakjoon, 2015, pp. 123–124.

3   The story is told in Paul Fischer, *A Kim Jong-Il Production*. New York: Thorndike Press, 2015.

4   Kim Hakjoon, 2015, pp. 118–119.

5   Lim, 2009, p. 196.

6   Cormac Ó Gráda, *Famine: A Short history*. Princeton, NJ: Princeton University Press, 2009, p. 257.

7   Daniel Goodkind, Daniel and Lorraine West, "The North Korean Famine and Its Demographic Impact," *Population and Development Review* 27, no. 2 (2001): 219–238; Marcus Noland, "North Korea as a "New Famine," in Stephen Deveraux (ed.), *The New Famines: Why Famines Persist in an Era of Globalization*. London: Routledge, 2007, pp. 197–221.

8   Daniel Goodkind, Loraine West and Peter Johnson, "A Reassessment of Mortality in North Korea, 1993–2008," Paper Annual Meeting of the Population Assn of America, March 31–April 2, 2011 Washington, DC.

9   Stephen Haggard and Marcus Noland, *Famine in North Korea: Markets, Aid and Reform*. New York: Columbia University Press, 2007, p. 73.

10   Haggard and Noland, 2007, p. 11.

11 See Gordon L. Flake and Scott Snyder (eds), *Paved with Good Intentions: The NGO Experience in North Korea*. Westport, CT: Praeger, 2004; Andrew S. Natsios, *The Great North Korean Famine*. Washington, DC: United States Institute of Peace Press, 2001; Cormac Ó Gráda, *Famine: A Short history.* Princeton, NJ: Princeton University Press, 2009.

12 Yim Sang-chŏl, *Pukhan nongŏp [North Korean Agriculture]*. Seoul: Tosŏ Ch'ulp'an Sŏil, 2000, p. 122.

13 Joo Hyung-Min, "Visualizing the Invisible Hands: The Shadow Economy in North Korea," *Economy and Society* 39, no. 1 (2010): 110–145.

14 Lankov, 2013, pp. 36–37.

15 Noland Marcus and Stephan Haggard, *Witness to Transformation: Refugee Insights into North Korea*. Washington, DC: Peterson Institute for International Economics, January 10, 2011, p. 48.

16 Yim Sang-chŏl, pp. 108, 120; Mun Woong Lee, p. 37.

17 Mun Woong Lee, p. 37.

18 Mun Woong Lee, pp. 45–46.

19 Noland, 2007, p. 200.

20 Natsios, p. 14.

21 Haggard and Nolan, 2007, pp. 31–32.

22 "Every Tree in this Green Land Carries His Love," *Korea Today* 223 (March 1975): 35.

23 Natsios, *The Great North Korean Famine*, p. 12.

24 Donald Oberdorfer, *The Two Koreas: A Contemporary History*. New York: Basic Books, 1998, p. 356.

25 Mun Woong Lee, p. 61.

26 Han S. Park, *North Korea: The Politics of Unconventional Wisdom*. Boulder, CO: Lynne Rienner, 2002, p. 93.

27 Chong-Ae Yu, "The Rise and Demise of Juche Agriculture in North Korea," 119–144 in Suh, Jae-Jung (ed.). *Origins of North Korea's Juche*. Latham, MD: Lexington Books, 2012.

28 Lim, 2009, p. 108.

29 Baik Bong, *Kim Il Sung Biography* (II). Tokyo: Miraisha, 1970, p. 97.

30 Ralph Hassig and Kongdan Oh, *The Hidden People of North Korea: Everyday Life in the Hermit Kingdom*. Latham, MD: Rowman & Littlefield, 2009, p. 113.

31 Hassig and Oh, 2009, p. 113.

32 Yim, p. 37; Hassig and Oh, 2009, pp. 112–114; Andrei Lankov, *North of the DMZ: Essays on Daily Life in North Korea*. Jefferson, NC: McFarland & Company, 2007, pp. 227–229; Kwon, pp. 83–85.

33 Lee Suk, p. 6.

34 Yim, p. 37.

35 Ralph Hassig and Kongdan Oh, *North Korea: Through the Looking Glass*. Washington, DC: Brookings Institution Press, 2000, p. 52.

36 Haggard and Noland, 2007, p. 48.

37 Lee Suk, p. 8.

38 Human Rights Watch, *North Korea: A Matter of Survival: The North Korean Government's Control of Food and the Risk of Hunger* 18, no. 3 (c) (May 2006): 8.

39 Heonik Kwon and Byung-ho Chung, *North Korea: Beyond Charismatic Politics*. Lanham, MD: Rowman & Littlefield, 2012, p. 168.

40 Pak, Sunyoung, Daniel Schwedendiek and Hee Kyoung Kim, "Height and Living Standards in North Korea, 1930s–1980s," *The Economic History Review* 64, no. 1 (2011): 142–158.

41 Kim Il-pyong, p. 90.

42 Haggard and Noland, 2007, p. 128.

43 Haggard and Noland, 2007, p. 93.

44 Haggard and Noland, 2007, pp. 87–88.

45 Bradley Martin, *Under the Loving Care of the Fatherly Leader*. New York: St Marin's Press, p. 622.

46 Kang Hyok, with Philippe Grangereau and Shaun Whiteside (translator), *This Is Paradise! My North Korean Childhood*. London: Little, Brown, 2007, pp. 121–125. See also Kang Chol-hwan and Pierre Rigoulot, *The Aquariums of Pyongyang*. New York: Basic Books, 2001, p. 173.

47 Barbara Demick, *Nothing to Envy: Ordinary Lives in North Korea*. Spiegel & Grau, 2009.

48 Natsios, p. 29.

49 Hassig and Oh, 2009, p. 118.

50 Haggard and Noland, 2007, p. 208.

51 Ó Gráda, pp. 257–258.

52 Haggard and Noland, 2007, p. 84.

53 Ó Gráda provides a good summary of modern famines. See also Frank Dikötter, *Mao's Great Famine: The History of China's Most Devastating Catastrophe, 1958–1962*. New York: Walker and Company, 2010; Robert Conquest, *Harvest of Sorrow: The Soviet Collectivization and the Terror-Famine*. New York: Oxford University Press, 1987.

54 Lim, 2009, p. 108.

55 Cha, p. 81.

56 Samuel S. Kim, "North Korea in 1999: Bringing the Grand Chollima March Back In," *Asian Survey* 40, no. 1 (January/February 2000): 151–163.

57 Kwon and Chung, pp. 83–85.

58 Kim Hakjoon, 2015, pp. 125–127.

59 Lim, 2009, p. 152.

60 Satterwhite, David H, "North Korea in 1996: Belligerence Subsiding, Hunger Worsens," *Asian Survey* 37, no. 1 (January 1997): 10–15.

61 Gi-Wook Shin, *Ethnic Nationalism in Korea: Genealogy, Politics, and Legacy.* Stanford, CA: Stanford University Press, 2006, p. 93.

62 This follows the interpretation given in Brian Myers, *The Cleanest Race: How North Koreans See Themselves-And Why It Matters.* Brooklyn, NY: Melville House, 2010.

63 Samuel S. Kim, "North Korea in 1999."

64 Yoshinori Takeda, "KEDO Adrift," Georgetown *Journal of International Affairs* 6, no. 2 (2005): 123–131.

65 NTI "North Korean's Missile Capacity," Nuclear Threat Initiative, May 1, 2010, http://www.nti.org/analysis/articles/north-korea-missile-capabilities/. Accessed June 2013.

66 Roehig, Terrence, "North Korea and the Northern Limit Line," *North Korea Review* 5, no. 1 (Fall 2009): 8–22.

67 Samuel S. Kim, "North Korea in 1999."

68 Samuel S. Kim, "North Korea in 2000: Surviving through High Hopes of Summit Diplomacy," *Asia Survey* 41, no. 1 (January/February 2001): 12–29.

69 Yinchay Ahn, "North Korea in 2002: A Survival Game," *Asia Survey* 43, no. 1 (January/February 2003): 49–63, 55.

70 Bank of Korea, *GDP of North Korea in 2002.* Seoul: Bank of Korea, 2002. http://www.nkeconwatch.com/nk-uploads/DPRK-GDP-2002.pdf. Accessed April 12, 2016.

71 David G. Brown, "North Korea in 1998: A year of Foreboding Developments," *Asian Survey* 39, no. 1 (January/February 1999): 125–132.

72 Koh, Dae-Won, "Dynamics of Inter-Korean Conflict and North Korea's Recent Policy Changes" An Inter-Systemic View," *Asian Survey* 44, no. 3 (May/June 2004): 422–441.

73 Young Chul Chung, "North Korean Reform and Opening: Dual Strategy and 'Silli' (Practical) Reform," *Pacific Affairs* 77, no. 2 (2004): 283–305.

74 Lim, 2009, pp. 123–124; Ken E. Gause, *North Korea Under Kim Jong-il: Power, Politics and Prospects for Change.* Westport, CT: Praeger, 2011, pp. 44, 47.

75 Cha, p. 144.

76 Marcus Noland, "Life in North Korea" June 5, 2003 Peter Institute for International Economics, https://piie.com/commentary/testimonies/life-north-korea

77 Kim Byung-Yeon and Song Dongho, "The Participation of North Korean checks in the Informal Economy: Size, Determinants and Effect," *Seoul Journal of Economics* 21, no. 2 (2008): 373.

78 See *Daily NK* dailynk.com for many reports on this.

79 Haggard and Noland, 2011, p. 79.

80 Martin Petersen, "The Downfall of a Model Citizen?: Family Background in North Korean Graphic Novels," *Korean Studies* 36 (2012): 83–122.

81 Daniel Tudor & James Pearson, *North Korea Confidential: Private Markets, Fashion Trends, Prison Camps, Dissenters and Defectors*. Tokyo: Tuttle, 2015, p. 223.

7

Failed Revolution, Enduring State
2005–2016

The DPRK regime survived famine and the death of Kim Jong Il in 2011 to continue into a third generation. It proved to be more enduring than many observers had expected. By a mix of pragmatism, oppression and relentless indoctrination of the general populace, the state and the elite families who dominated it maintained their grip on power. Yet, while North Korea was not a failed state, it presided over a failed revolution. The goal of the North Korean revolution to create a strong, prosperous state was pathetically unfulfilled, and its plan to reunify the country under its leadership abandoned. The regime's main objective was to hang on to power. For most non-elite North Koreans, their goal was to somehow get by; for a few, it was to get out.

Retreat from Reform

By 2005 North Korea had seemed to have survived the worst of the famine conditions. The government had carried out a few modest reforms, a partially market-based economy was emerging, and relations with the South, while still often tense, were improving. The first steps toward investment and tourism from the ROK led to the hope by Seoul and its allies that the North's economy would gradually be internationalized, modernized and at least partially integrated into the South's. The rigid, state-defined social order was cracking as was the information cordon that kept the population isolated. The long-term viability of the regime was still in doubt, but it appeared that in the near future it might follow the reformist path of its Asian communist neighbors. North Korea, however, did not pursue a path to economic or political reform. Rather with economic conditions easing somewhat, the regime began to curb private markets, reimpose some of the previous controls over society, ramp up tensions with the South as well as with the USA and Japan, and reaffirm the basic principles of its unique path to socialism. Indeed, the moderate reforms and concessions to private markets seemed to have been a tactical retreat; once the regime became more confident that it would weather the economic crisis it began to reimpose greater state control over the economy. However, North Korean society had changed and the pre-famine economic and social order could not be restored.

Curbing Private Markets

The first major step in the retreat from reform took place in the summer of 2005 when the old ban on the sale of grain in private markets was reimposed. First enacted in the 1950s the ban had ceased to be enforced with the famine. In October 2005, during the 60th anniversary of the founding of the Korean Workers' Party (KWP) the state announced it was reintroducing the public distribution system (PDS), supplying 15-day rations of basic food items twice a month.[1] In December 2006 men of working age were prohibited from trading in the markets. One year later, in December 2007, all women under 50 were also banned from trading. Thus, market activity was restricted to older women; all others were supposed to be at their assigned work units. Other restrictions limited the type and amount of items that could be sold. Bans were issued on the use of trucks for private trade. In January 2008 private markets were limited to operating just three days a month, once every ten days, and could not include industrial goods.[2] Regular inspections of *changmadang* (general markets) began that year.[3] To crack down on the markets and on corruption the government created Anti-Socialist Patrols. It tightened controls along the Chinese border in an effort not only to curb illegal crossings but to crack down on official corruption and bribery that made these crossings relatively easy. Officials carried out public executions of illegal cross-border traders. In 2008 there were 15 reported such executions.[4]

However, limiting the markets was difficult. This was because of widespread government corruption. Members of the elite, the military and the police were increasingly involved in black marketing and smuggling activities or taking bribes from those who were. Informal transportation systems, using military or civilian government vehicles or the railway, distributed food and black market goods. Even at the highest ranks there was involvement in these illegal activities. The market had become so lucrative for the country's elite that it was difficult for the state to control it. Furthermore, the reintroduction of the PDS was slow-going and it never was able to provide full rations; and there were reports of the PDS breaking down completely in places. As long as the state was unable to provide the basic nutritional needs of the people, individuals and families had to resort to the markets. Estimates in 2011 were that 40 percent of households were receiving almost all of their food from private markets and 95 percent at least some.[5] Another estimate at the time was that two-thirds of all households were receiving half or more of their income from private activities.[6]

One of the most extreme and disastrous efforts to control market forces was the December 2009 currency reform. Many North Koreans had begun saving cash. The supply of this cash, like the markets, limited the state's control over the economy. On November 30, 2009 the government suddenly announced new currency notes. The old notes were devalued by 99 percent. People were allowed to exchange only $40 of old notes for the new; the rest became worthless. By this measure the state was attempting to wipe out capital accumulation. A month later the authorities also banned the possession of foreign currencies. Suddenly people's savings vanished. The reaction was panic buying; wild inflation, with the price of staple foods soaring; and, most unusual, public displays of anger. Items of all kinds disappeared from shops and even the hard currency shops visited by the elite were closed. The government responded by raising the limit on money that could be converted. In an unprecedented move Pak Nam-ki, the 76-year-old official reportedly behind the policy, and Prime Minister Kim Yong-il made a public apology in

February 2010. Pak was forced to resign and according to some reports was charged with being a life-long American spy and executed.[7]

Reimposing Controls

The government began to enforce many of the controls over movement that had broken down during the famine. Other crackdowns were directed at illegal South Korean videos. Restrictions were placed on the ability of workers to leave failing state-owned enterprises to seek work elsewhere. Workers were forced to report at their jobs even if there was little work to do. Especially tragic were the plights of North Korean refugees. The border between North Korea and China was never hermetically sealed. During Mao Zedong's disastrous Great Leap Forward, which resulted in mass hunger in China, some ethnically Korean residents in Manchuria crossed into North Korea in search of food. With the famine in the late 1990s, thousands of North Koreans began crossing into China, walking across the frozen Tumen and Yalu rivers, bribing border guards and risking arrest to look for food and work in China. Many returned or made multiple trips, so the population was not stable, but at any one time there were as many as 200,000 North Koreans living in China, mostly near the border. With the greater enforcement of border controls, they faced arrest when returning; many were sent to prison camps. The remainder became caught in an uncertain limbo, fearing punishment if they returned but living miserable and dangerous lives as illegal aliens in China. Many of the women entering China became victims of human traffickers, working in brothels or becoming unwilling brides of Chinese men suffering from a shortage of women. Beijing refused to acknowledge them as political refugees or grant them asylum. China also denied NGOs seeking to offer assistance access to the North Korean community.

North Korea took steps to limit the information from the outside world. This was sometimes difficult with the influx of pirated South Korean videos, the importation of televisions and radios that could pick up foreign broadcasts, and as cell phones became available and those living near the Chinese border were able to make calls and gather information from outside the country. To deal with this potential threat to the regime, Kim Jong Il ordered stepped-up inspections to catch people with illegal videos. He created a special "Bureau 27" to control computers. In early 2011 he ordered an inventory of all the nation's computers, cell phones, flash drives and MP3 players, and created mobile riot squads. Security was tightened at the universities to prevent subversive ideas from entering.[8] South Korean-style haircuts were prohibited and it became more dangerous to play South Korean songs or watch DVDs; this may have hindered people but it did not stop them from continuing to do so.[9] Public executions increased in 2007, after becoming less common since 2000. According to unconfirmed accounts from defectors, entire stadiums were filled with spectators required to watch them. Meanwhile, there was no letup in political indoctrination. In 2007 the state launched a "Portrait Project," a campaign for citizens to clean the portraits of Kim Il Sung and Kim Jong Il. Those found with "illegal" frames in their homes and workplaces, bought on the private market, had to replace them.[10]

Knowledge of the outside world by a people who were told they were the envy of their southern cousins, however, continued to seep in via those who had traveled to China, through pirated videos, through South Korean stations that could be heard on imported radios being smuggled into the country and through cell phones. This along with the pervasive corruption by civilian and military authorities threatened to undermine whatever public support there was for the regime. It is difficult to determine how much skepticism or even hostility there was among the general population. Existence of widespread public cynicism was suggested by a series of interviews of refugees in China published in early 2008. The interviewers found that most of the refugees believed that officials regularly stole or otherwise denied food aid to those in need.[11] However, these refugees coming predominately from the northern borders areas may not have been fully representative of the general population. They were, of course, the people who took risks to leave, so it was not easy to gauge just how much cynicism, disillusionment or even latent hostility to the regime existed.

In the face of a struggling economy the DPRK government relied on such traditional but now pathetically inadequate measures such as a mass mobilization campaign to collect human feces from public and private toilets in order to mix it with ash to make fertilizer. Food rations were reduced even in the armed forces, where rank-and-file soldiers were restricted to two meals a day.[12] North Korea continued to blame the international situation on food shortages. The Great Leader was officially reported as duly concerned about the suffering this caused. Despite his portly frame he was presented in the media as skimping on meals as he traveled about the country giving on-the-spot guidance and commiserating with his people. Kim Jong Il, the *Rodong sinmun* reported on February 1, 2010, "My heart bleeds for our people who are still eating corn. Now what I have to do is feed our great people as much white rice, bread and noodles as they want." It assured its readers that Kim Jong Il planned to "implement definitively [Kim Il Sung]'s last testament ... so that the people can live a contented life as soon as possible."[13]

The Foreign Policy of Survival

Pyongyang's foreign policy reflect the changed situation from the 1990s. The regime was realistic enough to understand that reunification under its leadership was no longer possible. Its efforts focused on survival. This required some foreign exchange to keep its economy functioning, and to provide luxury goods for the elite to keep them loyal and contented, and imports of materials and equipment needed for the military. But foreign currency continued to be a problem. In the 2000s the activities of Room 39, the organization set up by Kim Jong Il in the 1970s as a means to earn foreign exchange, were a target of international efforts. Few things illustrate North Korea's lack of commitment to reform or adherence to international norms of behavior than this shadowy branch of government. It was a key part of the "court economy" that provided the foreign exchange to support Kim Jong Il, his family and his core supporters. Room 39, with its alleged headquarters at a KWP office near one of his villas, was believed to be overseeing the running of restaurants in foreign countries and conducting a variety of illegality activities, including the production and sale of heroin, crystal methamphetamine and knockoff premium brands of cigarettes; and the notorious counterfeiting of high-quality US$100 dollar bills called "superbills."[14] The USA and other countries took measures such as closing down the Banco Delta Asia bank in Macau, which was involved in money laundering for North Korea. But new schemes emerged. One was insurance fraud in which the government's Korean National Insurance Corporation would seek reinsurance from major Western firms such as Lloyds of London and then issue false claims. Since restrictions on entry into the country made it impossible to verify these claims the companies paid up. Gradually realizing they were involved in state-sponsored fraud major reinsurers began to sue in court and refused to take on new policies but only after admitting to losses totaling hundreds of millions of dollars.

The regime earned some foreign exchange from sending an estimated 20,000 workers to Russian timber camps on three-year contracts. This was the result of a 1967 agreement in which the profits were split with Russia. Working conditions were so harsh in the heavily guarded camps that they drew the attention of Russian human rights groups in the 1990s. In 1995 an agreement opened the camps to inspection but little changed. Perhaps another 25,000 worked in the Gulf states, Mongolia and Africa. Most lived and worked under extremely harsh conditions.[15] In addition, thousands of North Koreans labored in factories in the Dandong area of China just across the Yalu River, and 40,000 worked for South Korean firms at Kaesŏng.

Its efforts at survival included receiving as much aid from South Korea and the USA as possible. This meant making tactful gestures at reconciliation or at what appeared to be concessions in its weapons development program in exchange for aid. At the same time, Pyongyang needed to maintain tensions with the ROK and the USA, as this justified the existence of the regime as the protector of the North Korean people while providing an explanation and purpose for their hardships. The state needed to maintain a constant atmosphere of imminent war with imperialist forces – primarily the USA and its southern collaborators – that would crush the independence and violate the purity of the Korean people. Military strength was also a source of pride for a revolutionary regime that had so far failed in its goals to create a prosperous, unified state. At the same time, Pyongyang needed the support of China without getting so close that it would threaten its sovereignty. This then was the basis for its foreign policy. While it seemed at times irrational and erratic it was rational and consistent within its own logic of survival even if crudely and often clumsily executed.

A central element in that survival strategy was developing nuclear weapons and a delivery system including a missile with the capability to reach the USA. This was not only for domestic reasons but also as a means of protecting itself. The US invasion of Iraq in 2003 only reinforced the need to develop these. Evidence suggests that, despite some agreements to the contrary, the country worked continuously on its nuclear and missile projects. It test-fired a series of missiles, including on July 4, 2006, but its attempt to launch a long-range missile was unsuccessful. Later that year, on October 9, it detonated a nuclear weapon. This was a rather modest-sized detonation, suggesting that the weapon may have misfired. Nonetheless, it had the intended effect of making the country a nuclear power. The nuclear test was in violation of its 1991 agreement with South Korea, and outraged China and much of international society who had a hard time accepting that an impoverished state that was unable to feed its own people could devote scarce resources for this purpose. However, it was promoted as a great source of pride at home and increased Pyongyang's leverage in talks, as well as drawing US attention to the need to negotiate with the DPRK. When the six-party talks resumed in 2007, the USA showed more willingness to meet bilaterally with North Korean officials. Pyongyang's nuclear test had achieved its intended outcome.

Not long after becoming a nuclear power North Korea shifted to a more conciliatory tack, agreeing in February 2007 to shut down the nuclear reactor at Yongbyon and to permit IAEA inspectors to return. Pyongyang also agreed to "disable" all nuclear facilities and give a full accounting of all their nuclear programs. In exchange Washington agreed to return frozen assets held by the Banco Delta Asia in Macao, to supply heavy fuel oil and to move toward normalization. Another bargaining chip North Korea had was the fear by the USA and other nations that it would sell its nuclear technology abroad. That this was a real possibility was confirmed by a nuclear facility the North Koreans were helping Syria to construct until it was destroyed by an Israeli air strike in September 2007. North Korea soon after this, in the fall of 2007, promised not to transfer nuclear materials, weapons or weapons-making knowledge; in turn, the USA hinted at taking the country off the state sponsors of terrorism list. While Pyongyang allowed IAEA inspectors to return, and in 2008 the main nuclear cooling tower at Yongbyon was destroyed, it continued to clandestinely work on developing weapons of mass destruction. Tensions were again raised when Pyongyang launched a multistage rocket on April 5, 2009, in a trajectory that sent it over Japan; it was probably a failed attempt to launch a satellite. On May 25, 2009, North Korea tested a second and larger nuclear bomb. This second underground nuclear test was more successful than the first, and resulted in a larger explosion – though still smaller than that of Hiroshima or Nagasaki. The international reaction to it was stronger than for previous ones. This time China and Russia joined the USA, South Korea and Japan in strongly condemning the nuclear test. On June 12, 2009, the UN Security Council passed Resolution 1874. This imposed further economic and commercial sanctions on North Korea. It also authorized UN members to stop, search and destroy on land, sea and air any transport suspected of supplying or aiding its nuclear program.

North Korea's relations with the world now followed a pattern that has not changed as of the time of writing. The USA and other members pressured Pyongyang to give up its nuclear weapons and at the very least stop nuclear and missile tests. North Korea continued with its nuclear and missile program anyway. The UN responded to each test by imposing economic sanctions intended to make it difficult to import materials for weapons and to halt the flow of luxury goods for the elite. But these sanctions were largely toothless since at least three-quarters of the DPRK's imports and exports came through China which paid lip service to the sanctions but did not enforce them. China feared the collapse of North Korea if economic sanctions were too severe, a scenario that would mean chaos on its border and a wave of desperate refugees flooding its northeast provinces, and it did not like the prospect of a unified democratic Korea allied with the USA and Japan on its border.

Shortly before the missile launch and nuclear test, in March 2009, two American journalists, who had allegedly crossed into the DPRK when making a documentary about the trafficking of North Korean women, were arrested and tried. This led to the visit of former President Bill Clinton to Pyongyang in August 2009 where he met with Kim Jong Il.

Although Washington denied it, the North Korean officials claimed he was bringing an official message to Kim. Following the meeting, Kim Jong Il granted a pardon to the two journalists. A photo op released by the DPRK gives some insight into the propaganda purposes of North Korea's provocative actions. A proud Kim Jong Il was shown seated next to Clinton. In the background was a huge painting of stormy waves crashing against a rock. It was a symbol, easy for a Korean audience to decode, of the defiant resistance of their small country in the face of imperialist aggressors.

From Sunshine to Renewed Confrontation with the South

Pyongyang's relationship with South Korea was if anything more complicated and more fraught with danger to the regime than relations with the USA. South Korea became extremely important to the North Korean economy, second only to China. Not only did trade between the two Koreas expand, but South Korea became a principal supplier of food aid which provided a substantial amount of basic foodstuffs consumed in the North. It also supplied large quantities of fertilizers. Earnings from the Kaesŏng Industrial Complex and from South Korean tourism were a significant source of foreign exchange. However, the regime, while finding South Korean aid and some trade a useful economic lifeline, could not afford to allow the public to realize just how prosperous the South was. Perhaps even more threatening to its continued grip on power, it could not allow its people to learn the truth that the ROK was not a US puppet and its people had no interest in reunification under the leadership in Pyongyang. In fact, increasingly the younger generation of South Koreans had little interest in reunification at all, viewing the North as a backward society whose population would be an economic burden.

In October 2007 South Korean president Roh Moo-hyun, a strong advocate of continuing his predecessor's Sunshine Policy walked across the DMZ and held a second summit conference with Kim Jong Il. The election of Lee Myung-bak (1941–) as president of the ROK in December 2007, however, changed the tone of the relationship. Lee was firmly opposed to the Sunshine Policy. He was critical of the large but poorly monitored aid it was supplying and with DPRK's lack of significant political or substantial economic and social reform. Many in the South wondered if its generous aid was simply propping up the northern regime and providing it with a disincentive to reform. In the spring of 2008 the Lee Myung-bak administration began insisting on the same monitoring procedures that the UN World Food Program required. North Korea responded angrily, cancelling military agreements and ratcheting up tensions along the peninsula. It threatened to close down the industrial complex at Kaesŏng even though this would hurt it more than the ROK, and began to order South Korean businessmen to leave the country. The newly elected president, however, was not a cold warrior, rather he presented what he called "Vision 3000," a plan aimed at developing the North Korean economy, helping it to achieve a growth rate of 10 percent a year for a decade so that it would reach a GDP per capita of $3,000. This would be done through targeting aid toward industrial, infrastructural and educational development, and carrying out financial reforms – all to be financed by an international aid fund. Aid from this fund in turn would be tied to political and economic reforms. At the minimum Lee insisted that North Korea adhere to its 1991 agreement with the ROK, calling for a denuclearized peninsula. In other words, aid would be on the condition of the country abandoning its nuclear program.[16]

Pyongyang reacted to this plan with unsurprising hostility. On the same day Lee made his proposal before the South Korean National Assembly on July 11, 2008, a South Korean woman visiting the Kŭmgang complex was shot and killed by a North Korean guard when she strayed over the strictly enforced boundaries of the resort. It is not clear whether this shooting was intentional, perhaps part of an effort to ratchet up tensions to test the new ROK president, or whether it was an accident. The woman's death and Pyongyang's refusal to apologize outraged the South Korean public and contributed to doubts about whether the DPRK really wanted to have better relations. The Lee Myung-bak administration reacted to the incident by suspending all visits to the resort complex. The DPRK then confiscated the $200 million resort without compensation. It also imposed restrictions on the Kaesŏng Industrial Complex, ordering many of the South Korean managers to leave and raising fees for utilities and other expenses, but it did not close the industrial park. Relations soured and Seoul suspended food aid to the North, refusing to supply grain, fertilizer and other assistance until it saw progress toward abandoning its weapons of mass destruction programs. This suspension was a blow to the North's economy. China supplied some food aid but not enough to make up for the deficit. Still despite a decline in two-way trade, the ROK remained a major trading partner.

A Hurried Succession

In August 2008 Kim Jong Il suffered a stroke. This was kept secret but when on September 9 he failed to show up for a military parade commemorating the founding of the DPRK rumors floated about. When he did appear in public his gaunt pallor and loss of weight indicated poor health. His concern with and total control over the media suggested that by allowing himself to be shown this way he was preparing the public for the possibility of his own demise. At this time he began to prepare for his own successor.

It seemed almost a necessity that the succession would remain in the Kim family. The entire ideology of the state was so centered on the Kim Il Sung family that it was difficult to conceive of how anyone outside the family could comfortably serve as the legitimate leader. By the 2000s internal propaganda had presented the following: the Korean people were a unique, pure and virtuous race. After millennia of resisting foreign invaders and suffering under exploitive elites they were now independent, strong and were constructing a socialist paradise. However, half the nation was under repressive domination of foreign imperialists and their local collaborators who were feverish plotting to bring the free half under their control and crush its efforts toward socialist progress. Fortunately, a line of truly virtuous, brilliant and totally dedicated leaders from a family that embodied all that was best about Korea were protecting them. This virtuous family and the Korean people when united were invincible. It was a long "arduous march" but as long as the Kim family led and the people were united "with one mind" they would prevail to build a rich and strong country and liberate their cousins to the south. This narrative framework made succession within the family imperative. So while some analysts speculated on a powerful military person succeeding the ailing Kim Jong Il, he looked toward members of his immediate family.

The most obvious candidate was his eldest son, Kim Jong Nam (Kim Chŏng-nam). But he fell out of favor with his father. Allegedly this was because he was arrested in Tokyo in 2001 trying to enter Japan on a false passport, reportedly to visit Tokyo Disneyland. Later he moved to China where he was often seen at the casinos in Macau. The second son, Kim Jong Chul (Kim Ch'ŏng-ch'ŏl), was passed over, reportedly because his father found him too weak-willed and girlish.[17] Instead, Kim Jong Il designated his youngest son, Kim Jong Un (Kim Chŏng-ŭn), as his successor. Reports, most famously by his sushi chef, said that Kim Jong Il found his youngest son most like him. There were other possibilities. The succession could have gone to his sister Kim Kyŏng-hŭi's husband, Chang Sŏng-t'aek, much as Kim Il Sung had once serious considered his younger brother as his political heir; but it seems that Kim Jong Un was the first choice from 2008.[18]

Kim Jong Un was born either January 8, 1983, or 1984, the second son of the Japanese-born dancer Ko Young-hee, Kim Jong Il's third wife. Information about his early life is sketchy but he is known to have attended an English-language international school in Bern, Switzerland, for several years in his early adolescence, returning home in 1998. Later he attended his father's alma mater, Kim Il Sung University, where he received a degree in physics. He received another degree at the Kim Il Sung Military Academy. He was said to be a lover of sports, especially basketball. He looked strikingly like his grandfather Kim Il Sung. His hair was cut in a similar style, and some South Koreans rumored that he had plastic surgery to enhance this resemblance. As with Kim Jong Il's other children he was unknown to the public.

Kim Jong Un was gradually introduced to the public. In September 2009 school children were being taught a song praising "the Young General Kim Jong Un."[19] In June 2010 the Supreme People's Assembly made the young Kim vice chair of National Defense Commission. Meanwhile, Kim Jong Il made two trips to China in 2010, first in May and then in August. Since two such trips only months apart was unprecedented, he might have been seeking Chinese approval or at least making sure they would not create problems about the succession. It is believed that Kim Jong Un accompanied his father as he met the Chinese leaders. Visiting China, Kim Jong Il traveled to Manchuria where according to the *Rodong sinmun* he visited the places associated with his father.[20] Perhaps this too was to remind the people of the historic roots of the regime, roots inseparable from the Kim family.

At the end of September 2010 a party conference took place, the first since 1966. On September 28, 2010, just before the start of the Third Party Conference Kim Jong Un was made a four-star general. At the party conference he was appointed vice chairman of the KWP's Central Military Commission. For the first time the media mentioned him by name. Shortly after the conference the 65th anniversary of the founding of the KWP on October 10 was celebrated in grand style with him appearing prominently, making it a sort of coronation ceremony. Thereafter Kim Jong Un appeared regularly in public, most often at his father's side, although be made no public speeches. The young Kim now accompanied his father on frequent "on-the-spot guidance" tours, most often at military-related sites. In the media he was referred to as the "*yŏngmyŏng-han tongji*" (brilliant comrade). Meanwhile his eldest brother Kim Jong Nam, who lived in exile in China, dividing his time between Beijing and Macao, told an Asahi TV reporter on October 9, 2010: "Personally, I am opposed to the hereditary transfer to a third generation of the family."[21]

It was not clear how much if any involvement in policy making the young, inexperienced successor had but some speculated that his emergence might have been linked to two unusually provocative developments in 2010. On March 26 the South Korean ship *Cheonan* was sunk by what was believed to have been a North Korean torpedo; 46 ROK sailors were killed. On November 23 North Korean artillery shelled the South Korean inhabited island of Yeonpyeongdo killing two marines and two villagers. Could these acts have been carried out to demonstrate the Kim Jong Un toughness or military prowess? Were they intended to make him more acceptable to military hardliners? Whatever the case it seemed unpromising for the future.

On December 17, 2011 Kim Jong Il died, officially of a stroke, while riding on a train inspecting the countryside. Although he had been ailing for three years, he showed no signs of deteriorating health in previous months and had appeared to have had an active schedule so his death came with unexpected suddenness, much as his father's had. Kim Jong Il's death was a major milestone in the history of North Korea. He ruled the DPRK for 17 years. Compared with the nearly half-century reign of his father this was brief but it was much longer than many thought likely in 1994. His impact on the country was enormous. For two decades before coming to power he had been the second most powerful figure in the country, shaping its performing arts, its ideology, its security systems and its party structure. And he entirely dominated the country during the time he led it. State media portrayed him as a dedicated figure devoted to his people. Supposedly, he made a hundred inspection tours a year around the country with no time to eat more than a simple ball of rice.[22] Yet he was never the beloved figure his father had been. Lacking any personal charisma, reclusive, physical unimposing, he never gave public speeches and his often dour expression contrasted with the beaming, outgoing, gregarious nature of his father. Despite the massive indoctrination, which may have succeeded in making most citizens accept his rule as necessary, refugees from North Korea frequently displayed contempt for him while remaining respectful of his father. His rule was one of almost constant deprivation, which continued long after the horrific famine ended. The economic failure of the country and the chronic hunger of millions of its people continued to his last days.

North Korea Under Kim Jong Un

Initially the new transition in leadership resembled the previous one in 1994. No radical changes took place in policy and many familiar figures still populated the leadership ranks. On December 28, 2011, Kim Jong Un was declared Supreme Leader. Kim Yong-nam, North Korea's de facto head of state, declared: "Respected Comrade Kim Jong Un is our party, military and country's supreme leader who inherits great comrade Kim Jong Il's ideology, leadership, character, virtues, grit and courage." On December 30 the Politburo of the KWP formally appointed him Supreme Commander of the Korean People's Army. The media declared him to be an "outstanding leader of the party, army and people," and a "respected comrade who is identical to Supreme Commander Kim Jong Il." Within days of his succession the "Great Successor" was being given the same revered status of his father, with his picture ubiquitous, his name always set in bold type and his quotations appearing in print in a special font.[23]

Surrounding Kim Jong Un was an inner core of leaders thought to serve as the young son's mentors or regents. These included Kim Jong Il's sister, Kim Kyŏng-hŭi, and her husband, Chang Sŏng-t'aek. Kim Kyŏng-hŭi had long been close to her brother, and her husband at times had even been rumored as a possible successor. Kim Jong Un's sudden rise was accompanied by their rise as well. Both were more widely seen in public in 2010 than the young Kim. Kim Kyŏng-hŭi was also made a four-star general on September 28. She had also been elected to the Politburo and was in charge of light industry. Chang had long been prominent in the regime but fell out of favor in the period 2003–2006. Back in favor, he became an alternative member of the Politburo in 2010, as well as vice chairman of the National Defense Commission and was director of the KWP Administrative Department which gave him oversight over internal security offices. Chang was also involved in economic projects with China. He was seen standing beside Kim Jong Un at Kim Jong Il's funeral ceremony wearing a military uniform. Since their only child, a daughter, had died Chang and his wife, Kim Jung Un's aunt, posed no dynastic threat and were well placed to serve as guardians to the young, inexperienced leader. Another important figure was Ri Yŏng-ho a vice chairman of the Central Military Commission and former head of the Pyongyang Defense Command, a key military position in charge of the forces protecting the capital. Ri was promoted to vice marshal in September 2010 and ranked fourth on the funeral committee list. Another military man, General O Kuk-yŏl, was also considered an important person around the new designated successor.

Kim Jong Un's meteoric rise continued. In the days before the big event he was given new positions. On April 1, at the Fourth Party Conference he was appointed first secretary of the KWP. This was a new title. His father had served as general secretary, a position by which he had become more frequently referred to in the last few years of his rule. Khrushchev used the term "First Secretary" in 1953, to differentiate himself from the authoritarian rule of Stalin who had served as general secretary for

30 years. North Korea now adopted the title but for somewhat different reasons. Just as Kim Jong Il did not assume his father's position as president but declared Kim Il Sung the eternal president, his father became "the eternal general secretary." On April 13, the young leader became head of the National Defense Commission. He now assumed almost every post or its equivalent held by his predecessors. On July 18, Kim Jong Un became "Marshal of the Korean People's Army," a title that made him a rank higher than all others in the military.

However, there were some real changes under the new leadership. One was a move away from Kim Jong Il's Military-First policy. The top echelon of the party and state was now dominated by non-military men. Top military ranks were given to people with a more technocratic background. An example was Choe Ryong Hae (Ch'oe Ryŏng-hae), son of Ch'oe Hyŏn one of Kim Il Sung's guerilla comrades, who had a background in economics. Born in 1950 he was a relatively youthful 62 upon his appointment. Choe held various mid-level positions before rising rapidly in the ranks between 2010 and 2011, being promoted to the rank of general and made an alternate member of the Politburo. In April 2012 he was made a vice marshal and member of the Standing Committee.[24] The most dramatic change in leadership came in July 2012 when Ri Yŏng-ho, the highest ranking military man, was suddenly removed from his posts. A brief public announcement said he had resigned due to poor health. A new military man replaced him as the army's chief of staff. His sudden fall from power took observers by surprise since, up till then, he had featured prominently, standing by Kim Jong Un's side in public photos. The removal of the only military person in the inner circle along with the re-emergence of Pak Pong-ju, the head of the Ministry of Light Industry, which oversees the civilian economy, suggested a shift in emphasis from military to economic development. Pak was regarded by foreign observers as a more technocratic and reform-minded official. His removal from the cabinet in 2005 has previously been interpreted as a retreat from reform.

Overall the leadership was looking more civilian and technocratic. About 40 percent of the top 106 positions were held by graduates of Kim Il Sung University and 9 percent from Kim Ch'aek University of Technology. Among the cabinet about a quarter were Kim Ch'aek graduates. About 1 percent of the top leadership positions were held by Kim Il Sung Military Academy graduates. It was not, however, a major break with the past. Most of the top leaders were second-generation family members or related to family members of Kim Il Sung and his guerilla comrades. Nor was it a youthful leadership; the average age of party central committee members was 72 and for the cabinet a youthful 63. And it was overwhelmingly male. Women held only 2 percent of upper elite positions. This included, of course, Kim Kyŏng-hŭi, the sister of Kim Jong Il. A third were from the poor Hamgyŏng region in the northeast, including 16.3% from North Hamgyŏng province, near the area where Kim Il Sung had operated.[25] Since this was a region where many people of undesirable background were sent and often the most neglected part of the country this might seem odd, but it reflected the fact that so many guerillas before 1945 came from this region along the Manchurian border. They hardly appeared to be a group that would push radical change.

Consolidating Power

Perhaps because he was so young and inexperienced Kim Jong Un's ascension to power was followed by frequent purges and shake-ups among those in key positions. The most dramatic development was the removal of his uncle, Chang Sŏng-t'aek, from power. On December 8, 2013, he was shown on television being unceremoniously dragged from a Central Committee meeting. Publicly he was charged with plotting to overthrow the government and shot four days later. This was unprecedented in several ways: it was the first major purge of a top leader in decades, it was the first time a top official was publicly arrested or tried since the purges of the 1950s, and it was the first time someone so closely related to the ruling family was known to have been executed. Speculation arose about whether this meant Kim Jong Un was uncertain of his power – his father rarely purged top officials while he was in power – or did it represent a ruthless or even recklessness among the young leader? Unconfirmed reports suggested that the animosity between Kim and Chang arose over conflicts about access to foreign exchange between rival patronage groups, and that Chang had developed his own independent power base which was a threat to Kim's absolute authority.[26]

At about the same time Choe Ryong Hae, who briefly appeared to hold the number two position was demoted, supposedly because of money and women problems.[27] Rumored to have been purged he reappeared in late 2014 when he accompanied Hwang Pyong So (Hwang Pyŏng-sŏ) and Kim Yang-Gon (Kim Yang-gŏn), who headed the ruling party's United Front Department in charge of South Korea-related affairs, to a visit to the Asian Games in South Korea in October.[28] Hwang, a close aid to Kim Jong Un and an official in the powerful Organization and Guidance Department, emerged in 2014 as a key figure in the regime, serving as director of the KPA's political bureau, a vice marshal and a member of the Politburo. Purges continued during the first five years of Kim Jong Un's rule. Some of these moves seemed intended to clip the power of the military and to strengthen that of the KWP and the civilian bureaucracy. Several high-ranking military officers were removed from their posts – altogether 44 percent of the top 218 military officers in the KPA were removed.[29] However, the downgraded status of military leaders did not necessary mark a major shift in the ruling structure. The leadership had since the late 1950s consisted of Kim Il Sung, his family, his guerilla comrades and their families and clients. This elite had intermarried and was now in its third generation. Politics was often about rivalry between families and their patronage networks. Since, as mentioned, powerful families tended to have members in both the military and the party, as well as different sectors of the state apparatus, the military was not a separate caste. The politics of North Korea had evolved to become similar to the precolonial old dynastic state, with bitter factional disputes among members of the elite families, sometimes disguised or misinterpreted as policy issues.

Kim Jong Un attempted to strengthen his legitimacy and authority by situating it within the dynastic family or, as it was often termed, the "Paektu Bloodline." In the spring of 2014 the 94-year-old Kim Yŏng Ju, the younger brother of, and one-time possible successor to, Kim Il Sung was reappointed honorary vice chairman of the Supreme People's Assembly. A powerless post, it nonetheless served to underline the continuity of the Kim family. More special days were added to the calendar, including December 17, Kim Jong Il's death day, and December 26, the birthday of

Kim Chŏng-suk, Kim Jong Il's mother. Oddly, Kim Jong Un's own birthday, January 8, was not made a holiday. But even members of the "Paektu Bloodline" were not immune to Kim Jong Un's brutal elimination of all or potential rivals to his authority. On February 14, 2017 DPRK-employed agents assassinated his elder half-brother, Kim Jong Nam, an exile living in China, by putting a deadly poison on his face at Kuala Lumpur international airport.

Modest Changes in Style and More Tinkering with the System

The first focus of the new Kim Jong Un administration was preparing for the April 15, 2012 celebration of the centennial of Kim Il Sung's birth. For some time this date had been hailed as the point at which the DPRK would become a rich and powerful state. Throughout much of 2011, campaigns were carried out to complete various construction projects, such as new housing, by this special day. The preparations for the centennial followed the old pattern of constant exhortations, mass mobilizations and calls for extra human effort to meet targets that were almost never attainable. The idea that the impoverished society could possibly achieve this goal when it was making little headway in even dealing with chronic malnutrition, when electricity was often available only one or two hours a day and when even the limited improvements made by the existence of free markets was being undermined by efforts to curb them seem fantastical. The disconnect between reality and propaganda seemed to be so extreme as to question the credibility of the regime even to its own people. But it was not that different than in the past decades when grandiose and totally unrealistic plans were made along with claims that they had been met.

A notable change in governance under Kim Jong Un was in style. In contrast to his reclusive father, who never gave public speeches, Kim Jong Un spoke at the centennial ceremonies. While not a polished speaker he spoke comfortably, and often frankly and directly to the people. He showed his grandfather's outgoingness, traveling about and mixing with the people. On July 6 national television showed Kim Jong Un and other officials attending a concert with characters such as Mickey Mouse and Winnie-the-Pooh dancing on stage before them. Alongside the costumed characters there were screen projections of Disney characters such as Snow White and Dumbo. He was also depicted with a fashionably dressed young woman who was later, in July, identified as his wife Ri Sol Joo (Ri Sŏl-ju), a popular singer. Since Kim Il Sung's wife Kim Kyŏng-ae was dropped from the media's attention in the early 1970s, spouses of the inner circle were rarely seen or mentioned in public. The pictures of Kim and his wife, whispering, smiling and talking to each other, were a break from the past, an attempt to humanize and soften the image of the leader. The direct appeal to the people, the more playful style and his wife's fashionable clothes all suggested a difference – a possible liberalization.

Liberalizing reforms, however, were as superficial such as permission for women to wear shorter skirts. A movie that opened in the Toronto Film Festival in the fall of 2012 "Comrade Kim Goes Flying," a romantic comedy about a girl who joins the circus and a boy who falls in love with her, contained no overt propaganda. Yet these modest developments were accompanied by continual calls about being vigilant against the seductions of the imperialist aggressors. In fact, in many ways the authoritarian nature of the regime increased, suggested by the tightening of its borders. Rather than opening more to the outside world, the state took measures to prevent illegal crossings into China. The central government launched a crackdown on border guards notoriously open to bribes, on black marketers and on those seeking to leave. About 20,000 troops were dispatched to the border. Guards were punished if caught accepting bribes and frequently rotated. Not only defectors but also their families were now punished. Those who crossed to buy food, medicine and other goods were no longer treated with leniency. The result was that the flow of refugees was reduced from 2,000 a year to perhaps less than a tenth of that. There were also a renewed crackdown on South Korean videos, CDs and DVDs. The regime continued the practice of forging internal unity by creating a sense of being under siege from outside forces.

A bizarre campaign was carried out in the summer of 2012 urging the population to be vigilant against a plot by the US imperialists and South Korea. Media in the DPRK reported that the Lee Myung-bak regime had created a so-called Statue Demolition Society, and with the support of

ROK and US intelligence were sneaking agents into the country to destroy statues of Kim Il Sung. A former defector, Jon Yong Chol (Chŏn Yong-ch'ŏl), was arrested on July 19, 2012 re-entering the country as part of this plan. Meetings were held to deal with this threat and citizens formed guard watches from 7 pm to 7 am to protect statues of Kim Il Sung as well as History Museums, Towers of Eternal Life and Kim Il Sung and Kim Jong Il Revolutionary Ideology and Research Institutes.[30] Meanwhile, there were no ideological changes. There was less interest in *juche* thought than in the past, a trend that had begun under Kim Jong Il when his Military-First policy pushed *juche* into the background. Kim Jong Un did not even mention the term in his 2013 or 2014 New Year's Addresses.[31] In 2013 meetings were held at all levels to introduce the modifications to the Ten Principles for the Establishment of the Monolithic Ideological System. These amounted to merely adding the name Kim Jong Il after that of Kim Il Sung. For example, the second principle, "We must honor Great Leader comrade Kim Il Sung with all our loyalty," was amended to "We must honor Great Leader comrade Kim Il Sung and General Kim Jong Il with all our loyalty,"[32] an emendation that suggested there was no change, only continuity. In October 2012 the *Rodong sinmun* declared, "The imperialists see the young as the main target of their cultural and ideological invasion scheme." It went on to say, "This reality demands that we wake up to the imperialists' plan to undermine our youth."[33]

There were some moves to economic reform. On June 28 a new set of guidelines entitled "One establishing a new economic management system in our own style" was promulgated among officials. Called simply the June 28 Policy this was to be implemented from October 1, 2012. The policy, details of which were not made public, gave more authority to local managers. A more significant change was in the policy on agriculture. Experimenting with several counties the plan allowed farmers to keep 30 percent of their produce and have the state collect only 70 percent. This would be in addition to anything they produced that was above the quota. Farmers would be free to sell this 30 percent of the crop. This would be an improvement over the past, although it was not clear how effectively it would be implemented since officials were known to collect as much from farmers as possible, as was the case in the 1990s when the military was sent in to collect the harvest. The *punjo*, the basic production unit on the cooperatives, was to be reduced from 10–25 to only 3–4 members. And procurement prices were to be "realistically" adjusted to match market prices.[34] While this was an important reform it was far short of the Vietnam model let alone the Chinese.

The June 28 measures of 2012 were put into practice in 2013 and resulted in good harvests. In 2014 the state announced the "May 30 Measures" to be implemented in 2015. These would go even further giving "production teams" up to 60 percent of the crop. Production teams were reduced to household units. Furthermore, they would increase the size of private family plots to 3,300 square meters up from the tiny kitchen plots of only 100 square meters. Industry would be reformed by the introduction of a "direct responsibility system" in which factory managers would be given far more freedom to buy and sell materials. They would also be given the power to hire and fire workers and determine pay scales. Implementation of these changes was slow and did not signal a change from the official commitment to a command economy. DPRK officials in the media and in conversations with foreigners stressed that the country would not abandoned its socialist path. One official was quoted by the Korean Central News Agency as saying that calls for reform were a "hallucination" by South Korea's "hostile forces." To expect policy change and reform in the North "is nothing but a foolish and silly dream, just like wanting the sun to rise in the west, " he said.[35] State media blamed foreigners for economic hardships and urged citizens to be self-reliant rather than look to outsider powers for assistance. "Dry bread at home is better than roast meat abroad," a Korean Central News Agency editorial proclaimed.[36] The harshness of everyday life was suggested by the new requirement that students bring firewood to school to heat the classroom stove. Previously this was supplied, when available, by the local government.[37]

More fundamental than these "measures" was the continued trend toward a semi market-oriented economy – described by journalists Daniel Tudor and James Pearson as "self-reliance by hook-by-crook capitalism."[38] Salaries and the PDS could not meet the needs of those beyond the elite. Most people made do with sideline jobs, by trading, by any way possible. The army and officialdom also depended on private trade and bribes from those engaged in it to supplement their income. The result was a complex, factionalized, corrupt system that combined markets and trade with socialism. North Korea had become especially dependent on foreign trade to keep the economy from collapse. The actual scale of foreign trade is modest, only a tiny fraction of South Korea's trade, but it remains a crucial lifeline to the impoverished state.

North Korea and the Outside World

In foreign affairs, the international community at first looked to the new leadership for changes in policy, but what transpired was continuity. Kim Jong Un followed what was essentially a revival of the "equal emphasis" policy inaugurated in the early 1960s. He called the "new strategic line" a policy of simultaneously increasing the country's military capabilities while pursuing economic growth. He pursued his nuclear and missile program with renewed energy. At first quiet negotiations with Washington in Beijing, which had begun toward the end of Kim Jong Il's reign, continued. On February 29, a breakthrough took place. Under the "leap year agreement," North Korea would halt its nuclear program, open its nuclear facilities to international inspections, refrain from new missile tests and agree to return to the six-party talks. In return the USA would supply 240,000 tons of nutritionally rich foodstuffs such as biscuits. These special foods would alleviate the food shortage and would avoid the problem of monitoring where the food aid went since there was little market value for these foods and they would not by coveted by the elite as would be rice. The agreement was a verbal commitment, subject to somewhat different interpretations by the two sides, yet regarded as an important breakthrough. Almost immediately North Korea violated it when it announced plans for a missile test during the centennial celebration. Pyongyang announced it would be launching a new *Kwangmyŏng-sŏng* ("Brilliant Star") satellite, from a multistage rocket. This appeared to be another attempt to test a long-range missile capable of reaching parts of the USA. Two previous attempts in 1998 and 2009 had both failed, although the state media declared them successful. North Korea took the unusual step of allowing foreign journalists to witness the missile launch. Journalists from 21 foreign media organizations in the USA, Japan,

Britain, France, Germany, Russia, Brazil and South Africa attended. The missile launch took place on Friday, April 13, which proved an unlucky day when the rocket disintegrated 90 seconds after blast-off. The launch, besides embarrassing the regime, ended the February 29 agreement. The regime went on to test a nuclear weapon on February 12, 2013, another one on January 6, 2016, and a large one on September 9, 2016. UN sanctions were passed but without China's active enforcement their impact was limited.

Besides nuclear weapons and missiles the DPRK invested in cyber-warfare, creating Unit 121 for that purpose. Despite the fact that North Korea was the only nation on earth not significantly connected to the World Wide Web and access was limited to a tiny number of trusted officials, it made some headway in this field. Its capabilities came as a surprise when in late 2014 it hacked Sony Pictures, an American affiliate of the Japanese corporation. This was in response to a movie, *The Interview*, a comedy about two Americans who assassinate Kim Jong Un. North Korea denied it carried out the hacks but had warned the studio of the consequences of releasing the film. Following more threats, the movie was distributed on a limited basis after most theaters were afraid to show it. This internet attack and blackmail raised a disturbing new form of terrorism. North Korea also attacked South Korean internet sites and attempted, with only limited success, to hack into the country's nuclear power stations.

Kim Jong Un sought not openness but crises to continue the siege mentality that served the regime well. During the spring of 2013 he created one with South Korea. Using the regularly scheduled joint military exercises between US and ROK forces, Pyongyang began to accuse Washington and Seoul of planning aggression toward the DPRK. There was nothing new in these charges but the rhetoric was more heated than usual. On March 7, Pyongyang threatened to launch a preemptive nuclear strike against the USA, calling it the "sworn enemy of the Korean people." The following day it announced that it was cancelling its non-aggression pacts with South Korea, closing the border crossing and disconnecting the hotline. On March 13, it announced that it was unilaterally ending the 1953 Armistice. At the end of the month it actually cut the hotline, declaring on March 30 that it was at "a state of war" with

South Korea. The DPRK declared that it "exercises the right to launch a preemptive nuclear strike in order to destroy strongholds of the aggressors."[39] Propaganda videos showed missiles destroying US cities, and one that showed Obama in flames became an internet hit. The DPRK withdrew 53,000 workers at the Kaesŏng Industrial Complex, even though this was an important source of foreign exchange. On May 18 and 19 it fired four short-range guided missiles into the waters off the coast. The level of violent rhetoric went beyond that of the past. Yet despite the talk of war, observers in Pyongyang saw little evidence of the country being on a war footing. Soldiers seen in the capital in April were mainly busy planting flowers and sprucing up the city for Kim Il Sung's birthday. And, in early June, the rhetoric died down, and Pyongyang announced it was to open the first dialogue in years with the South. In the several months that followed the two sides began negotiating an agreement to arrange another family meeting, which was unilaterally cancelled by the North, and the Kaesŏng Industrial Complex was reopened in September 2013, only to be closed again in 2016, this time by Seoul after relations again soured.

The state continued to be increasingly dependent on China. Since trade statistics published by the People's Republic of China were unclear on the matter, it was a not certain just how extensive the trade between the two countries was. According to one estimate, by 2010 China was providing North Korea with 80 percent of its imported consumer goods and 45 percent of its imported food.[40] Overall, the volume of trade with China grew while from 2009 that with South Korea declined, although in 2012 the ROK was still North Korea's second largest trading partner. In 2011, according to South Korean analysts, North Korea's exports and imports with China reached US$5.63 billion, up 60 percent from the previous year. China accounted for 70 percent of the DPRK's total foreign trade.[41] The Chinese were particularly interested in the DPRK's considerable mineral resources. For a small country, North Korea is well endowed with minerals. One US Geological Survey report estimated the market value of exploited minerals as being enormous, in excess of 1 trillion dollars.[42] Other estimates range as high as $10 trillion.[43] It has globally significant deposits of iron ore, coal, limestone, magnesite, copper, lead, graphite, tungsten, zinc, molybdenum and some gold. It may also have significant deposits of rare earths. These minerals attracted the attention of Chinese investors, mainly from the two bordering provinces of Jilin and Liaoning. Chinese investments in North Korea were rare until after 1997. Only after 2004 did these involve minerals. Between that year and 2010, 138 Chinese firms established joint ventures with North Korea.[44] The biggest attractions were the extractive industries. Most of these were small-scale private enterprises with only four known state-owned enterprises and only two major firms participating.

Beijing had begun to see North Korea as useful for its plans to develop the relatively poor northeastern region. This region, known to the West as Manchuria, had long been linked with Korea, and was where Kim Il Sung grew up and the base for his guerilla warfare against the Japanese. By the late twentieth century, what had once been the most industrialized region of China had become its rust bucket of old, heavy industry plants. It had failed to attract the modern foreign investment of the southern coastal provinces. Trade and investment in North Korea was part of the answer. North Korea also provided access to the sea for the landlocked Jilin province. The largely forlorn Rasŏn Special Economic zone in the extreme northeast corner of the country began to receive greater attraction as an outlet to the sea since the port of Rajin was only 50 kilometers from the border. To encourage commerce in Jilin and to link it with North Korea, in 2009 the government launched a Changchun–Jilin–Tumen Regional Economic Pilot Zone or Changjitu with the goal of tripling income in the region by 2020.[45] As they invested in infrastructure they saw Rasŏn port as a key component. In the summer of 2012 Chinese tourists arrived in enough numbers that the previously empty hotels were overbooked on the weekends.[46] More than half of all foreign trade went through the city of Dandong across the Yalu from the DPRK city of Sinŭiju. The contrast between the bright lights of Dandong and the darkness on the North Korean side was striking. It is estimated that in 2015 a quarter of Dandong's labor force is employed in businesses linked with North Korea. Besides the steady flow of trucks across the bridge connecting the two countries an estimated 13,000 North Koreans work in grim, unheated factories in the Chinese city.[47]

So a combination of geography and the growing demand in China for mineral resources encouraged investment in North Korea. This followed a broader pattern where China in its search for minerals, energy and commodities invested in pariah states where Western firms could not because of sanctions or because of high risks – countries such as Sudan, Zimbabwe, the Democratic Republic of Congo and Myanmar. But doing business in North Korea was not easy. As other investors found there was little rule of law, corruption was rampant and regulations were subject to sudden and arbitrary change. Many Chinese firms lost heavily and all complained about the difficulties of doing business there.

However, China's economic ties with North Korea had a character different from other states. Its proximity, its historical ties to China and the special geopolitics of the region all led to concerns that it was becoming what the South Korean press called "the fourth Northeast province" (the other three being the Manchurian provinces of Liaoning, Jilin and Heilongjiang; the first two form the border with the DPRK). These concerns were reinforced by China's "Northeast Borderlands and Chain of Events Research Project," known simply as the "Northeast Project." Funded by the Chinese government in 2002 its task was to investigate the ancient history of the region. Scholarship focused on the ancient Koguryŏ kingdom which flourished from the first to the seventh century. It was based in southern Manchuria and in what is now North Korea, eventually moving its capital from Manchuria to Pyongyang. Conclusions by some scholars that this state was part of Chinese history caused outrage in South Korea in the 2000s. In 2004 the government promised Seoul that these claims would not appear in the textbooks. But suspicions remained in South Korea that the historical research could be used in the event of the collapse of North Korea to justify its annexation. This would follow the pattern taken by the Japanese government in the early twentieth century when it sponsored historical and archaeological research that promoted the claim that Korea was once part of the Japanese polity in ancient times, a claim used to justify the annexation of Korea.

As good nationalists, North Korea's rulers were no doubt fully aware of this and had no desire to become a Chinese satellite. In fact, North Korea viewed Koguryŏ as the real ancestor of modern Korea. In 2001 it applied to UNESCO to have the tombs which it was restoring registered as the country's first "world heritage" site.[48] According to the interpretation given by North Korean histories, after an interlude when the southern-based Silla ruled, the descendants of Koguryŏ created the Koryŏ state which achieved the first real unification of the country since Silla had to share some of what constitutes Korea today with the Manchurian-based Parhae state. This differed from the view in Seoul where the Silla, whose boundaries roughly coincide with the modern South Korean state, is seen as the unifier of the peninsula, possessing a culture that formed the foundations for later Korean society.

Since both South Korea and increasingly North Korea looked to ancient times to lay the basis of their competing claims to being the mainstream, and torchbearers, of Korean nationalism both viewed China's interest in North Korea with suspicion. The southern boundaries of Koguryŏ were roughly where the boundaries between the two Koreas are today. So it did look suspiciously as though China were laying the basis for some sort of contingency to take over the North in the event of a collapse. South Koreans were concerned that a unified Korea, under Seoul, posed a threat to China since it would mean an open, democratic state allied to the USA, and perhaps Japan, would be on their border. Chinese officials may have also been concerned by irredentist claims to parts of Manchuria, sometimes made by ultra-nationalists in the South and the existence of nearly 2 million ethnic Koreans near the Chinese border with North Korea. Some South Koreans, including lawmakers, called for the abrogation of the 1909 treaty between China and Japan which demarcated the boundary, since it left out the predominantly ethnically Korean Kando (Chinese: Jiando) area which became part of Jilin province. Any claim by a borderland ethnic group from China had unacceptable implications for the country which had contentious minorities covering huge portions of its outer territories – notably the Uighurs in the northwest and the Tibetans in the southwest. Whatever China's intentions, it was clear that North Korea had no intention of being the "fourth Northeast province" or being a tributary state of Beijing. Thus, it limited the amount of Chinese involvement in linking its infrastructure with that of Manchuria.

As humiliating as it might be for the fiercely independent regime, the DPRK had found itself by the 2010s dependent on China for survival. It needed Beijing's support or at least tolerance since with UN sanctions in place the vast majority of its international trade, important to its survival, was with or went through China. The lack of high-level visits between the two countries was an indication of how frosty relations were. Still, China deemed even a difficult and dangerous North Korea better than chaos or a Western-allied Republic of Korea or even US troops on its border. Nonetheless, Beijing often signaled its displeasure with Pyongyang's nuclear and missile program, for example banning coal imports, the DPRK's most important export in the February 2017 in response to a series of missile tests.

Prospects for unification seem to become ever less promising. In North Korea, even with tightening measures under Kim Jong Un, South Korean culture penetrated the North. Reports were that in 2010 the two biggest hit TV dramas in South Korea were both known and popular in the North. Girls Generation, a K-Pop all-girls group was also popular.[49] But in South Korea attitudes toward the North among the younger generation had changed from a fashionable admiration by many college students and younger intellectuals to a disdain for what they regarded as backward and brainwashed cousins. Between 1990 and 1994 there were only 86 defectors; from 1994 to 2000, 100 a year; and then over a 1,000 a year in 2002. The number began to taper off after 2011.[50] By early 2017 there were 30,000 North Korean refugees living in the South. They were smaller in stature, less healthy, less well educated and suffered from discrimination. South Koreans associated them with laziness, irresponsibility, drunkenness, criminal activity and seeking government handouts. Many wondered if the two Koreas had grown too far apart to be easily unified even if the situation made this possible.

Reviving the Past, Moving to an Uncertain Future

The Seventh Party Congress

On October 20, 2015 the DPRK announced that a Seventh Congress of the KWP would be meeting in the spring. The announcement was particularly surprising as it had been 36 years since the last party congress met in 1980. Such a move, along with the great attention that was given to it, could have signaled a major shift in policy. There was nothing new in the preparations for the gathering. It was preceded by the usual mass mobilization campaign – a "Seventy-Day Battle" (*ch'il sip-il il chŏnt'u*) in which citizens of the capital were rounded up to spruce up the streets. As in the past, for important meetings the exact dates and even the venue for the congress were kept secret. The five-day congress opened on May 6, 2016 with 3,500 delegates and 1,500 observers attending. One hundred foreign journalists were also invited but were not allowed to watch but rather only allowed inside for a few minutes. There were no official foreign delegations; this was a purely internal affair.

Rather than initiating bold reforms the Seventh Party Congress was instead an expression of continuity with the past. Kim Jong Un became chairman of the KWP, reviving a post that had been abolished a half-century earlier. He also became chairman of the new Commission for State Affairs that replaced the National Defense Commission. Thus, both of these changes as well as the congress itself appeared to be a revival of some of the forms and atmosphere of the Kim Il Sung era. There were no major changes in leadership. The same family members held the top positions, including the "royal" Kim family. Kim Jong Un's younger sister, Kim Yŏ-jŏng, was appointed to the Central Committee. The meeting took place in the April 25th Building, named after the anniversary of the founding of the North Korean army and perhaps symbolizing the continued importance of the military. Yet the locus of power seemed to be recentered back in the party.

As his grandfather had done Kim Jong Un provided a lengthy main speech; his was 14,000 words. He began his speech with a eulogy to the revolutionary comrades who had passed away since the last congress. The list included almost all the members of the first generation of Manchurian partisans, underlining that the revolution had passed to newer generations. Kim referred to the period since the last congress as a time of "grim struggle," implying that was now over.[51] Much of the attention of his speech was devoted to his *byungjin* (pyŏngjin, "equal emphasis") policy, giving equal emphasis to economic and military development. This too was hardly new, but rather a continuation of the policy formulated at the December 1962 Party Plenum. His father had shifted this policy from the double emphasis on economic progress and military strength as the basis of legitimacy to a single reliance on military strength.

Kim Jong Un was bringing the focus back to where it had been before the economic disasters. The congress appeared to be about reasserting the past, not breaking with it.

Kim Jong Un called for self-sufficiency in food production, for increased energy production and for an increase in foreign trade. Nothing here was new. Even the call for foreign trade focused on increasing the production of minerals and not special economic zones or the development of export industries. For outside observers looking for signs of economic reform the congress was a disappointment. In an obvious and insulting reference to China Kim Jong Un declared: "Despite the filthy wind of bourgeois liberty and 'reform' and 'openness' blowing in our neighborhood, we let the spirit of sŏn'gun rifles fly and advance according to the path of socialism that we had chosen."[52] Thus making it clear that North Korea had no intention of emulating its reform-minded communist neighbor. One important announcement was of a new five-year plan for 2016–2020. Not only was it the first new five-year plan since 1956, but it was the first economic plan of any defined length in over two decades. Since the economic crises of the 1990s North Korea had broken with the tradition of socialist economies by not having any central plans with their specific if often unrealistic targets. Rather, North Korea had simply improvised and limped on in a strange hybrid of socialism and de facto market economics. Now it appeared that the intention was to bring the DPRK back to its pre-1990s normalcy – a normalcy in which the party was supreme, the economy was centrally coordinated and the emphasis would be on growth. This return to normalcy was further reinforced by hints that there would be an eighth party conference, perhaps in five years, at the end of the new economic plan.

For ordinary North Koreans too the immediate future appeared to be more of the same. To highlight this, within days after the congress officials announced the start of a 200-day "loyalty campaign" to fulfill the new five-year plan. It was yet another effort at calling upon the citizens to work harder to achieve party goals. There was no hint of liberalization of any kind.

Yet so much had changed since the last congress in 1980 that North Korea could not go back to "normalcy." In 1980 there was still an international socialist movement that the DPRK could align itself with. North

Korea had a powerful ally and benefactor – the Soviet Union. China, its other ally, had just begun to move away from Maoist policies. Pyongyang could attempt to be a leader of the Third World; it was not yet an international pariah. South Korea was a military dictatorship that was undergoing an economic crisis, and not the vibrant first world democracy it now was. There was no internet, cell phones nor smuggled DVDs of the globally popular South Korean pop music videos and TV soap dramas. And, of course, the economic crisis and the famine of the 1990s had not yet turned much of the bureaucracy, the military and a hungry under-employed population into entrepreneurs. In 1980 there was still hope for the regime that North Korea would become a strong, prosperous state that could win over the people of the South and reunify the country under its leadership. In 2016 the best the leadership could hope for was to make some modest improvements in the poor, aid-dependent country's economy.

North Korea in 2017

After the Seventh Party Congress the economy did improve modestly, with significant growth in 2016 which continued into 2017. Most of the benefits of this prosperity went to the elite. In 2017 Pyongyang was experiencing a construction boom with luxury apartments, supermarkets and stores springing up selling imported goods. Despite UN sanctions designed to restrict exports of luxury goods for the upper echelons of society, the number of new BMWs and Mercedes-Benzes on the streets was increasing. The role of the private market continued to grow, symbolized by the appearance of street vendors for the first time in many decades. Economic growth was fueled by exports of coal, iron and increasingly textiles. The latter were manufactured in North Korea and then shipped to China where they were labeled "Made in China." While most of the foreign exports, perhaps 90 percent, were with or went through China, an illicit trade with Russia was also expanding. The modest agricultural reforms and the gradual enlarging of the private sector were probably also a contributing factor in the improving economy. But the country still ranked among the world's poorest countries, suffered food shortages and needed international aid.

As he promised at the party congress, Kim Jong Un expanded the country's military strength. His main focus was on accelerating missile and nuclear weapons development. The 68th anniversary of the DPRK on September 9, 2016, was marked with the country's fifth nuclear test, the second in that same year. More impressive was the sixth nuclear test on September 3, 2017, far larger than the previous ones and causing earth tremors in adjacent regions of China and Russia. North Korea claimed plausibly that it was a hydrogen bomb. Missile development took a quantum leap with the successful test of an intercontinental ballistic missile capable of reaching Alaska, launched provocatively on July 4, 2017. A second successful test of a missile capable of reaching most of the continental USA took place three weeks later on July 28. On August 29 and September 15, 2017 Pyongyang fired missiles over northern Japan.

Kim Jong Un appeared to be deliberately demonstrating his country's power and creating international tensions. Both purposes served domestic audiences, keeping the country in a state of military vigilance and fulfilling his pledge to strengthen the military. A public exchange of personal insults with American President Trump and the latter's threat to "totally destroy" the DPRK reaffirmed Pyongyang's warning to its people of the aggressive intentions of imperialists, aggressive intentions that only its military might and steadfast leadership were able to thwart. He appeared to have no desire to improve relations with the South but rather seemed intent on keeping the two Koreas apart. In May 2017 South Korea elected a new liberal president, Moon Jae-in, who had hoped to abandon the hardline stance of his two conservative predecessors and resuscitate the Sunshine Policy. Kim's lack of interest in cooperating with the new administration and his nuclear and missile tests and rhetoric forced Moon to shift quickly to a policy emphasizing the ROK's military preparedness. South Korean public opinion was increasingly hostile and impatient with the North.

China, in the face of tightening international sanctions, seemed to be more crucial to the survival of the regime than ever. However, Kim Jong Un did little to improve the frosty relations between Pyongyang and Beijing. Some of his actions seem defiant and insulting. In February 2017 he assassinated Kim Jong Nam, despite that fact that his half-brother was living under Chinese protection, and he tested a nuclear weapon in September 2017 as President Xi Jinping was presenting a key foreign policy speech boasting of his efforts to promote global harmony. China, however, despite its clear frustration with North Korea, did not fully comply with the economic sanctions fearing the economic collapse of the regime and its unification under the US-allied South.

By 2017 the North Korean state had survived but its revolution had failed. Modern revolutions more often than not fall short of achieving their aims but few have failed as much as had North Korea's. A revolutionary state, which once carried out a radical egalitarian agenda, had developed into one of the most inequitable societies on the face of the earth, a land where most led desperate lives of hunger, darkness and deprivation while a tiny elite lived in luxury. A state founded on the universal beliefs of Marxist-Leninist socialism had become a cult society based on an ideology of racial-nationalism. A revolutionary regime that sought to be at the vanguard of human progress presided over an impoverished, isolated society, the only major one not connected to the World Wide Web. A revolutionary state whose aim was to achieve national unity became the chief obstacle to that unity. A regime that once sought international respect was universally reviled. Seven decades after its founding, the main accomplishment of Kim Il Sung's state was that it had managed not to disintegrate into chaos as some outsiders had expected.

The failure of the North Korean revolution is a tragedy for the 25 million people that have led hard lives of endless labor campaigns, harsh living conditions, food shortages, malnutrition, starvation and political oppression on an almost unprecedented scale and degree, and who have been cordoned off from the outside world. The extent of this tragedy is clear when their lives are contrasted with those of their fellow Koreans in the South who enjoy what to most North Koreans must be unimaginable prosperity and personal freedom. In fact, the gap in living standards and the difference in lifestyles among North Koreans and South Koreans is probably the greatest between any two neighboring societies in the world. Yet they share the same cultural heritage, and they were part of the same ethnically homogeneous nation until suddenly, unexpectedly divided by an arbitrary line drawn up in 1945 by outside powers. The history of North Korea is also the story of its ordinary men and women. They have not simply been passive or faceless masses carrying out the will of the leader, but have helped shape its history. At times they enthusiastically embraced the goals of the state. Most at least came to accept the system. When it failed them they refashioned it, not through rebellion, but out of necessity. The people of North Korea made so many sacrifices, endured so much suffering, under the leadership and direction of those who ill-served them.

Notes

1   Andrei Lankov, "Pyongyang Strikes Back: North Korean Policies of 2002–08 and Attempts to Reverse 'De-Stalinization from Below'," *Asia Policy* 8 (July 2009): 47–71; Gause, p. 81.

2   Lankov, 2009; Stephan Haggard, and Marcus Noland, "Sanctioning North Korea: The Political Economy of Denuclearization and Proliferation," *Asian Survey* 50, no. 3 (May/June 2010): 539–568.

3   Haggard and Noland, 2011, p. 10.

4   Haggard and Noland, 2011, p. 11.

5   Haggard and Noland, 2011, pp. 50–51.

6   Haggard and Noland 2011, p. 59.

7   "North Korean Tecnhnocrat Executed for Bungled Currency Reform: Yonhap News Agency, 18 March 2010, http://english.yonhapnews.co.kr/northkorea/%26/0401000000AEN20100318004400315F.HT

8   Reporters Without Borders, "North Korea: The Web as a Pawn with Power Game" (March 2014), http://12mars.rsf.org/2014-en/tag/bureau-27/. Accessed April 29, 2015.

9   Cha, 445.

10 Joo, Hyung-Min, "Visualizing the Invisible Hands: The Shadow Economy in North Korea," *Economy and Society* 39, no.1 (2010): 110–145.

11 *Washington Post*, March 6, 2009; Yoonok Chang, Stephan M. Haggard, Marcus Noland, "Exit Polls: Refugee Assessments of North Korea's Transition," (Washington, DC: Peterson Institute for International Economics, January 2008), Working Paper No. 08-1,https://piie.com/publications/working-papers/exit-polls-refugee-assessments-north-koreas-transition

12 Yoonok Chang, Stephan M. Haggard, Marcus Noland, "Exit Polls: Refugee Assessments of North Korea's Transition," (Washington, DC: Peterson Institute for International Economics, January 2008), Working Paper No. 08-1./?

13 *Daily NK*, February 2, 2010.
14 For a counter view that argues these charges of criminality are exaggerated see Smith, 36–39.
15 Aiden Foster-Carter, "Keys to the Kingdom: North Korea's Economic heritage and Prospects After Kim Jong-Il's Death," Korean Economic Institute, *On Korea 2013* 6 (2013): 23–47.
16 Aidan Foster-Carter, "Lee Myung Bak's Nordpolitik: A U-Turn in the Pipeline?" *38North* (September 11, 2011), http://www.38north.org Accessed April 12, 2016.
17 Fujimoto, pp. 136–137, 227.
18 Na Chong-il, *Chang Sŏng-t'aek ŭi Kil* [Chang Sŏng-t'aek's Road]. Seoul: Alda, 2016, pp. 231–232.
19 Beck, Peter M, "North Korea in 2010," *Asian Survey* 51, no. 1 (January/February 2011): 33–40.
20 Beck, 2011, pp. 33–40.
21 Peter Foster, "Kim Jong Il's Oldest Son Against Dynastic Succession," *Daily Telegraph*, October 12, 2010.
22 Lim, 2015, 113.
23 Beck, 2011, pp. 33–40.
24 *North Korea Leadership Watch*, April 21, 2012.
25 *Daily NK*, July 17, 2012.
26 *New York Times*, December 13, 2013.
27 *Daily NK*, July 9, 2014.
28 Kim Yang Gon was reported to have been killed in a car accident in 2015 and was given a state funeral. "North Korean Official Dies in Car Accident," *Choson ilbo*, December 31, 2015,http://english.chosun.com/site/data/html_dir/2015/12/31/2015123101249.html
29 Hong Yung Lee, "North Korea in 2013: Economy, Executions, and Nuclear Brinkmanship," *Asian Survey* 94, no. 1 (January/February 2014): 89–100.
30 *Daily NK*, July 25, 2012.
31 Myers, 2015, 214.
32 *Daily NK*, August 9, 2013.
33 *Daily NK*, October 19, 2012.
34 *Daily NK*, July 11, 2012.
35 *New York Times*, September 4, 2012.
36 Huffington Post, June 12, 2012.
37 *Daily NK*, October 8, 20132.
38 Daniel Tudor and James Pearson, *North Korea Confidential: Private markets, Fashion Trends, Prison Camps, Dissenters and* Defector, (Tokyo: Tuttle, 2015), 16.

39 *New York Times*, March 11.
40 Drew Thompson, *Silent Partners, Chinese Joint Ventures in North Korea*, U.S. Korea Institute at SAIS, February 2011. http://uskoreainstitute.org/research/ special-reports/silent-partners-chinese-joint-ventures-in-north-korea/.
41 *South China Morning Post* December 28, 2012.
42 US Geological Survey John C. Wu, "The Mineral Industry of NK," 2005 *Minerals Yearbook: North Korea*, US Geological Survey (June 2007): 15.1.
43 Aiden Foster-Carter, "Keys to the Kingdom: North Korea's Economic heritage and Prospects After Kim Jong-Il's Death," Korean Economic Institute. *On Korea 2013* 6 (2013): 23–47.
44 Thompson, *Silent Partners*.
45 Thompson, *Silent Partners*.
46 Andray Abrahamian, "A Convergence of Interests: Prospects for Rason Special Economic Zone," 69–80.
47 *The Washington Post*, 14 March 2015.
48 Peter Hays Gries, "The Koguryo Controversy, National Identity, and Sino-Korean Relations Today," *East Asia* 22, no. 4 (2005): 3–17.
49 Woo Young Lee and Jungmin Seo, "'Cultural Pollution' from the South?," in Kyung-Ae Park and Scott Snyder, editors, *North Korea in Transition: Politics, Economy and Society*. Lanham, MD: Rowman & Littlefield, 2013, pp. 195–207.
50 International Crisis Group, *Strangers At Home: North Koreans in the South* Report No.208 Brussels: International Crisis Group, 2011, pp. 14–15.
51 Stephan Haggard, "Kim Jong Un Doubles Down I: The Opening Speech and the Central Committee Report. *Petersen Institute for International Economics* (May 9, 2016) https://piie.com/blogs/north-korea-witness-transformation/ kim-jong-un-doubles-down-i-opening-speech-and-central Accessed July 28, 2016.
52 Frank Ruediger, "The 7th Party Congress in North Korea: A Return to the New Normal" *38th North* (May 20, 2016) http://38north.org/2016/05/ rfrank052016/ Accessed July 29, 2016.

Glossary of Korean Terms

anjŏn powibu State Safety and Security Department

Anjŏnbu "safety bureau" term often used for the political police sometimes translated as State Security Department

banhŭi neighborhood associations in South Korea

byungjin see *pyŏngjin*

changgun general

changmadang general markets

ch'il sip-il il chŏnt'u "Seventy-Day Battle"

Ch'inaehan Chidoja "Dear Leader" (Kim Jong Il)

Choch'ongnyŏn (Japanese Chosoren) Korean Association in Japan

Chojikbu Organization and Guidance of the Korean Workers' Party

chosaek nongmin chohap "red peasant unions" communist peasant organizations

choktae kyech'ŭng "hostile" class in North Korean society used to designate least trustworthy of the three main social classes

Ch'ŏllima mythical flying horse, movement to speed up product in North Korea

chŏngbo unit of land (approximately 2.5 acres or one hectare)

ch'ongde ch'ŏlhak "barrel-of-the-gun philosophy"

chonghap sichang "general markets" used for private markets in North Korea from 1990s

Ch'ŏngsan-ri munbŏp "Ch'ŏngsan-ri Method" method for increasing output of collective farms

Ch'ŏng'udang Young Friends' Party

chŏnmin mujanghwa "arming the whole people"

Chosŏn lit. "Land of the Morning Calm," name of an early kingdom and of the Korean state from 1392–1910, used as the common term for Korea in North Korea

Chosŏn kŏn'guk chunbi wiwŏnhoe Committee for Preparation of Korean Independence

Chosŏn Minjujuŭi Inmin Konghwaguk Democratic People's Republic of Korea (official name of North Korea since 1948)

Chosŏn kongsandang Puk Chosŏn punguk North Korea Branch Bureau of the Korean Communist Party

Chosŏn Rodong-dang Korean Workers' Party official name of the North Korean Communist Party

chuch'e See juche
chuch'e sasang "juche thought"
ch'ulsin "origins" refers to family background
(chusŏk) "president" used in North Korea
Ch'usŏk the Korean fall thanksgiving
haeksim kyech'ŭng "core class" or loyal class in North Korean society
hanbok tradition Korean dress
Han'guk "Korea," most commonly used term for Korea in South Korea
han'gŭl the indigenous Korean alphabet (lit. "Korean writing")
hanmun Chinese characters, also called *hanja*
hansik holiday 105 days after the winter solstice
hwan'gap sixtieth birthday celebration
hyŏngmyŏngjŏk kagye "revolutionary family heritage" used for family of Kim Il
     Sung
hyŏngmyŏnghwa kuyŏk "revolutionization zones" rehabilitation wings of prison
     camps
hyŏnji chido "on the spot guidance"
Hyŏpdong nongjgang kŏmsa wiwŏnhoe inspection committees on a state farm
hyŏpdonghwa "cooperativization" North Korean term for collectivization of
     agriculture
indŏk chŏngch'i "a politics of love and trust" between the leader and his people
ingonggi (or People's Republic flag) flag of North Korea
inmin "the people"
inmin wiwŏnhoe people's committees
inminban neighborhood associations in North Korea
inminbanjang head of *iniminban*
juche (chuch'e) North Korean ideology based on the thought of Kim Il Sung,
     sometimes translated "self-reliance"
Kapsan kongjak wiwŏnhoe (Kapsan Operations Committee) logistical support
     organization for Manchurian guerillas
kayagŭm a Korean zither
kiŏp tongnip ch'aesanje the enterprise responsibility system
kokutai "national essence" (Japanese term) pre-1945 Japanese nationalist
     ideology
konan ŭi haenggun "Arduous March" term used for Kim Il Sung's escape from
     march from Japanese pursuers and for the 1990s famine
Koryŏ name of Korean state from 935 to 1392, another name for Korea
kotchebi "swallows" term for children abandoned in 1990s famine
kukka chŏngch'i powibu State Political Security Department

kukka powibu State Security Department
külloja hakkyo night schools teaching adult literacy
külloja chunghakkyo two-year workers' middle schools
kunsa wiwŏnhoe Military Committee
kwahakhwa "scientific transformation"
kwalliso North Korean political prisoner camps sometimes translated as "administrative and control centers"
(Kwangbok ŭi ch'ŏlli kil) the "One Thousand *Ri* Journey for Liberation."
Kwangmyŏngsŏng "Brilliant Star" satellite
kyech'ŭng "class" the three classes of North Korean society
Kyŏtkaji "side branch" refers to Kim Il Sung's family by his third wife
minjok "people" or "nation"
Minjudang Democratic Party
minjung "the masses" or "the people"
mip'ung yangsok "beautiful customs and virtues"
Munhwabu "Department of Culture" propaganda bureau aimed at South Korea
na sŏn "four lines" military preparedness policy in North Korea
nodong kyohwaso labor correction centers for more serious offenses
nodong kyoyangso labor education centers for more short term prisoners
nodong tallyŏndae labor training centers for minor offences
Nongjangwon members of a state collective farm
nongmin sijang farmer's markets
Nonong chŏkwidae Worker-Peasant Red Guards
ŏbŏi suryŏng "parental leader" term for Kim Il Sung
Odo haengjŏngguk Five Provinces Administrative Bureau
ogajo "five-household team"
oho tamdangje (five households-in-change system) of neighborhood collective security
Paeum ŭi ch'ŏlli kil "One Thousand *Ri* Journey for Learning"
pando lit. "half island," peninsula
pangch'ang a technique of offstage singing in operas
pibaegŭp sidae "age of non-distribution" [of food]
pŏp cooked rice
puin wife or married woman
punjo sub-work team on a state farm
Puk Chosŏn minju ch'ŏngnyŏn tongmaeng Democratic Youth League
Puk Chosŏn minjujuŭi t'ongil chŏnsŏn United Democratic National Front
Pukchosŏn minju yŏsŏng tongmaeng North Korean Democratic Women's League
Pulgŭn Ch'ŏngnyŏn Künwidae Young Red Guards

p'umassi-ban (agricultural) mutual aid teams

punjo subteams on collective farms

pyŏngjin "equal progress" or "equal emphasis" policy of emphasizing both military and economic development Also *byungjin*

sadaejuŭi "flunkyism" or the blind subservience to a great power

saenghwal ch'onghwa self criticism meetings

Samdae hyŏngmyŏng sojo undong the Three Revolutions Small Team Movement

samuwŏn term for white collar workers in North Korea

silli "practical benefits"

simhwajo "deep investigation team"

Sinmindang New Democratic Party

sŏngbun grades in which society is divided (North Korea)

sŏn'gun "Military First" policy of North Korea

Sonyŏndan Children's Union

sukpak kŏmyŏl midnight home visits in North Korea

Taeanŭi saŏpch'ekye Taean Work System

t'aegukki flag of Korea before 1910 and of South Korea since 1948

Taehan Min'guk Republic of Korea (Official name of South Korea since 1948)

Taenam yŏllakpu South Korean Liaison Bureau

Taeoe chŏngbo chosabu Department of External Intelligence Inquires often known as the "35th office"

Taeanŭi saŏpch'ekye Taean Work Section

taet'ongnyŏng "president" used in South Korea

tang chungang "Party Center" euphemism for Kim Jong Il

Tano (Dano) the fifth day of the fifth lunar year

t'ongbokwa notification system

t'onghaengjŭng travel permit

t'ongil p'ojŏn "unification fields" farm plots

Tongnip ch'aesanje independent accounting system

t'ongyo kyech'ŭng "wavering" class in North Korean society the middle ranking of the three main classes that North Korean society is divided into

tongmu "comrade"

tŏlgyŏk undong "assault movement"

t'ŏtpat family farm plot

ŭibyŏng "righteous armies," resistance bands during the Japanese invasions of Korea

urisik sahoejuŭi "our style of socialism"

waeguksaram "foreigners"

wanch'ung ŭi hae "year of readjustment"

wanjŏn t'ongje kuyŏk "total control zones" sections of political prison camps

Widaehan Chidoja "Great Leader" (used for Kim Jong Il)

Widaehan Ryŏngdoja "Great Leader" (term used for Kim Jong Il)

Widaehan Suryŏngnim "Great Leader" (term used for Kim Il Sung)

wŏn unit of currency

yangban "two sides," the aristocratic elite of Korea

yanggwŏn coupons for food and other essentials

yŏngmyŏnghan tongji "brilliant comrade" used for Kim Jong Un

yŏsŏng "woman"

yuilsasangch'egye "Monolithic Ideological System of Thought"

yuhun t'ongch'i "governance based on the teaching left behind" (by Kin Il sung)

xiafang "downward to the village" (Chinese term) sending officials to farms

Bibliography

Books

Armstrong, Charles K. *The North Korean Revolution, 1945–1950*. Ithaca, NY: Cornell University Press, 2003.

Armstrong, Charles. *Tyranny of the Weak: North Korea and the World, 1950–1992* (Studies of the Weatherhead East Asian Institute). Ithaca, NY: Cornell University Press, 2013.

Armstrong, Charles K., Gilbert Rozman, Samuel S. Kim, and Stephen Kotlin (eds). *Korea at the Center: Dynamics of Regionalism in Northeast Asia*. Armonk, NY: M.E. Sharpe, 2006.

Baik, Bong. *Kim Il Sung Biography*. Tokyo: Miraisha, 1970.

Bermudez, Joseph S. Jr. *The Armed Forces of North Korea*. London: I.B. Tauris, 2001.

Brazhanova, Nadia, *Koro e sŏn Pukhan kyŏngje* [North Korean Economy at a Crossroads], trans. Yang Chun-yong, Seoul: Han'guk Kyŏngje Sinmunsa, 1992.

Buzo, Adrian. *The Guerilla Dynasty: Politics and Leadership in the DPRK 1945–1994*. Sydney: Allen & Unwin, 1999.

Buzo, Adrian. *The Making of Modern Korea*. New York: Routledge, 2007.

Cha, Victor. *The Impossible State, North Korea, Past and Future*. New York: Ecco, 2012.

Chen, Jian. *China's Road to the Korean War: The Making of the Sino-American Confrontation*. New York: Columbia University Press, 1994.

Chŏng, Ch'ang-yŏng. *Kyŏt esŏ pon Kim Chŏng-il* [Close to Kim Jong Il]. Seoul: Kimyŏngsa, 2000.

Chung, Chin O. *Pyŏngyang Between Peking and Moscow: North Korea's Involvement in the Sino-Soviet Dispute, 1958–1975*. Tuscaloosa, AL: The University of Alabama Press, 1978.

Crane, Conrad C. *American Airpower Strategy in Korea, 1950–1953*. Lawrence, KS: University of Kansas Press, 2000.

Cumings, Bruce. *The Korean War: A History*. New York: The Modern Library, 2010.

Cumings, Bruce. *Origins of the Korea War*, Vols I and 2. Princeton, NJ.: Princeton University Press, 1981, 1990.

Demick, Barbara. *Nothing to Envy: Ordinary Lives in North Korea*. New York: Spiegel & Grau, 2009.

Deveraux, Stephan (ed.). *The New Famines: Why Famines Persist in an Era of Globalization*. London: Routledge, 2007.

Eberstadt, Nicholas. *The North Korean Economy: Between Crisis & Catastrophe*. New Brunswick, NJ: Transaction Publishers, 2007.

Flake, Gordon L. and Scott Snyder (eds). *Paved with Good Intentions: The NGO Experience in North Korea*. Westport, CT: Praeger, 2004.

Fujimoto Kenji. *Kim Chŏng-il uui yorisa* [Cook of Kim Jong Il], trans. Sin Hyŏn-do. Seoul: Wŏlgan Chosŏnsa, 2003.

Gause, Ken E. *North Korea Under Kim Jong-il: Power, Politics and Prospects for Change*. Westport, CT: Praeger, 2011.

Grzelczyk, Virginie. *North Korea's New Diplomacy: Challenging Political Isolation in the 21st Century*. London: Palgrave Macmillan, 2017.

Haggard, Stephan and Marcus Noland. *Famine in North Korea: Markets, Aid, and Reform*. New York: Columbia University Press, 2007.

Haggard, Stephan and Marcus Noland. *Witness to Transformation: Refugee Insights into North Korea*. Washington, DC: Peterson Institute for International Economics, 2011.

Harrison, Selig S. *Korean Endgame: A Strategy for Reunification and U.S. Disengagement*. Princeton, NJ: Princeton University Press, 2002.

Hassig, Ralph and Kongdan Oh. *The Hidden People of North Korea: Everyday Life in the Hermit Kingdom*. Lanham, MD: Rowman & Littlefield, 2009.

Hassig, Ralph and Kongdan Oh. *North Korea: Through the Looking Glass*. Washington, DC: Brookings Institution Press, 2000.

Hwang Chang-yŏp. *Na nŭn yŏk-sa ŭi chilli rŭl poatta* [I saw the truth of history]. Seoul: Hanul, 1999.

Jaeger, Sheila Miyoshi. *Brothers at War: The Unending Conflict in Korea*. New York: Norton, 2013.

Jang Jin-sung. *Dear Leader: Poet, Spy, Escapee – A Look Inside North Korea*, trans. Shirley Lee. New York: Atria Books, 2014.

Kang Chol-hwan and Pierre Rigoulot. *The Aquariums of Pyongyang*. New York: Basic Books, 2001.

Kang Hyok, with Philippe Grangereau and Shaun Whiteside (trans). *This Is paradise! My North Korean Childhood*. London: Little, Brown, 2007.

Kim, C.I. Eugene and B.C. Koh (eds). *Journey to North Korea: Personal Perceptions*. Berkeley, CA: University of California Press, 1983.

Kim Ha-yong. *Kukche Chuŭi sigak esŏ pon hanbando* [The Korean Peninsula from an International Perspective]. Seoul: Ch'aek Pŏllae, 2002.

Kim Hae-wŏn, *Pukhan ŭi Nambukhan chŏngch'i hyŏpsang yŏn'gu* [Research on North Korea's Political Negotiations with South Korea], Seoul: Sŏnin Publications, 2012.

Kim, Ilpyong J. Kim. *Historical Dictionary of North Korea*. Lanham, MD: The Scarecrow Press, 2003.

Kim, Joungwon Alexander. *Divided Korea: The Politics of Development, 1945–1972*. Cambridge, MA: Harvard University Press, 1975.

Kim Kwang-un. *Pukhan Chŏngch'i yŏn'gu 1* [Studies of North Korean Political History] *1: History of the Establishment*]. Seoul: Sŏnin, 2003.

Kim Sŏng-bo. *Pukhan ŭi yŏksa 1: Kŏn'guk kwa inminjujuŭi ŭi kyŏnghyŏm* [North Korean History Vol 1: Establishment and Experience of the People's Democracy]. Seoul: Yŏksa Pip'yŏngsa, 2011.

Kim Sŏng-bo. *Pukhan ŭi yŏksa 2: Chuch'e Sassang kwa yuilch'eje* [North Korean History: Juche and the Monolithic Ideological System]. Seoul: Yŏksa Pip'yŏngsa, 2011.

Kim, Sun Joo (ed.). *The Northern Region of Korea: History Identity Culture*. Seattle, WA: University of Washington Press, 2010.

Kim, Suzy. *Everyday Life in the North Korean Revolution, 1945–1950*. Ithaca, NY: Cornell University Press, 2013.

Kim, Yongho. *North Korean Foreign Policy: Security Dilemma and Succession*. Lanham, MD, Lexington Books, 2011.

Koh, Byung-chull. *The Foreign Policy of North Korea*. New York. Prager, 1969.

Koh, Byung-chull. *The Foreign Policy Systems of North and South Korea*. Berkeley, CA: University of California Press, 1984.

Kwon, Heonik and Byung-ho Chung. *North Korea: Beyond Charismatic Politics*. Lanham: Rowman & Littlefield, 2012.

Lankov, Andrei. *From Stalin to Kim Il Sung: The Formation of North Korea, 1945–1960*. New Brunswick, NJ: Rutgers University Press, 2002.

Lankov, Andrei. *North of the DMZ: Essays on Daily Life in North Korea*. Jefferson, NC: McFarland & Company, 2007.

Lankov, Andrew. *The Real North Korea: Life and Politics in the Failed Stalinist Utopia*. Oxford: Oxford University Press, 2013.

Lee, Chong-sik. *The Korean Workers' Party: A Short History*. Stanford, CA: Stanford University, Hoover Institution Press, 1978.

Lee, Hy-Sang. *North Korea: A Strange Socialist Fortress*. Westport, CT: Praeger, 2001.

Lee, Jungsoo. *The Partition of Korea After World War II: A Global History*. New York: Palgrave Macmillan, 2006.

Lee, Mun Woong. *Rural North Korea Under Communism: A Study of Sociological Change*. Houston, TX: Rice University Press, 1976.

Lee Suk. *The DPRK Famine, 1994–2000*. Seoul: Korean Institute for National Unification, 2005.

Lim Jae-Chon. *Kim Jong Il's Leadership of North Korea*. London: Routledge, 2009.

Lim, Jae-Cheon Lim. *Leader Symbols and Personality Cult in North Korea*. London: Routledge, 2015.

Martin, Bradley. *Under the Loving Care of the Fatherly Leader*. New York: St Marin's Press.

Millet, Alan R. *The War for Korea, 1950–1951*. Lawrence, KS: University of Kansas Press, 2010.

Morris-Suzuki, Tessa. *Exodus to North Korea: Shadow from Japan's Cold War*. Lanham, MD: Rowman & Littlefield, 2007.

Myers, Brian. *The Cleanest Race: How North Koreans See Themselves-And Why It Matters*. Brooklyn, NY: Melville House, 2010.

Na Chong-il. *Chang Sŏng-t'aek ŭi Kil*. [Chang Sŏng-t'aek's Road]. Seoul: Alda, 2016.

Nam, Koon Woo. *The North Korean Communist Leadership, 1945–1965: A Study of Factionalism and Political Consolidation*. Tuscaloosa, AL: University of Alabama Press, 1974.

Natsios, Andrew S. *The Great North Korean Famine*. Washington, DC: United States Institute of Peace Press, 2001.

Oberdorfer, Donald. *The Two Koreas: A Contemporary History*. New York: Basic Books, 1998.

Ó Gráda, Cormac. *Famine: A Short History*. Princeton, NJ: Princeton University Press, 2009.

Pak Hyŏnsŏn. *Hyŏndae Pukhan sahoe wa kajok* [Contemporary North Korean society and family]. Sŏul: Hanul, 2003.

Park, Han S. Park. *North Korea: The Politics of Unconventional Wisdom*. Boulder, CO: Lynne Rienner, 2002.

Park, Kyung-Ae and Scott Snyder (eds). *North Korea in Transition: Politics, Economy and Society*. Lanham, MD: Rowman & Littlefield, 2013.

Park, Philip H. *Self-Reliance or Self-Destruction?: Success and Failure of the Democratic People's Republic of Korea's Development Strategy of Self-reliance "Juche."* New York: Routledge, 2002.

Robinson, Michael. *Cultural Nationalism in Colonial Korea, 1920–25*. Seattle, WC: University of Washington Press, 1988.

Salisbury, Harrison. *To Peking and Beyond: A Report on the New Asia*. New York: Quadrangle Books, 1973.

Scalapino. Robert A. (ed.). *Korea Today*. New York: Praeger, 1963.

Scalapino, Robert A. and Jun-Yop Kim (eds). *North Korea Today*. Berkeley, CA: University of California Press, 1983.

Scalapino Robert A. and Hongkoo Lee (eds). *North Korea in a Regional and Global Context*. Berkeley, CA: University of California Press, 1986.

Seiler, Sydney. *Kim Il-Soong 1941–1948: The Creation of a Legend, the Building of a Regime*. Lanham, MD: University Press of America, 1994.

Shin, Gi-Wook. *Ethnic Nationalism in Korea: Genealogy, Politics, and Legacy*. Stanford, CA: Stanford University Press, 2006.

Shin, Gi-wook. *Peasant Protest and Social change in Colonial Korea*. Seattle, WC: University of Washington Press, 2014.

Shen, Zhihua and Danhui Li. *After Leaning to Once Side: China and Its Allies in the Cold War*. Stanford, CA: Stanford University Press, 2011.

Smith, Hazel. *North Korea: Markets and Military Rule*. Cambridge: Cambridge University Press, 2015.

Sŏ Chae-jn. *Kim Il-sŏng hangil mujang t'ujaeng ŭi sinhwahwa yŏn'gu* [A Study of the Mythicization of Kim Il Sung's Anti-Japanese Military Struggle]. Seoul: Korean Institution for National Reunification, 2006.

Sŏ Tong-man. *Puk chosŏn yŏn'gu* [Studies on North Korea]. Paju, Republic of Korea: Han'guk wŏnsik, 2010.

Son Ho-ch'ŏl (ed.). *Han'guk chŏnchaeng kwa nampukhan sahoe ŭi kuchojŏk pyŏnhwa* [The Korean War and Structural Change in North and South Korean Society]. Seoul: Kyŏngnam Taehakkyo kungnipdong munje yŏn'gyso, 1991

Sŏng, Hye-rang *Tŭngnamu chip: Sŏng Hye-rang Chasŏjŏn* [Wisteria House: The Autobiography of Song Hye-rang]. Seoul: Chisiknara, 2000.

Stueck, William. *The Korean War: An International History*. Princeton, NJ: Princeton University Press, 1995.

Suh, Dae-Sook. *Kim Il Sung: The North Korean Leader*. New York: Columbia University Press, 1988.

Suh, Dae-sook (ed.). *Korean Studies: New Pacific Currents*. Honolulu: University of Hawaii, Center for Korean Studies, 1994.

Suh, Jae-Jung, (ed.). *Origins of North Korea's Juche*. Lanham, MD: Lexington Books, 2012.

Szalontai, Bazacs. *Kim Il Sung in the Khrushchev Era: Soviet-DPRK Relations and the Roots of North Korean Despotism, 1953–1964*. Stanford, CA: Stanford University Press, 2006.

Tudor, Daniel, James Pearson. *North Korea Confidential: Private markets, Fashion Trends, Prison Camps, Dissenters and Defectors*. Tokyo: Tuttle, 2015.

Wada Haruki. *Kim Il-sŏng kwa Minju hangil chŏnchaeng* [Kim Il Sung and the Manchurian Anti-Japanese War]. Seoul: Ch'anggak, 1992.

Wada Haruki, *The Korean War: An International History*. Lanham, MD: Rowman & Littlefield, 2014.

Worden, Robert L. (ed.). *North Korea: A Country Study* (Area Handbook Series). Claitor's Law Books and Publishing Division, 2009.

Yang, Sung chul. *The North and Southern Political Systems: A Comparative Analysis*. Elizabeth NJ.: Hollym, 1994.

Yim, Dongwoo. *North Korean Atlas*. Seoul: Kyeonwon Suh, 2014.

Yim, Sang-chöl. *Pukhan nongöp* [North Korean Agriculture]. Seoul: Tosö Ch'ulp'an Söil, 2000.

Articles and Other Sources

Abrahamian, Andray. "A Convergence of Interests: Prospects for Rason Special Economic Zone," 69–80.

Ahn Yinchay. "North Korea in 2002: A Survival Game," *Asia Survey* 43, no. 1 (January/February 2003): 49–63.

Armstrong, Charles "Centering the Periphery: Manchurian Exile(s) and the North Korean State," *Korean Studies* 19 (1995): 1–16.

Armstrong, Charles, K. "'Fraternal Socialism': The International Reconstruction of North Korea, 1953–62," *Cold War History* 5, no. 2 (May 2005): 161–187.

Armstrong, Charles. "The Origins of North Korean Cinema: Art and Propaganda in the Democratic People's Republic," *Acta Koreana* 5, no. 1 (January 2002): 1–19.

Baldwin, Frank. "Participatory Anti-Imperialism: The 1919 Independence Movement," *Journal of Korean Studies* 1, no. 1 (1979): 123–162.

Bank of Korea. *GDP of North Korea in 2002*. Seoul: Bank of Korea, 2002.

Beck, Peter M. "North Korea in 2010," *Asian Survey*, 51, no.1 (January/February 2011): 33–40.

Beck, Peter. "North Korea in 2011: The Next Kim Takes the Helm," *Asian Survey*, 52, no.1 (January/February 2002): 65–71.

Brown, David G. "North Korea in 1998: A year of Foreboding Developments," *Asian Survey*, 39, no. 1 (January/February 1999): 125–132.

Buoc, Allan. "A Visit to North Korea," *New York Times*, June 14, 1971

Chang, Yoonok Chang, Stephan M. Haggard, Marcus Noland. "Exit Polls: Refugee Assessments of North Korea's Transition," (Washington, DC: Peterson Institute for International Economics, January 2008), Working Paper No. 08-1.

Chen, Cheng, and Ji-Yong Lee. "Making Sense of North Korea: 'National Stalinism' in Comparative-Historical Perspective," *Communist and Post-Communist Studies* 40, no. 4 (2007): 459–475.

Chen Jian. "Limits of the 'Lips and Teeth' Alliance: An Historical Review of Chinese-North Korean Relations," Asia Program Special Report No. 115 Washington DC, Woodrow Wilson International Center for Scholars, September 2003.

Cho, Soon Sung. "North and South Korea: Stepped-Up Aggression and the Search for New Security," *Asian Survey*, 9, no. 1 (January 1969): 29–32.

Cho Ŭn-hŭi "Pukhan ŭi tapsa haenggun ŭl t'onghae pon hyŏnghae pon hyŏngmyŏng chŏnt'ong ŭirye mandŭlgi [North Korea's Making the Ritual of the Revolutionary Tradition Through visits to Revolutionary Sites]," *Hyŏndae Pukhan yŏn'gu* [Modern North Korea Studies], 10, no. 2 (2007): 100–147.

Choe, Yong-ho. "Christian Background in the Early Life of Kim Il-song," *Asian Survey* 26, no. 10 (1986): 1082–1091.

Choe, Yong-ho. "Reinterpreting Traditional History in North Korea," *Journal of Asian Studies*, 45, no. 3 (May 1981): 503–517.

Choi, Hyungsub. "Rationalizing the Guerilla State: North Korean Factory Management Reform, 1953–61," *History and Technology* 20, no. 1 (March 2004): 53–74.

Choi, Jinwook. "The North Korean Domestic Situation and its Impact on the Nuclear Crisis," *Ritsumeikan Annual Review of International Studies*, 5 (2006): 1–18. www.ristumeikan.ac.jp/acd/cg/ir/college/bulletin/evol.5/CHOI.pdf

Chung, Joseph S. "Economic Planning in North Korea," in Robert A. Scalapino and Jun-Yop Kim (eds). *North Korea Today*. Berkeley, CA: University of California Press, 1983, pp. 164–188.

Chung, Young Chul. "North Korean Reform and Opening: Dual Strategy and 'Silli' (Practical) Reform," *Pacific Affairs*, 77, no. 2 (2004): 283–305.

Clemens, Walter. "North Korea's Quest for Nuclear Weapons: New Historical Evidence," *Journal of East Asian Studies*, 10, no. 1 (2010): 1–27

Clippinger, Morgan E. "Kim Jong IL in the North Korean Mass Media: A Study of Semi-Esoteric Communication," *Asian Survey*, 21, no. 3 (March 1981): 289–309.

Collins, Robert. *Marked for Life: Song North Korea's Social Classification System.* Washington, DC: Committee for North Korean Human Rights http://www.hrnk.org/uploads/pdfs/HRNK_Songbun_Web.pdf. Accessed on April 24, 2015.

David, Benedict S. "Visitor to North Korea Describes Vast Building Drive," *New York Times*, August 10, 1971.

David-West, Alzo. "Nationalist Allegory in North Korea: The Revolutionary Opera 'Sea of Blood,'" *North Korean Review* 2, no. 2 (2006): 75–87.

Do Jein. "Nuclear Weapons as Ideology: The Formation of North Korean Nuclear Independence, 1962–1964," *Seoul Journal of Korean Studies*, 28, no. 2 (December 2015): 181–212.

Feffer, John. "North Korea and the International Politics of Famine," *Japan Focus* (October 2006).

Foster-Carter, Aiden. "Keys to the Kingdom: North Korea's Economic Heritage and Prospects After Kim Jong-Il's Death," Korean Economic Institute. *On Korea 2013* 6 (2013): 23–47.

Foster-Carter, Aidan. "Lee Myung Bak's Nordpolitik: A U-Turn in the Pipeline?," *38North* (September 11, 2011), http://www.38north.org. Accessed on April 12, 2016.

Gabrousenko, Tatiana. "North Korean "Rural Fiction" from the Late 1990s to the Mid-2000s: Permanence and Change," *Korean Studies* 33 (2009): 69–100.

Ginsburgs, George. "Soviet Development Grants and Aid to North Korea, 1945–1950." *Asia Pacific Community* 18 (Fall 1982): 42–63.

Goodkind, Daniel and Lorraine West. "The North Korean Famine and Its Demographic Impact," *Population and Development Review* 27, no. 2 (2001): 219–238

Gries, Peter Hays. "The Koguryo Controversy, National Identity, and Sino-Korean Relations Today," *East Asia*, 22, no. 4 (2005): 3–17.

Hamisevicz, Nicholas. "10 People You Need to Know for the Transition in North Korea," KEI.

Han, Hongkoo. "Colonial Origins of Juche: The Minsaengdan Incident of the 1030s and the Birth of the North Korea-China Relationship," in Suh, Jae-Jung (ed.). *Origins of North Korea's Juche*. Lanham, MD: Lexington Books, 2012, pp. 33–62.

Han, Monikka (2003) '1960 nyŏntae Pukhan-ŭi kyŏngche kukpang pyŏng-chin nosŏn-ŭi ch'aet'aek-kwa taenam chŏngch'aek [North Korea's choice of the simultaneous economic-military strengthening strategy and its policy towards South Korea]', *Yŏksa-wa hyŏnsil [History and Reality]*, 50: 133–164.

Han, Sung-joo. "North Korea's Security Policy and Military Strategy," in Robert A. Scalapino and Jun-Yop Kim (eds). *North Korea Today*. Berkeley, CA: University of California Press, 1983, pp. 144–163, 155.

Haggard, Stephan, and Marcus Noland. "Sanctioning North Korea: The Political Economy of Denuclearization and Proliferation," *Asian Survey*, 50, no. 3 (May/June 2010): 539–568.

Harden, Blaine. "North Korea's Extreme Makeover," *Foreign Policy*, (July 26, 2012), on line.

Hong Tack Chun. "The Second Economy of North Korea," *Seoul Journal of Economics* 12.21. (1992): 173–194.

Human Rights Watch. *"North Korea: A Matter of Survival: The North Korean Government's Control of Food and the Risk of Hunger,"* 18, no. 3 (c) (May 2006)

International Crisis Group. *Strangers At Home: North Koreans in the South* Report No. 208 Brussels: International Crisis Group, 2011.

Joo, Hyung-Min. "Visualizing the Invisible Hands: The Shadow Economy in North Korea," *Economy and Society* 39, no. 1 (2010): 110–145.

Jorganson, John. "Tan'gun and the Legitimization of a Threatened Dynasty: North Korea's Rediscovery of Tan'gun," *Korea Observer* 27 (1996): 273–306.

Kang Chŏng-gu. "Han'guk chŏnchange kwa pukhan sahoechuŭi kŏnsŏl," [The Korean War and the construction of North Korean Society] in Son Ho-ch'ŏl (ed). *Han'guk chŏnchaeng kwa nampukhan sahoe ŭi kuchojŏk pyŏnhwa* [The Korean War and Structural Change in North and South Korean Society]. Seoul: Kyŏngnam Taehakkyo kungnipdong munje yŏn'gyso, 1991, pp. 159–201.

Kang, Jin Woong. "The 'Domestic Revolution' Policy and Traditional Confucianism in North Korean State Formation: A Socio-cultural Perspective," *Harvard Asia Quarterly* 10 (2006): 34–45.

Kang, Jin Woong. "Historical Changes in North Korean Nationalism," *North Korean Review* 3, no. 1 (2007): 86–104.

Kang, Jin Woong. "The Patriarchal State and Women's Status in Socialist North Korea," *Graduate Journal of Asia-Pacific Studies* 6, no. 2 (2008): 55–70.

Kang, Jin Woong. "Political Uses of Confucianism in North Korea," *Journal of Korean Studies* 16, no. 1 (Spring 2011): 63–87.

Kihl, Young Whan. "North Korea in 1983: Transforming "The Hermit Kingdom"," *Asian Survey* 24, no. 1 (January 1984): 100–113.

Kihl, Young Whan. "North Korea in 1984: 'The Hermit Kingdom' Turns Outward!," *Asian Survey* 25, no. 1 (January 1985): 65–79

Kim, Byung-Yeon, Suk Jin Kim and Keun Lee. "Assessing the Economic Performance of North Korea, 1954–1989: Estimates and Growth Accounting Analysis," *Journal of Comparative Economics* 35, no. 3 (2007): 564–582.

Kim Byung-Yeon and Song Dongho. "The Participation of North Korean Households in the Informal Economy: Size, Determinants and Effect," *Seoul Journal of Economics* 21, no. 2 (2008): 373.

Kim, C.I. Eugene. "Introduction: A Long Journey," in Kim, C.I. Eugene, and B.C. Koh (eds). *Journey to North Korea: Personal Perceptions*. Berkeley: University of California Press, 1983, pp. 1–23.

Kim, Chu-wal. "Interview: With North Korea's Highest Ranking Military Defector," *New Focus International* 4 January 2014, newfocusintl.com/exclusive-conversation-north-koreas-highest-ranking-military-defense.

Kim Gwang-Oon. "The Making of the North Korean State," *Journal of Korean Studies* 12, no. 1 (2007): 15–42.

Kim, Gwang-Oon. "The Making of the Juche State in Postcolnial North Korea," in Suh, Jae-Jung (ed.). *Origins of North Korea's Juche*. Lanham, MD: Lexington Books, 2012, pp. 63–87.

Kim Hakjoon. "The Hereditary Succession from Kim Jong-il to Kim Jong-un: Its Background, Present Situation, and Future," in Sang-hun Choe, Gi-Wook Shin, and David Straub (eds). *Troubled Transition: North Korea's Politics, Economy, and External Relations*. Stanford, CA: Walter H. Shorenstein Asia-Pacific Research Center, 2013, pp. 229–259.

Kim, Samuel S. "North Korea in 1999: Bringing the Grand Chollima March Back In," *Asian Survey*, 40, no. 1 (January/February 2000): 151–163.

Kim, Samuel S. "North Korea in 2000: Surviving through High Hopes of Summit Diplomacy, *Asia Survey* 41, no. 1 (January/February 2001): 12–29.

Kim Seong-bo. "The Decision-Making Process and Implementation of the North Korean Land Reform," in PNF Kie-Chung and Michael D. Shin (eds). *Landlords, Peasants and Intellectuals in Modern Korea*. Ithaca, NY: Cornell University Press, 2005, pp. 207–241.

Kim, Sung-chull. "Fluctuating Institutions of Enterprise Management in North Korea: Prospects for Local Enterprise Reform," *Harvard Asia Quarterly*: 10–33.

Kim Young C. "The Democratic People's Republic of Korea in 1975," *Asian Survey* 16, no. 1 (January 1976): 82–94.

Kim, Young C. "North Korea 1979: National Unification and Economic Development," *Asian Survey* 20, no. 1 (January 1980): 53–62.

Koh, Byung-chul. "Ideology and Pragmatism in North Korean Foreign Policy," in Dae-Sook Suh (ed.). *Korean Studies: New Pacific Currents*, Honolulu, HI: Center for Korean Studies, 1994, pp. 207–226.

Koh, Byung Chul. "The Impact of the Chinese Model on North Korea," *Asian Survey* 18, no. 6 (1978): 626–643.

Koh, Byung Chul. "North Korea in 1987: Launching a New Seven-Year Plan," *Asian Survey* 28, no. 1 (January 1988): 62–70.

Koh, Byung Chul. "North Korea: Old Goals and New Realities," *Asian Survey* 14, no. 1 (January 1974): 36–42.

Koh, Byung Chul. "Unification Policy and North-south Relations," in Robert A. Scalapino and Jun-Yop Kim (eds). *North Korea Today*. Berkeley, CA: University of California Press, 1983, pp. 264–308, 266, 269.

Koh, Dae-Won. "Dynamics of Inter-Korean Conflict and North Korea's Recent Policy Changes: An Inter-Systemic View," *Asian Survey*, 44, no. 3 (May/June 2004): 422–441.

Koo, Bon-Hak. "Political Economy of Self-Reliance: Juche and Economic Development," in *North Korea, 1961–1990*. Seoul: Research Center for Peace and Unification of Korea, 1992, p. 85.

Korea Newsreview, October 16, 1993, 30–31.

Kotlin, Stephen and Charles K. Armstrong. "A Socialist Regional Order in Northeast Asia After World War II," in Charles K. Armstrong, K. Gilbert Rozman, Samuel S. Kim, and Stephen Kotlin (eds). *Korea at the Center: Dynamics of Regionalism in Northeast Asia*. Armonk, NY: M.E. Sharpe, 2006, pp. 110–125.

Lankov, Andrei N. "The Demise of Non-Communist Parties in North Korea (1945–1960)," *Journal of Cold War Studies* 3, no. 1 (Winter 2001): 103–125.

Lankov, Andrei. "Pyongyang Strikes Back: North Korean Policies of 2002–08 and Attempts to Reverse "De-Stalinization from Below"," *Asia Policy* 8 (July 2009): 47–71.

Lankov, Andrei. "North Korea is No Stalinist Country," *Korea Times* October 9, 2011.

Lee, Chong-sik. "Land Reform, Collectivization and the Peasant in North Korea," in Robert A. Scalapino (ed.). *Korea Today*. New York: Praeger, 1963, pp. 65–81.

Lee, Chong-sik. "Why Did Stalin Accept the 38th Parallel?," *Journal of Northeast Asian Studies* 4, no. 4 (Winter 1985): 67–74.

Lee, Hong Yung. "North Korea in 2013: Economy, Executions, and Nuclear Brinkmanship," *Asian Survey*, 94, no. 1 (January/February 2014): 89–100.

Lee, In-ho. "The Soviet Military Government in North Korea," *Korea Observer* 23, no. 4 (1991): 521–548.

Lee, John H. "By Any Standards Industry is Powerful," *New York Times* June 4, 1972.

Lee Mun Woong. "Rural North Korea under Communism: A Study of Sociological Change," Ph. D Dissertation, Rice University, 1975.

Lee, Suk. "Reliability and Usability of the DPRK Statistics: Case of Grain Statistics in 1946–2000," *International Journal of Unification Studies* 15, no. 1 (2006): 132–172.

Lee, Woo Young and Jungmin Seo "'Cultural Pollution' from the South?," in Kyung-Ae Park and Scott Snyder (eds). *North Korea in Transition: Politics, Economy and Society.* Lanham, MD: Rowman & Littlefield, 2013, pp. 195–297.

Lerner, Mitchell. *"Mostly Propaganda in Nature" Kim Il Sung, the Juche Ideology and the Second Korean War.* Washington, DC: Woodrow Wilson International Center for Scholars, 2011.

Lim, Jae-Cheon. "Institutional Change in North Korean Economic Development Since 1984: The Competition Between Hegemonic and Non-hegemonic Rules and Norms," *Pacific Affairs* 82, no. 1 (Spring 2009): 9–27.

MacDonald, Callum A. "So Terrible a 'Liberation': The U.N. Occupation of North Korea," *Bulletin of Concerned Asian Scholars,* 23, no. 2 (1991): 6–7, 17.

Mansourov, Alexandre. "Stalin, Mao, Kim and china's Decision to Enter the Korean War, September 16–October 15, 1950," *Cold War International History Project,* 6–7 (Winter 1995): 94–107.

Merrill, John. "North Korea in 1993: In the Eye of the Storm," *Asian Survey,* 34. no. 1 (January 1994): 10–18.

Michishita, Narushige. "Calculated Adventurism: North Korea's Military-Diplomatic Campaigns," *Korea Journal of Defense Analysis* 16, no. 2 (Fall 2004): 188–197.

Miller, Owen. "North Korea's Hidden History," *International Socialism* 109 (2006): 153–166.

Myers, Brian. "The Watershed that Wasn't: Re-evaluating Kim Il Sung's "Juche Speech" of 1955," *Acta Koreana* 9, no. 1 (January 2006): 89–115.

Nam, Koon Woo. "The Purge of the Southern Communists in North Korea: A Retrospective View," *Asian Forum* 5, no. 1 (1973): 43–54.

Nam Sung-wook. "Chronic Food Shortages and the Collective Farm System in North Korea," *Journal of East Asian Studies* 7 (2007): 93–123.

Natsios, Andrew. *The Politics of Famine in North Korea* (Special Report) U.S. Institute of Peace (August 2, 1999) http://www.usip.org/oc/sr/sr990802.

Niksch, Larry A. Niksch. *The Collapse of the February 29 Agreement: Is Denuclearization of North Korea Still a Credible Policy Objective?* Washington, DC: Institute for Corean-American Studies, ICAS Lectures February 14, 2012.

Noland, Marcus. "Life in North Korea" June 5, 2003 Peter Institute for International Economics, https://piie.com/commentary/testimonies/life-north-korea

Noland, Marcus. "North Korea as a "New Famine," in Stephen Deveraux (ed.). *The New Famines: Why Famines Persist in an Era of Globalization* London: Routledge, 2007, pp. 197–222.

Paige, Glen D. "Korea Creates the Future," *Asian Survey*, 7, No. 1 (January 1967): 21–30.

Pak, Sunyoung, Daniel Schwedendiek and Hee Kyoung Kim. "Height and Living Standards in North Korea, 1930s–1980s," *The Economic History Review* 64, no. 1 (2011): 142–158.

Park, Kyung-ae. "North Korea in 2003: Pendulum Swing between Crisis and Diplomacy," *Asia Survey* 44, no. 1 (January/February 2004): 139–46.

Park, Kyung Ae. "Women and Revolution in North Korea," *Pacific Affairs* 65, no. 4 (Winter 1992–93): 527–545.

Peterson, Martin. "The Downfall of a Model Citizen?: Family Background in North Korean Graphic Novels," *Korean Studies* 36 (2012): 83–122.

Petrov, Leonid. "Turning Historians into Party Scholar-Bureaucrats: North Korean Historiogrpahy from 1955–1958," *East Asian History* 31 (June 2007): 101–119.

Reilly, James. "The Curious Case of China's Economic Aid to North Korea," *Asian Survey* 54, no. 6 (November–December 2014): 158–183.

Reporters Without Borders. "North Korea: The Web as a Pawn with Power Game" (March 2014), http://12mars.rsf.org/2014-en/tag/bureau-27/. Accessed on April 29 2015.

Robinson, Joan. "Korean Miracle," *Monthly Review* 16, no. 9 (January 1965): 541–549.

Roehig, Terrence. "North Korea and the Northern Limit Line." *North Korea Review* 5, no. 1 (Fall 2009): 8–22.

Ruediger, Frank. "Money in Socialist Economies: The Case of North Korea," *The Asia-Pacific Journal*, 8-2-10, February 22, 2010.

Ruediger, Frank. "The 7th Party Congress in North Korea: A Return to the New Normal," *38th North* (May 20, 2016) http://38north.org/2016/05/rfrank052016/. Accessed on July 29 2016.

Sakai, Takashi. "The Power Base of Kim Jong Il: Focusing on Its Formation Process," in Han S. Park (ed.). *North Korea Ideology, Politics, Economics*. Englewood Cliffs, NJ: Prentice Hall, 1996, pp. 105–122.

Satterwhite, David H. "North Korea in 1996: Belligerence Subsiding, Hunger Worsens," *Asian Survey*, 37, no. 1 (January 1997): 10–10.

Scalapino, Robert. "Korea the Politics of Change," *Asian Survey*, 3, no. 1 (January 1963): 31–40, 63.

Schaeler, Bernd. *North Korean "Adventurism" and China's Long Shadow, 1966–1972*. Washington, DC: Woodrow Wilson International Center for Scholars, pp. 5, 9.

Shimotomai, Nobuo. "Pyeongyang in 1956," *Cold War International History Project* 16 (Fall 2007–Winter 2008): 455–463.

Simmons, Robert. "North Korea: Silver Anniversary," *Asian Survey*, 11, no. 1 (January 1971): 104–110.

Simmons, Robert R. "North Korea: The Year of the Thaw," *Asian Survey* 12, no. 1 (January 1972): 25–31.

Shin Jongdae. "North Korean State-Makin: Process and Characteristics," in Michael Seth (ed.). *The Routledge Handbook of Modern Korean History*. London: Routledge, 2016, pp. 197–210.

Sŏ Tongman. "Pukchosŏn ŭi yugyo tamnon e kwanhayŏ: Kim Chŏngil ŭi t'ongch'i tamnon ŭl chungsim ŭro" [On Confucian discourse in North Korea: Focused on Kim Jong Il's ruling discourse]. In *Pukchosŏn yŏn'gu* [North Korea research], edited by Sŏ Tongman chŏjakjip kanhaeng wiwŏnhoe, 269–331. P'aju: Ch'angbi, 2010

Sŏ Tongman. "Pukhan sahoejŭui esŏ kŭndae wa chŏt'ong" [Modernity and tradition in North Korean socialism]. In *Han'guk ui 'kŭndae' wa 'kundaesŏng' pip'an* [A critique of the modern age and modernity in Korea], edited by Kang Man' gli et al., Sŏul: Yŏksa Pip'yŏngsa.

Suh, Dae-Sook. "Arms and the Hammer and Sickel: Kim Ils Sung and the Rise of the Partisan Generals," *The Korean Journal of Defense Analysis* 1, no. 2(1989), pp. 217–239.

Suh, Dae-sook. "North Korea 1978: The Beginning of the Final Push," *Asian Survey* 19, no. 1 (January 1979): 51–57.

Suh, Sang-chul. "North Korean Industrial Policy and Trade," in Robert A. Scalapino and Jun-Yop Kim (eds). *North Korea Today*. Berkeley, CA: University of California Press, 1983, pp. 197–229.

Sung, Chul Yang. "A Study of North Korea's Ruling Elite, 1946–1990: Based on A Background Analysis of the Members of the Korean Workers' Party Central Committee," *Vantage Point* 14, no. 4 (April 1991): 1–15; 145 (May 1991): 1–13.

Szalontai, Balazs. "'You have No Political Line of Your Own': Kim Il Sung and the Soviets, 1953–1964," *Cold War International History Project Bulletin* 14, no. 15 (Winter 2003/Spring 2004): 87–137.

Takeda, Yoshinori. "KEDO Adrift," Georgetown *Journal of International Affairs* 6, no. 2 (2005): 123–131.

Thompson, Drew Thompson. *Silent Partners, Chinese Joint Ventures in North Korea* U.S. Korea Institute at SAIS, February 2011. http://uskoreainstitute. org/research/special-reports/silent-partners-chinese-joint-ventures-in-north-korea/

Weathersby, Kathryn. "Korea, 1945–50, To Attack, or Not to Attack?: Stalin, Kim Il Sung, and the Prelude to War," *Cold War International History Project Bulletin* 5 (Spring 1995): 1–9.

Weathersby, Kathryn. "New Russian Documents on the Korean War," *CWHIP Bulletin*, 6, no. 7 (Winter 1995/1996): 77. http://www.wilsoncenter.org/sites/default/files/CWIHP_Bulletin_6-7.pdf

Wu, John C. "The Mineral Industry of NK," 2005 *Minerals Yearbook: North Korea*, U.S. Geological Survey (June 2007): 15.1.

Yook, Youngsoo. "Historiography and the Remaking of North Korea's Ideology in the Age of Globalization: Interpreting the Revised Edition of *Ryeoksa sajeon*," *Korea Journal* 50, no. 1 (Spring 2010): 133–159.

Yu, Chong-Ae. "The Rise and Demise of Juche Agriculture in North Korea," in Suh, Jae-Jung (ed.). *Origins of North Korea's Juche*. Lanham, MD: Lexington Books, 2012, pp. 119–144.

Zagoria, Donald S. and Young Kun Kim. "North Korea and the Major Powers," in William J. Barnds (ed.). *The Two Koreas in East Asian Affairs*. New York: New York University Press, 1976, pp. 177–189.

Index